FLOATING DEATH-TRAPS!

That is what the American merchant seamen of World War II called Hitler's Q-Boats!

And that is what these ingeniously-disguised secret raiders proved to be to Allied shipping in the three most dangerous years of the war—for they sank *nearly three times* the total tonnage accounted for by the entire German surface navy!

"Dramatic, authoritative, objective . . . despite the fact that they were our enemies, one is forced into a certain amount of admiration for them and for what they accomplished against tremendous odds."
—*New York Times*

"Immensely readable."
—*The New Yorker*

"A stirring and ferocious documentary of warfare on the high seas."
—*Boston Herald*

"Dramatic sea stories—all authentic."
—*Minneapolis Tribune*

"High adventure . . . thoroughly absorbing."
—*U.S. Coast Guard Magazine*

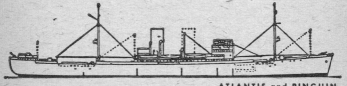

ATLANTIS and PINGUIN

The story of the German armed merchant raiders in the Second World War.

THE
SECRET
RAIDERS

DAVID WOODWARD

Complete and Unabridged

AVON PUBLICATIONS, INC.
575 Madison Avenue — New York 22, N. Y.

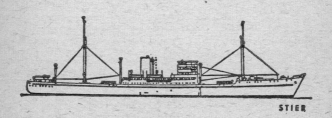

STIER

CONTENTS

Operational Areas

C.CHELIUSKIN
C.DICKSON

MAUG
LAMOTREK

AILINGIAP
NAURU
EMIRAU Is.

GALAPAGOS Is.

TUAMOTO Arch.

CHAGOS Arch.

Siberia

SHARK BAY

FIJI

Balbo

Romulus

IELEN

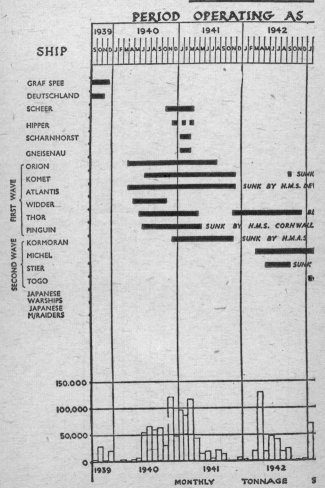

SURFACE RA

PERIOD OPERATING AS

	1939	1940	1941	1942

SHIP

GRAF SPEE
DEUTSCHLAND
SCHEER
HIPPER
SCHARNHORST
GNEISENAU

FIRST WAVE
ORION
KOMET   ⊞ SUNK
ATLANTIS   SUNK BY H.M.S. DE
WIDDER
THOR   BL
PINGUIN   SUNK BY H.M.S. CORNWALL

SECOND WAVE
KORMORAN   SUNK BY H.M.A.S
MICHEL
STIER   SUNK
TOGO

JAPANESE WARSHIPS
JAPANESE M/RAIDERS

150.000
100.000
50.000
0

1939   1940   1941   1942

MONTHLY   TONNAGE   S

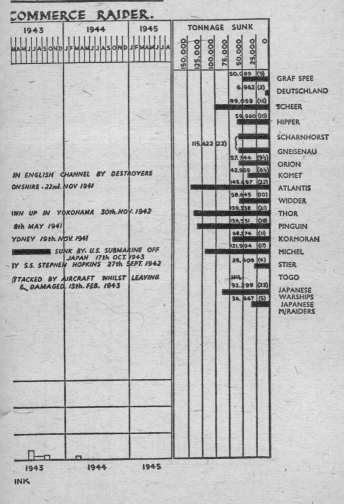

IDERS 1939-45.

COMMERCE RAIDER.

1943	1944	1945
MAMJJASOND	JFMAMJJASOND	JFMAMJJA

TONNAGE SUNK

150,000	125,000	100,000	75,000	50,000	25,000	0

Tonnage	Ship
50,089 (9)	GRAF SPEE
6,962 (2)	DEUTSCHLAND
99,059 (16)	SCHEER
59,960 (10)	HIPPER
115,622 (22)	SCHARNHORST
	GNEISENAU
57,744 (9½)	ORION
42,959 (6½)	KOMET
145,697 (22)	ATLANTIS
58,645 (10)	WIDDER
139,330 (21)	THOR
136,551 (28)	PINGUIN
68,274 (11)	KORMORAN
121,904 (17)	MICHEL
29,409 (4)	STIER
NIL	TOGO
92,299 (23)	JAPANESE WARSHIPS
30,867 (5)	JAPANESE M/RAIDERS

IN ENGLISH CHANNEL BY DESTROYERS

ONSHIRE · 22nd. NOV 1941

WN UP IN YOKOHAMA 30th. NOV. 1942

8th MAY 1941

YDNEY 19th. NOV. 1941

SUNK BY U.S. SUBMARINE OFF
JAPAN 17th OCT. 1943
Y S.S. STEPHEN HOPKINS 27th SEPT. 1942

TTACKED BY AIRCRAFT WHILST LEAVING
& DAMAGED. 13th. FEB. 1943

1943	1944	1945

INK

I

Introduction

Between 1940 and 1943 there were at sea a total of nine German armed merchant raiders (converted freighters), and between them they sank more than 130 Allied or neutral merchant vessels, totalling over 850,000 tons. This was nearly three times the total tonnage of merchant shipping sunk by the German surface warships, whose names were so well known—*Scharnhorst, Gneisenau, Admiral Graf Spee* and the others. Altogether, the surface raiders sank as many ships as did the mines, laid by the German navy and air force, which were such a grave danger to the Allies at the most critical stage of the war.

The raiders sailed the seas of the world; they operated in the Arctic, in the Antarctic, in the Atlantic, the Pacific and the Indian Ocean. The most successful of all raiders in any war was the *Atlantis*, at sea continuously for twenty-one months, during which time she sank twenty-two ships. The *Komet*, a tiny vessel, hardly bigger than a cross-channel steamer, passed from the North Cape, north of Siberia, into the Pacific. The *Pinguin* raided the Allied whaling fleets in the Antarctic, and the *Thor* drove off two British armed merchant cruisers of greater size, and sank a third.

Two of the raiders were lost in single ship actions so fierce that both the German vessel and her opponent were sunk; the *Kormoran* sank and was sunk by the Australian cruiser *Sydney,* and the *Stier,* similarly, sank and was sunk by the American freighter *Stephen Hopkins.* Altogether, of the nine armed merchant raiders all but two were sunk, but it took the Allied navies three and a half years to accomplish this, at a time when every one of their ships was desperately needed to defeat the submarine menace and to prepare for the liberation of occupied Europe and Asia.

This struggle against the German raiders has been over now for twelve years, but its story cannot be considered simply as so much history, for it is upon the fast ocean-going raider that the Russians are laying the greatest emphasis in their rebuilding of a first-class surface navy, and the problems presented by these raiders are something which the NATO forces must still bear in mind, despite the development in the past ten years of aircraft, submarines and guided missiles.

The fact that by 1957 Russia is expected to have some thirty large cruisers designed as raiders gives an idea of the scale on which this problem might arise once again. As a comparison it may be noted that during World War II the Germans operated as raiders a total of nine armed merchant vessels, four capital ships, three pocket battleships and two heavy cruisers.

The first stage in the preparation for the campaigns of World War II against Allied merchant shipping was begun in 1927, when the Weimar Republic was near the height of its power, and the German navy reduced, in theory, to a token force by the disarmament clauses of the Treaty of Versailles.[1]

This first stage of rearmament was one of planning. What was required was an organisation in neutral ports which would, in time of war, be able to buy supplies locally, load them on board German merchant ships and get those ships to sea through a possible enemy blockade in order to revictual raiders which had broken out from home waters. In addition, it was to be the duty of these branches of the organisation, called by the German *Etappen,* to provide any commercial or shipping intelligence which might be of value either to raiders or to the German naval staff. Furthermore, the *Etappen* agents—unpaid volunteers in time of peace—were supposed also to carry out small-scale operations of economic warfare,

[1] The total permitted force from 1921 to 1935, when the disarmament clauses of the Treaty of Versailles were abrogated by Hitler, was six old battleships (two in reserve), six light cruisers (with two in reserve), twenty-four destroyers and torpedo boats (with eight in reserve). No submarines or naval or military aircraft were permitted.

chiefly by manipulation of the local stock exchange through the spreading of rumours.

This system of *Etappen* had worked well during the early stages of World War I, when one of the officers in charge of it in the United States had been Captain von Papen, later Chancellor of the Reich and Hitler's ambassador to Turkey.

In 1928 Admiral Erich Raeder was appointed Commander-in-Chief of the German navy. He was to hold that office until 1943, when he resigned, following a disagreement with Hitler over the use of surface vessels in support of the U-boat campaign against Allied shipping. Raeder was responsible for the rebuilding of the German navy and for the planning of its strategy in World War II. He had distinguished himself during World War I on the staff of Admiral Hipper, who commanded the battle-cruisers of the High Sea Fleet at Jutland, and he came to the highest post in the navy with very definite ideas on cruiser warfare. These ideas he had developed while writing the first two volumes of the German official history of the war at sea, dealing with cruiser operations in foreign waters. Three years after the planning of the *Etappen* had begun, the work of these organisations reached the point where money was clandestinely included for them in the naval estimates.

In 1934, also clandestinely, provision was made for the building of four auxiliary cruisers (disguised as merchant vessels), but these ships were not built because the German army would only agree to release to the navy twenty-four 5.9-inch guns for their armament. This led, in naval circles, to bitter jokes on the theme of "Guns or Butter," it being said that Goering had the butter, the army had the guns, and the navy had nothing.

Raeder had tried to get these disguised merchant vessels built because he believed that it would be impossible to use ordinary warships as raiders at sea so long as Germany or her allies had no bases. The raiders used would have to be disguised as cargo ships because liners, which had been employed as raiders in the early part of World War I, were far too conspicuous, especially from the air.

The result of Raeder's failure to get guns for his four ships

13

in 1934 was that by 1939 the German navy had no auxiliary cruisers either building or being converted; but there had been a successful dress rehearsal of the *Etappen* system in the crisis of September 1938.

With no armed merchant raiders available, Raeder had after all at the beginning of World War II to rely on his warships, and accordingly, just before the attack on Poland, the pocket battleships *Deutschland* and *Admiral Graf Spee* were sent to sea. If sighted they could be at once identified as German ships, but their diesel engines meant that they would be able to operate for long periods without refuelling.

While the Germans were very short of surface raiders, the British and French navies were far from being able to protect Allied merchant vessels against the raiders which did get to sea. Such protection could only have been given by a convoy system on all principal trade routes, and for this sufficient cruisers did not exist.

Without convoys, the only possible alternative was, firstly, the patrol of focal areas through which shipping had to pass; secondly, the diversive routing of ships, which meant that in order to take a track away from areas in which raiders were suspected they had to use fuel and time making a detour. Finally, there were created hunting groups of capital ships, cruisers and aircraft-carriers which might be able to catch raiders when it was known in what area they were operating. Altogether there were, in the first months of the war, nine of these groups, mixed British and French, comprising four capital ships, fourteen cruisers and five aircraft-carriers. The total British and French strength at this time was only twenty-three capital ships and eight aircraft-carriers. Thus the proportion of the Allied forces used at this time to deal with two raiding pocket battleships will be seen to be very great indeed, and shows clearly the serious situation in which the Allies would have been if Hitler had given Raeder the time for which he asked to develop a first-class surface fleet.

Raeder had planned to have this force ready by 1944–5, and its planned operations were based entirely on the conduct of cruiser warfare on a vast scale, supported by a submarine fleet of over 100 boats. For surface warfare Raeder planned to have the following fleet:

6 battleships of 56,000 tons, 8 16-inch guns
2 battleships of 42,000 tons, 8 15-inch guns
2 battleships of 31,000 tons, 9 11-inch guns
3 battle-cruisers of 31,000 tons, 6 15-inch guns
3 pocket battleships of 14,000 tons, 6 11-inch guns
2 aircraft-carriers of 20,000 tons, 40 planes
8 heavy cruisers of 14,000 tons, 8 8-inch guns
9 light cruisers of 6,000-8,000 tons, 8 or 9 5.9-inch guns
   together with destroyers and other light craft.

These ships were to have been divided into three groups. The smaller battleships *Bismarck, Tirpitz, Scharnhorst* and *Gneisenau* were to remain in home waters to pin down a proportion of the British fleet; then the battle-cruisers, the pocket battleships, cruisers and carriers would have been sent to sea as commerce raiders. This, it was anticipated, would have led to the dispatch of British heavy ships and cruisers to hunt them down, and these in turn would have been hunted by the 56,000-ton battleships working in two groups of three ships each.

The change from these grandiose plans to the control by the German naval staff (the SKL or *Seekriegsleitung*) of the movements of only two pocket battleships was indeed something of an anticlimax, but Raeder, after one gloomy memorandum of protest, set to work to make war with what means he had.

He needed both ships and bases. As far as bases were concerned, he hoped to operate from Russian, Italian (East African) and Japanese ports, although all these countries were then neutral. Use of these ports would avoid the necessity of his ships having to pass and repass the British blockade line between Scotland and Norway every time they had to enter or leave the ocean; this blockade line was composed of some twenty-five armed liners, which had been taken over with twenty-five similar ships and placed in service on the trade routes at the outbreak of the war.

As soon as the war started the conversion was begun by the Germans of a number of merchant vessels as raiders—the activities of these ships form the subject of this book. As has been said, there were nine of them; one more never got through the English Channel, and two were converted but never sailed. It may seem surprising that out of a merchant marine which in 1939 totalled 250 ships between 5,000 and 10,000 tons in size only ten ships were converted into raiders, but it will be seen that special characteristics were required for such a conversion to be successful, and that of those actually converted several were quite unsatisfactory.

None of these conversions was finished before the end of March 1940. A little later it was clear that the armed merchant raiders would at first, at least, have to replace rather than reinforce the big warships which had been required for the Norwegian campaign, in the course of which the *Scharnhorst* and *Gneisenau* had suffered damage, and the heavy cruiser *Blücher*, sister ship of the *Admiral Hipper* and the *Prinz Eugen*, had been sunk.

The first winter of the war had been marked only by the cruises of the *Admiral Graf Spee* and *Deutschland*, and a sortie by the *Scharnhorst* and *Gneisenau* in which the armed merchant cruiser *Rawalpindi* had been sunk. At the beginning of the second winter of the war the situation was very different, although up to that point the raiders altogether had only sunk eleven merchant ships of 59,000 tons. Following the fall of France and the entry of Italy into the war, British resources were stretched very nearly to breaking point. Most of the capital ships, and many other vessels as well, which had been operating against raiders on the high seas had been recalled to deal with the situation in the Mediterranean. In the protection of ships on the sea lanes first priority went to the troop convoys which in the exposed waters of the North Atlantic were given full cover—that is to say, they were accompanied throughout their voyage by heavy ships which could have stood off any raider. This was essential, but it meant that there were few ships left to provide full cover for the convoys carrying food and war materials. These had accordingly to depend chiefly on distant covering forces and hunting groups.

So thin on the sea were the British forces at the worst period of the war that only two aircraft-carriers and five cruisers were available for the North Atlantic, the Home Fleet, and Force H at Gibraltar. The North Atlantic troop convoys were reasonably protected but all the other troop convoys in the world were defended by one "R" class battleship (obsolete), eight cruisers and one armed merchant cruiser, whilst one more "R" class battleship and a handful of armed merchant cruisers had to look after all the trade convoys. This meant, in practice, that ships either sailed without convoy, and it will be seen that almost all the 130 or more ships sunk by the armed merchant raiders were sailing alone, or else they sailed in a convoy with an entirely inadequate escort. An example of what could happen in the latter case was provided in November 1940 when the pocket battleship *Admiral Scheer* became the first of the German heavy ships to operate in the oceans of the world since her sister ship the *Graf Spee* had been destroyed ten months before.

The *Scheer,* commanded by Captain Krancke, left Brunsbuttel, at the North Sea end of the Kiel Canal, on October 23, passed round the north of Iceland in misty weather and was then ready to carry out the simple order which had been given her captain: "Attack the North Atlantic convoys."

German naval intelligence informed the *Scheer* that a large homeward-bound convoy had left Halifax on October 27, and the pocket battleship steered to intercept it. On the afternoon of November 5 convoy HX 84 was sighted. It was composed of thirty-seven ships escorted by the armed merchant cruiser *Jervis Bay* commanded by Captain E. S. F. Fegen, R.N.

It was getting dark as the *Scheer* attacked; she was a large, fast and armoured ship, with six 11-inch guns and eight 5.9-inch guns with up-to-date fire-control equipment, as opposed to the obsolete 6-inch guns, controlled in a very rudimentary fashion, of the slow and unarmoured *Jervis Bay*.

As soon as he sighted the enemy Captain Fegen informed the Admiralty, ordered the convoy to scatter, and, trailing a smoke-screen across them as they did so, he headed towards the enemy at full speed, hoping to delay the *Scheer* until the ships in his charge had escaped into the dark. As for the

17

action between his ship and the raider, that, he knew, could have only one result.

The *Scheer* opened fire at 18,000 yards—well outside the range of the *Jervis Bay*—straddled her at once and then began to hit her heavily and to keep on hitting. Within an hour the British ship was ablaze from stem to stern, her fire control gone, although the guns which would still bear continued firing independently. At 2000 the *Jervis Bay* sank, her captain being among the 200 officers and men who perished. Meanwhile, the *Scheer* had gone off as fast as she could in pursuit of the scattered merchant ships—but it was dark, they were hard to find, and the raider had little time, for Krancke knew that the *Jervis Bay* had given the alarm and that planes and big warships might be upon him very soon. Such was his need for haste that he had time to find and sink only five of the thirty-seven ships for which he was looking. One of these ships which arrived safely in the United Kingdom was the tanker *San Demetrio*, which had been abandoned by her crew after having been set on fire by the raider's shells. Led by the tanker's second officer, a boatload of the crew afterwards returned on board, put out the fire and brought her home in triumph to the United Kingdom.

To sink 47,000 tons of shipping on this occasion the pocket battleship had expended one-third of the ammunition for her main armament, and half that for her secondary guns.

But the effect on the North Atlantic convoys was very nearly shattering; the entire system was disorganised for twelve days, and no convoy arrived in Britain for a whole week. This was the only occasion during the war in which there was a delay of this length. A vast amount of shipping space and time was lost and for five weeks hunting groups searched in vain for the raider, which had gone into the Indian Ocean. Finally, having had several rendezvous with the armed merchant raiders and their oilers, the *Scheer* returned to Germany after a cruise lasting 161 days, during which she had sunk sixteen ships of 99,000 tons.

Following the encouraging news of the *Scheer's* attack on convoy HX 84, the heavy cruiser *Admiral Hipper* was also sent into the Atlantic. Her engines were turbines and not diesels, as had been those of the *Scheer*, which meant that she required about two and a half times as much fuel. In addition, her turbines, of a new type, were not satisfactory, and it was soon discovered that this splendid-looking great ship was not dependable unless she had a supply vessel within 600 miles. However, on Christmas Eve she sighted a troop-carrying convoy 700 miles west of Cape Finisterre; she shadowed it, attacked during the night with torpedoes, all of which missed, and was driven off by the escorting cruisers *Berwick* and *Bonaventure*. Two days later she entered Brest, where she remained until February 1, when she sailed again into the Atlantic. She found a slow convoy of nineteen unescorted ships on the way to Freetown, and sank seven of them, about 200 miles east of the Azores. This was on February 12. Two days later, her captain being worried about his engines and a shortage of fuel and ammunition, she returned to Brest.

It was during the month of February 1941 that the raiders, warships and armed merchant vessels were at their most active; at that time there were at sea the two battleships *Scharnhorst* and *Gneisenau*, the *Scheer*, the *Hipper* and six of the armed merchant raiders.

The *Scharnhorst* and *Gneisenau* in a two-months cruise together accounted for twenty-two ships of 115,622 tons. They started off with a narrow escape from interception by the Home Fleet, and then continued on to the Halifax convoy route, stopping to refuel at various Arctic and sub-Arctic rendezvous from tankers sent to meet them.

On February 8th they found convoy HX 106, but were driven off by the battleship *Resolution*, as Admiral Lütjens was unwilling to risk the damage to his ships that might be expected from the 15-inch guns of the obsolete British battleship, although Hoffmann, the captain of the *Scharnhorst*, suggested that he attack the British battleship while the *Gneisenau* dealt with the unprotected merchant ships. But Lütjens, who shortly afterwards lost his life in the *Bismarck*, had very much in his mind that even comparatively little damage might mean the disablement or loss of one of his big ships, far as they were from any friendly base.

After this failure Lütjens headed further west, believing that closer to the American coast British convoys were dispersed and single unprotected ships could easily be attacked. Five of these ships were in fact found, and sunk, but the alarm was given and the German battleships made off far southward, where they encountered another British convoy, again protected by a single battleship—the *Malaya*. Again they did not attack for the same reason that applied when they had met the *Resolution*.

After refuelling, Lütjens returned to the Halifax route and once more was successful in-sinking a number of unescorted merchantmen from convoys which had been dispersed for lack of escort vessels.

After a very brief encounter with the British battleship *Rodney*, which, with most of the Home Fleet, was searching for them, the two German ships went to Brest, there to wait until the *Bismarck* was ready for sea, when the three ships were to operate together against the North Atlantic convoys.

This was the high point in the activities of the large German surface warships, and Raeder was pleased with the work of his ships.

"Decisive offensive warfare against merchant ships is the only way to conquer Britain," he said on July 25th, 1941.

"German surface forces may gradually be destroyed, but this must not prevent them operating against shipping."

The losses of which Raeder spoke had begun with the sinking of the *Bismarck;* just afterwards the R.A.F. immobilised the *Scharnhorst* and *Gneisenau* in Brest, so that they were unable to leave French waters until the famous dash up the Channel took place in February 1942.

The R.A.F.'s intervention at Brest caused a lull in the heavy-ship operations which lasted from the sinking of the *Bismarck* to the completion of the *Tirpitz*. An additional obstacle to the use of the big ships was that by the end of December 1941 the German fuel-oil situation had become very bad, since virtually all imports from Rumania had stopped. The German synthetic oil plants were able to produce the petrol required for the Luftwaffe and the diesel oil needed for the submarines, but the production of fuel oil for the big ships was a different matter, and Raeder had to introduce a strict

20

system of rationing, which had the result of confining the *Tirpitz* to the Norwegian fiords for the whole of her life, except for a very occasional sortie.

Henceforward the surface war against Allied shipping was left to the armed merchant raiders, though the German heavy ships were to tie up great Allied forces to watch them until the *Tirpitz* was sunk by the R.A.F. in November 1944.

The damage that the big ships might have done had they gone to sea again is clearly illustrated by the comment which the author of *British Official History of the War at Sea*, Captain S. W. Roskill, R.N., makes on the cruise of the *Scharnhorst* and *Gneisenau*.

The ships had ". . . for a time, completely dislocated our Atlantic convoy cycles, with serious consequences to our vital imports. Their depredations forced the wide dispersal of our already strained naval resources. . . . Their foray had been skilfully planned, well co-ordinated with the movements of other raiders and successfully sustained by their supply ships sent out for the purpose."

By the time the *Scharnhorst* and *Gneisenau* had been immobilised there were six merchant raiders at sea, and one had returned to Germany after a successful cruise.

The first six raiders sailed between March 31 and July 9, 1940. They were the *Atlantis, Orion, Widder, Thor, Pinguin* and *Komet*. These ships were referred to as "The First Wave."

The seventh raider, *Kormoran*, which sailed on December 3, 1940, had been the first ship of "The Second Wave," and she was followed by the *Stier, Michel, Komet* (sunk at the beginning of her second cruise), *Thor* (on her second cruise), and, finally, the *Togo* (which never passed Boulogne).

In addition two other raiders were got ready to sail, but the efficacy of Allied watch by air and sea was so great that after the failure of the *Togo* to break out the plan was abandoned. These ships were the *Hansa* (ex-British *Glengarry*) and the *Coburg* (ex-Dutch *Amerskerk*).

II
1914-18

THE STORY of the operations of the German surface raiders in the First World War had in it much that was of value to Raeder and his officers in the second round of their struggle with Britain for the command of the sea, and not a little that is still of value today. Apart from the squadron of Spee, which steamed half-way round the world and defeated a British squadron on the way, there were six ships which were of particular importance. First, both in time and importance, where the *Goeben* and *Breslau,* whose escape into the Dardanelles in 1914 led to Turkey entering the war against the Allies. This cut direct communications between the Allies and Russia, so that the Russians were unable to receive arms and ammunition at a time when their troops were fighting against the Germans with fists and sticks and stones. To re-establish communications the Dardanelles campaign was fought, and when this failed there came after another year of hopeless struggle, the collapse of which led to the Bolshevik revolution.

Then there was the *Königsberg*, which, having been driven by a force of some eighty British warships to take refuge up a remote river in German East Africa, scuttled herself. Her crew and her guns went ashore and carried on a campaign in co-operation with the German land forces already there involving German and British East Africa, and Rhodesia and the Portuguese and Belgian possessions as well. The remains of the German naval and military forces under General von Lettow-Vorbeck did not surrender until a fortnight after the German revolution had broken out and the Armistice had been signed in Europe.

It will be seen in the next chapter of this book that Rogge, the most successful German raider captain of World War II, had this campaign very much in his mind. In the event of his ship being unable to continue her career as a raider he wished to take her to some British possession, there land his men and carry on a war of his own for as long as possible.

The lessons of both the *Goeben* and the *Königsberg* are clear today; one or two large Russian vessels arriving at some place of strategic importance in which there was already a strong Communist movement could bring the arms and technical assistance sufficient to start anything from an incident to a full-scale campaign which would be extremely embarrassing, if not extremely dangerous, to the cause of the Western allies. If such a thing were done the ships themselves would probably be lost in a short time, but the loss might be considered as worthwhile if they had been successful in starting a big enough diversion.

After the escape of the *Goeben* and *Breslau* the next German warship to become famous was the *Emden*, a comparatively slow and weakly armed light cruiser whose appearance in the Indian Ocean sufficed by itself to bring most of the seaborne trade in the area to a stop. At that time, as in World War II, it was hardly ever the actual sinkings and captures effected by a raider which caused the heaviest losses, but the delays occasioned by the stoppage of trade, the organisation of convoys, and the provision of escorts. This loss was not simply financial. Vital materials did not arrive in Allied ports because the ships carrying them could not sail, and because of delays and re-routings six ships might be required to do the work normally done by four. In that way—for the time being, at least—the two extra ships might be almost counted as lost, since they were not available for other purposes. The provision of heavy escorts, especially during the first months of the war, was as desperate a business in World War I as in World War II. The Grand Fleet always had to be ready to meet a sortie in full strength by the German High Sea Fleet—but the Grand Fleet could never be at full strength itself. There would always be some ships away refitting or repairing—probably about one in five unless the British had suffered an exceptional stroke of bad luck, which was always possible and did on occasion happen.

At the outbreak of war the comparative dreadnought battleship strength of the British and German fleets in home waters was such that there was never a great deal, from the British point of view, to spare. The detachment of three battle-cruisers to the Mediterranean to look after the *Goeben* and one ship in the Pacific to protect Australian troop convoys was a very grave matter at the beginning of the war. In the same way, later, four battle-cruisers were operating in such widely separated places as the Pacific, West Indies and the South Atlantic to catch the German raiding squadron commanded by Graf Spee. This was when the German battle-cruisers were making a series of raids on British coastal towns, and at that time only battle-cruisers could catch battle-cruisers.

After the *Goeben* had taken refuge in Turkish waters and other German surface warships outside home waters had been sunk or put out of action, the Germans converted merchant ships into raiders, as they did again in World War II, and a pair of these ships, the *Möwe* and *Wolf*, in three long cruises showed what this type of ship could accomplish.

Another merchant ship converted to raider which had a brilliant career was the sailing vessel *Seeadler*. Equipped with an auxiliary engine and commanded by the famous Luckner, she sailed half-way round the world on a career of destruction which was only ended by an accidental stranding in the South Pacific.

The *Goeben's* appearance in history—probably the most important ever made by a single ship—began on the evening of June 28, 1914. The battle-cruiser lay off Haifa. Her admiral, Souchon, commanding the German Mediterranean division, and most of her officers were attending a reception given in their honour by the German colony. A message was brought to the admiral, announcing the assassination of the Archduke Franz Ferdinand. Souchon's first thought was that this might mean war, and his second thought was for his boiler tubes, which were in such a state that his splendid ship was nearly crippled, being capable of only seventeen knots against a designed speed of twenty-seven knots.

The *Goeben* broke off her cruise and returned to the

Austrian naval base of Pola, where she was met by engineers and workmen sent from Germany in response to a request from Souchon. In the days of dead calm which followed the first stunning shock of the assassination, and in the days during which the European tension came to its head, bursting through an international structure which was the product of nearly half a century of mending, patching, compromising and hoping for the best, the *Goeben* was being prepared.

Before this crisis elaborate conversations had taken place between Souchon and his colleagues, the admiral's commanding the Austrian and Italian navies—Germany's partners in the Triple Alliance, on the subject of joint operations in the event of a war against France or against France and Britain. From these talks Souchon formed the conclusion that the Italians had little desire and the Austrians little ability to help him and that, if war came, he would have to look after himself. His first duty, he believed, would be to interfere with the mobilisation of the French army, an important part of which was in North Africa and which would have to be taken to France as quickly as possible to help stop the German advance on Paris.

Just in time, as the declarations of war were beginning, and with his repairs not quite finished, Souchon left Pola and steamed down the Adriatic into the Mediterranean. As he came he ordered to his flag the only other German seagoing ship in his division, the light cruiser *Breslau*. This ship had been part of an international naval force lying off the port of Durazzo to give support to the King of Albania, William of Wied, recently chosen by the great powers without the approval of Albania's neighbours or of the Albanians. As the Sarajevo crisis developed the international force broke up. The last two ships to go where the *Breslau* and the British light cruiser *Gloucester*, which had been "chummy ships" together. About a fortnight after the two crews had been playing water polo together, they were in action against each other.

On board the German light cruiser were two officers destined to rise to the top of their profession. One was Sub-Lieutenant Dönitz, later C.-in-C. of the German navy, and

25

last Chancellor of the Third Reich, now (1955) coming to the end of a sentence of ten years' imprisonment in the International Military Prison in Spandau as a war criminal. The other was his rival for command of the German navy in 1943, General Admiral Carls, at that time a lieutenant.

The international force left Durazzo almost at the same time as Albania's new king, after a reign of a few days over a few square miles. But the issue was no longer the creation of a small state in the Balkans in the hope of preserving an uneasy peace. The issue was now the future existence of all the countries in the Balkans and of most of the countries of Europe.

Souchon entered the Mediterranean and steamed west towards the French convoy routes; as he went he received warning that war with Britain was probable. At this time Britain, as has been said, maintained three battle-cruisers in the Mediterranean, the *Indomitable, Inflexible* and *Indefatigable*, principally to deal with the *Goeben*. They were slightly older, slightly slower and much less well protected than the German ship, but from what was known then it seemed that any two of them could overwhelm Souchon's flagship.

The French Mediterranean fleet at this time was greatly superior in number and gunpower to the British ships, but it included no large fast vessels such as would be required to overtake and sink the *Goeben*.

Souchon proposed to begin his campaign against the French by a bombardment of Bône and Philippeville. On the morning of August 4 he approached Bône flying a large Russian ensign, while the *Breslau* went to Philippeville.

As the two ships neared their objective they received an order from Berlin, telling them to make for the Dardanelles, but Souchon was determined to carry out his bombardment first.

German colours having been hoisted, a brisk bombardment took place; the French, learning that the Germans were on the edge of the western Mediterranean, postponed the sailing of their transports.

Steaming away from Algerian waters in the direction of the Dardanelles on that same morning of August 4, some twelve hours before Britain declared war on Germany, the *Goeben* was met by the *Indomitable* and *Indefatigable*. The minds of the German admiral and the senior British naval officer, Captain Kennedy, were both working fast on two planes of thought infinitely remote from each other. Kennedy reflected that it was his duty to salute the German admiral so long as war had not broken out. Souchon believed that one of the ships steaming to meet him was the flagship of Admiral Sir Berkeley Milne, the British commander-in-chief. He was an officer of greater seniority than Souchon, and accordingly the German owed him a salute—but the difficulty was that after the bombardment the *Goeben* had reloaded her guns with live ammunition and therefore was in no position to fire salutes of courtesy. For a moment Souchon played with the idea of sending a signal to the British ships explaining the position, but, as he discarded it, he saw that neither of them was flying an admiral's flag; Kennedy saw that Souchon's flag was not flying either. The ephemeral business of an exchange of salutes disappeared and the two commanders were faced with a very strange and very dangerous situation.

Kennedy asked for orders from London and at the same time let the *Goeben* go past him so that he would be between that ship and the French transports. He did not know that the French had suspended their sailing, although orders had been coming through from London fairly continuously. First, he had been told that he was to attack the Germans whether or not war had broken out between Britain and Germany if they attacked French ships. Then this order was cancelled and he was told that war was imminent and that he should keep in contact with the *Goeben*.

The three ships steamed eastward together, the *Goeben* leading and the two British ships behind, one on each quarter. The engines of all three ships were giving less than their contract speed, but the *Goeben* was still the faster ship, in fact as she was on paper, and she was able to draw away slowly, so that by the time Britain and Germany were at war she was out of sight, off to Messina—Italy being neutral —to coal and to meet the *Breslau*.

The two German ships coaled in Messina in the middle of

a combination of an Italo-German political crisis and an un-official *festa* organised by the citizens of the town, who crowded round the ship in small boats selling everything they could, including highly coloured accounts of how the Germans were on the verge of annihilation at the hands of the superior British squadron which was known to be waiting outside Italian territorial waters.

The Germans coaled in desperate haste and in tropical conditions; they sailed and slipped past Milne's squadron, which had not clearly understood its orders to pass through the Straits of Messina, Italian territorial waters, in pursuit. A short time after this Sir Berkeley Milne was transferred from his command. But if the Germans had dodged the British battle-cruisers, there was still another British force which might intercept them. This was a squadron of four armoured cruisers—smaller, weaker and slower ships than the *Goeben*—accompanied by eight destroyers, which was at the entrance to the Adriatic under Rear-Admiral Troubridge. Troubridge, in view of the weakness of his ships, did not close the Germans—an action for which he was afterwards courtmartialled, and acquitted but transferred to a shore command. Certainly it appeared immediately after the event, and so still appears to this day, that, in view of the immense harm the *Goeben* was capable of doing, Troubridge should have attacked, hoping that even if his cruisers were knocked out, his destroyers, with their torpedoes, might at least have damaged the German battle-cruiser.

This unsatisfactory incident had a sequel which vitally affected the war against German raiders on the other side of the world. One of the officers who wrote to Troubridge to sympathise with him after the incident was Rear-Admiral Cradock, then commanding in the South Atlantic and on the look-out for Spee's squadron. This, at the time, was believed to be heading from the Far East across the Pacific into the Atlantic on its way home. Cradock told Troubridge that it was clear from the Admiralty's attitude towards the escape of the *Goeben* that if he were to meet Spee with his considerably inferior squadron it would be his duty to engage him whether or not there seemed any chance of success, and this is exactly what was to happen a little later at the Battle of Coronel, off the coast of Chile.

Meanwhile the *Goeben* and *Breslau*, followed only by the *Gloucester* in hot pursuit, were escaping towards the Dardanelles. The *Gloucester* was a ship no bigger than the *Breslau*, and the heavy guns of the *Goeben* kept her at a distance, which meant that in the night it was easy for the faster German ships to get away. After a brief action they reached the Dardanelles and steamed towards the Turkish batteries, their guns trained upon them and their crews at action stations. Souchon has since said that he was determined to enter the Straits even if he had to force his way in; in fact that was not necessary, for the German military mission with the Turkish army was able to persuade Enver Pasha to allow the ships to enter peacefully. This was all kept very secret, so that the first that diplomatic circles in Constantinople knew of the affair was when an American tourist, daughter of the American ambassador, arrived in the city and said she had seen an action between the *Gloucester* and the *Goeben* and *Breslau*.

The German ships were almost immediately sold, in theory, to the Turkish navy, but retained their German officers and crew. In order that the ships should have a more Turkish look about them than that bestowed by hoisting the red flag with the white crescent upon it, half the crews were ordered to wear the fez. Unfortunately the first consignment of fezes, taken from a German merchant ship, proved to be of an unfashionable and un-Turkish pattern and caused great scandal when worn.

From the time the German ships reached Constantinople, they, their crews and German experts brought down through the neutral Balkans in plain clothes busied themselves with preparing Turkey for war against the Allies. There was much that needed to be done.

In the first place the Turkish navy had just lost its two largest vessels, battleships of the greatest size and power which had been built in Britain, part of the funds for their construction being provided by public subscription to which thousands of the poorest people in Turkey had willingly or otherwise contributed. When war became probable the two ships were taken over for the British navy; as has already been pointed out, the numerical superiority of the British over the German battle fleet was not a comfortable one, and it was clear in London that it was not simply a question of these ships passing from British control to a neutral country but that in fact there was a very great danger of Turkey coming into the war against the British.

Accordingly the two big ships were taken over, and the *Goeben* and the *Breslau* had to take their places, as far as that was possible.

The remaining ships of the Turkish navy were in poor state. For years Sultan Abdul Hamid had maintained a considerable fleet, which spent its entire time at anchor off Constantinople, since the Sultan was afraid that if ever he let it out of his sight it would revolt against him. These decades of virtual internment had rotted the ships, though they were always kept smartly painted, and discouraged officers and men, so that what was left of the navy in 1914 was in a very low state of efficiency, despite some years of work by a British naval mission. The Germans dealt with this situation by appointing their own officers to command the Turkish ships or to act as advisers to the more competent Turkish officers, and the effect of this measure, together with the natural fighting ability of the Turks when uninhibited by the whims of the Sultan, made the force a valuable one.

From before the beginning of the war the Germans had determined to have a strong naval force in the Dardanelles, being convinced that its influence would help or cause Enver to throw in his country's lot with the Central Powers. At the beginning of August, in co-operation with the Austrian Ministry of Foreign Affairs, they had tried to compel the Austrian naval command to transfer the best vessels of the Austrian navy from the Adriatic to the Sea of Marmora, but the Austrian commander-in-chief, Admiral Haus, had refused. From the point of view of the Central Powers it is probably a pity that the Austrian fleet was not moved—always supposing that it would have been possible to keep it supplied with ammunition and coal. In view of the great difficulty in looking after the *Goeben* and *Breslau* in this respect it is hard to see what could have been done for the Austrian navy, and it would seem that the Germans treated the Austrian navy as expendable in return for a temporary but very great advantage.

Even without the Austrians, by the end of October 1914 the Germans were ready for their next move. Without telling a single Turk—with the probable exception of Enver—Souchon hoisted a signal reading "Do your best for the future of Turkey" and took his ships to sea, flying the Turkish flag. Although Turkey was still neutral, they carried out bombardments of the Russian Black Sea coast and there was war between the Allies and Turkey.

The Dardanelles compaign and those in Mesopotamia, Egypt, Palestine and the Caucasus followed.

In so far as they could be kept in fighting trim and supplied with fuel, the *Goeben* and *Breslau* conducted a lively war against the Russian Black Sea fleet, and after the Russian revolution were able once again to turn their attention to the western exit from the Marmora. In January 1918 they made a sortie into the Mediterranean and sank two British monitors. The *Breslau* was mined and sunk on the way back, and the *Goeben* ran aground in the Dardanelles. She was the target for submarine torpedoes and over 100 bombs—a great total for those days—were dropped round her, only two of which hit.

She was finally got off her sandbank by the action of the only surviving Turkish battleship, which went as close alongside her as she dared and by use of her propellers pushed the sand away from under the keel of the grounded ship, so that she floated free.

After this the *Goeben* went back to the Black Sea, in which she had several months' cruising as undisputed mistress after the surrender or scuttling of the Russian fleet and the German occupation of the well-equipped naval base at Sevastopol.

At the end of the war the *Goeben* was really turned over to Turkey and has served in the Turkish navy ever since under the name of *Yavuz*. She was laid down over forty-five years ago and she can hardly be regarded as an effective warship, but she has played a tremendous part in history, and by her mere existence spans the gap between the first German navy of Tirpitz and the Kaiser and the beginnings of the formation of the third German navy in 1955.

Mention has been already made of the only concentration of German warships outside European waters in 1914, the East Asiatic Squadron commanded by Spee, and consisting of the two armoured cruisers *Scharnhorst* and *Gneisenau* and the three light cruisers, *Emden, Nürnberg* and *Dresden*. When a world war appeared possible, Spee left his base at Tsingtau, on the Chinese mainland, and disappeared into the Pacific amongst the islands which were to serve as bases for German and Japanese warships in the Second World War, which were to be the scene of fierce fighting and are, at the present time, proving grounds for atom and hydrogen bombs.

At the outbreak of war Spee sent the *Emden* into the Indian Ocean to raid independently, and slowly steamed across the Pacific, stopping to bombard the French port of Papiti, in Tahiti. On the way he picked up another light cruiser, the *Leipzig,* which had been stationed in American waters, and then headed southward towards Cape Horn. For three months the entire Japanese navy, together with British, Australian and French warships, looked for him in vain. On November 1 he encountered Admiral Cradock off Coronel, sank his two strongest ships and drove off the two weaker, without suffering any loss himself. A month later he planned an attack on the Falkland Islands, in the South Atlantic, and he arrived there just twenty-four hours after the British battle-cruisers *Inflexible* and *Invincible*. His force was as inferior to the British as Cradock's had been to his own, and after a long day's chase towards the Antarctic the *Scharnhorst, Gneisenau, Leipzig* and *Nürnberg* were all sunk. The *Dresden* escaped, but was caught in March of the following year off Juan Fernandez, and scuttled herself.

She was the last of the regular German surface warships at large on the oceans. The most famous of these had been the *Emden*. Her captain, Müller, was one of those Germans whom the British public, with a certain amount of reason, is prepared to admire almost unreservedly. The case of Rommel in the Second World War is fresh in the mind, although it is not quite parallel, since Müller was a comparatively junior officer and there was in his case none of the political consideration which arose in the case of the Field-Marshal. Had the British public in World War II ever heard of Rogge, the captain of the *Atlantis*, they would, no doubt, have regarded him in much the same light as previously they had done the captain of the *Emden*.

Müller's ship had a career of destruction which lasted three months; in this time she sank or captured 101,182 tons of shipping, and, as has been said, practically brought trade in the Indian Ocean to a standstill. In addition Müller made two sensational attacks on important seaports, first bombarding the oil tanks at Madras on September 22, then, a month later, entering Penang Harbour under a British flag, which he hauled down at the last moment as he torpedoed and sank first a Russian light cruiser, and then a French destroyer.

At this time Allied warships had been hunting the German raider. One of them, a Japanese cruiser, was deceived by Müller, who hoisted a dummy funnel and a White Ensign and pretended successfully to be the British cruiser *Hampshire*. After this, however, the captain of the raider made his fatal mistake, for he decided to attack the British cable station at Cocos Keeling to cut the cable. Before he could get his landing party ashore the signal station gave a warning which had been picked up by the mixed British, Australian and Japanese escort of an Australian troop convoy passing nearby. From this convoy H.M.A.S. *Sydney* was detached. She was considerably more powerful than the *Emden*, and the German raider was soon forced aground and surrendered. To this day, forty years later, her rusty hull can still be seen above the surface of the ocean. Her landing party, in a small and cranky sailing boat, made for Java, where they picked up a German merchant ship which had taken refuge there at the beginning of the war. They took this merchant ship and sailed to the coast of Arabia, where they contacted the nearest Turkish troops and made their way on camel back up the entire length of Arabia to Constantinople.

Another raider of 1914, whose wreck can still be seen, lies some miles up the Rufiji River in Tanganyika; this was the *Königsberg*, destroyed in her refuge after a brief career, in the course of which she sank the British light cruiser *Pegasus* and one merchant vessel.

To drive the *Königsberg* up the Rufiji had been the work of a great concentration of warships, and to destroy her once she was there was the work of some nine months, special shallow-draught monitors mounting the 6-inch guns being brought all the way from the United Kingdom. There two incidents in these operations were of interest; for very nearly the first time an aircraft was used for spotting the guns of the British ships as the *Königsberg* lay hidden in the vast mangrove swamps, and the second was the sinking of a blockship in the river so that there was no chance of the raider slipping out to sea while the monitors were on their way to the scene.

Finally, in July 1915 the raider was definitely out of action and her crew, with those guns of the ship which were still serviceable, set out to take part in the East African campaign.

The survivors from the *Königsberg* fought on, their numbers diminishing through death, disease and capture, but some of them survived at liberty until Lettow-Vorbeck's final surrender a fortnight after the Armistice and were sent back to Berlin as free men, where they met with a triumphant welcome in the dark days of March 1919, when the Berliners were recovering from a Communist coup d'état and getting nearer a Fascist one.

One other German light cruiser had three successful months commerce-raiding before being sunk by accident.

This was the *Karlsrühe*, which operated in the West Indies and that part of the Atlantic north of the Equator. Two days after the outbreak of war she had a narrow escape from British cruisers searching for her and only got away because her chief pursuer, the light cruiser *Bristol*, was not able to make her full speed.

34

The *Karlsrühe* was finally destroyed off Trinidad (B.W.I.) by an accidental explosion in her forward magazine which blew off her bows, so that she sank in a few minutes; casualties were heavy, as the explosion took place in the evening, during a standeasy, while a large number of the crew were on the forecastle listening to the ship's band.

The survivors were picked up by one of the *Karlsrühe's* prizes which was with her and taken back to Germany.

Apart from the warships which were already overseas at the beginning of the war, the Germans also had available for use as raiders a number of large and fast liners specially fitted for the purpose. Before war it had been planned to arm a large number of these, but in fact only one of these ships was sent to sea, and one, later in the war, as a minelayer. The others were laid in German or neutral ports. The reason for this was that, just as in 1939, the German authorities did not believe that England was going to declare war until it was too late for them to do anything about it. Accordingly the *Kaiser Wilhelm der Grosse,* the oldest of the big German Atlantic liners, was the only one of her type to appear, albeit very briefly, as a raider. Later, the *Berlin* was equipped as a minelayer, and laid the mines on which the brand-new battleship *Audacious* was lost in October 1914.

The latter success, of course, was worth far more to the Germans than all the time and trouble that they took preparing the raiders, but it was not the way in which it had been expected by either British or Germans that the big liners would be employed in wartime.

For twenty years or so before World War I it had been generally expected that in the next big naval war the large liners would be equipped as auxiliary cruisers—the German ships to raid commerce, the British ships to protect it. In those years, up to about 1905, the liners were much faster than any warships afloat except small craft such as destroyers and torpedo boats, and in the Russo-Japanese war the Japanese had used converted liners successfully for scouting purposes—the Russian fleet at Tsushima, for example, was first spotted by an armed liner operating as a cruiser on the fringes of Togo's fleet. But in the decade before 1914 warships increased greatly in speed through the introduction of the turbine; and whereas, when they were first built, the Cunard liners *Lusitania* and *Mauretania* were knots faster than the fastest cruiser likely to be able to sink them, by the time the war broke out this was no longer the case. Accordingly, although preparations had been made to equip them with fourteen 6-inch guns—the armament of a 10,000-ton cruiser of those days—it was soon clear that much smaller enemy vessels would be able to catch them and tear apart their great unarmoured steel sides with even the comparatively light armament which they carried.

In addition, these very large ships needed an enormous amount of coal; even if money were of no object, coaling these ships on the high seas was extremely difficult. Thus, it was that within a few weeks after the outbreak of war neither side was using their big liners as warships—the British transformed theirs into transports and hospital ships, and the Germans laid theirs up.

On the other hand, smaller merchant vessels were invaluable as warships; the British commissioned as auxiliary cruisers a great number of middle-sized and small liners, while the Germans took a number of inconspicuous freighters for use as commerce raiders—as they were to do in 1939–45.

However, before the Germans came finally to regard the larger liners as unsuitable for work as armed merchant raiders, four of them had been in operation between August 1914 and March 1915.

The *Kaiser Wilhelm der Grosse*, after her breakout from German home waters, had a comparatively short career of only three weeks off West Africa and the Canaries before she was sunk. One episode alone is noteworthy. Off Teneriffe on August 15 and 16 she stopped the British liners *Arlanza* and *Galician*, both carrying passengers. After dismantling their wireless so that they could not give the alarm they were allowed to proceed on the ground that the raider had nowhere to put the British passengers and crew. Setting people adrift in open boats or adopting a policy of "sunk without trace" was not considered possible in those days, but within a few months the Germans had begun the devaluation of international law with unrestricted submarine warfare and the bombardment of open towns, which has ended for the time being at least, in the International Military Tribunal at Nuremburg. However, although the unrestricted U-boat warfare in 1915–18 did produce a small number of people found guilty of war crimes by the Germans themselves, the captains and crews of the surface raiders of World War I came through the war with as clean a sheet as is possible for any group of fighting men in desperate war.

The *Kaiser Wilhelm der Grosse* was specially armed and sent out from Germany, but the other three liners received a very light armament while at sea from German warships, and although the armament of these raiders was very weak it was sufficient to stop an unarmed Allied merchant ship.

These liners were the *Cap Trafalgar* (18,710 tons), *Kronprinz Wilhelm* (14,908 tons) and *Prinz Eitel Friederich* (8,787 tons). The *Cap Trafalgar* was sunk in September 1914 by the British armed merchant cruiser *Carmania*, and the other two ships were interned by the Americans when, in the spring of 1915, they sought refuge in Newport News after having been at sea since the outbreak of the war.

The *Kaiser Wilhelm der Grosse* had had a much shorter career, being sunk off the Rio de Oro by the British light cruiser *Highflyer* on August 28, 1914. An interesting point of the conversion of the *Kronprinz Wilhelm* from a liner to a raider was that the work was carried out at sea, within two hours, by the liner's own crew and a party from the *Karlsrühe*.

In addition to these raiders there were two more which were interned in the Pacific by the Americans in the early stages of the war; these were the ex-Russian steamer *Ryazan*, converted into a German raider under the name of *Kormoran* by the *Emden*, and a sloop, the *Geier*.

While the raiders that had been at sea when war broke out were being sunk or driven to take refuge in neutral ports, the question arose as to how they were best to be replaced, and the idea of using conventional freighters, slow but inconspicuous and economical of fuel, was first put forward by a reserve lieutenant named Theodor Wolff, who was drowned shortly afterwards, but who goes down to history as the father of the armed merchant raiders of both world wars.

The first of these converted freighters was the famous *Möwe*, an ex-banana ship, which made two cruises—the first from December 1915 to March 1916, and the second from November 1916 to March 1917. Both cruises were for the most part in the southern and central Atlantic, but on the way out on her first cruise the *Möwe* laid mines off the north of Scotland on which the British battleship *King Edward VII* was lost.

The *Möwe's* two cruises were far surpassed in length by the single voyage of the *Wolf*, which was 445 days at sea, operating in the Atlantic, the Indian Ocean and the Pacific between November 1916 and February 1918.

Two other raiders, the *Greif* and *Leopard*, were sunk by British patrol forces on their way through the blockade lines—the *Greif* in February 1916, in an action in which her opponent, the British armed merchant cruiser *Alcantara*, was also sunk, and the *Leopard* in February 1917 by the cruiser *Achilles* and the armed boarding steamer *Dundee*.

I
Atlantis • SHIP 16

THE WINTER OF 1939–40 was of such extraordinary severity that the Second World War was nearly frozen stiff. Eleven times the great German offensive in the west had to be postponed because of the terrible weather. Air activity was at a minimum, and only at sea were British and French forces fully extended, by the handful of U-boats, by the German mining offensive and by operations of the raiding battleships and cruisers.

But bad weather had its effects on the naval war, also, for ice in the Baltic interfered with training and trials both of the new submarines and of the former merchant ships being fitted out as auxiliary cruisers.

The first of these, Ship 16—the *Atlantis*—was commissioned on December 19, 1939, but her trials were interrupted by ice and bad weather and she did not sail until March 31, a month later than intended. To get the raider out of the Baltic and into the North Sea it was necessary to send the former battleship *Hessen,* then serving as a radio-controlled target ship, to act as an ice-breaker. The *Hessen* had been launched in 1903, and had fought at Jutland, but her ageing plates and frame were still strong enough for the job. With some difficulty she forced a passage for herself, for the *Atlantis,* for Ship 21—the *Widder*—and for Ship 36—the *Orion*—which were also almost ready, into the North Sea. The month that had been lost by bad weather was very precious to the Germans, because by the time the ships were ready the Equinox had passed, and with it the long nights which would have given cover for the escape of the raiders into the Atlantic. In addition there was another point which worried the SKL. Usually the waters of the Far North are deserted, but soon the German attack on Norway was to begin and then the British Home Fleet would be drawn to the very waters through which the raiders were to escape, it had been hoped, unobserved.

The *Atlantis* got away less than a week before the German forces sailed, escorted by the submarine *U 37*. She was disguised as a Russian auxiliary warship, the *Krim*, with the seaplane on her deck painted with Russian markings, and with her crew in uniforms which, at a distance, at least, would pass muster as Russian.

Her troubles began at once; she missed her destroyer escort and set off in bad weather with *U 37* across the British convoy route to Scandinavia. German reconnaissance planes spotted three British cruisers in the neighbourhood which could only be avoided by the *Atlantis* heading north at full speed, but this the weather prevented. For four hours the raider crashed through heavy seas expecting the British to appear at any moment. Patrolling planes were sighted, and as it was not known whether they were British or German the ship's appearance was altered by setting two high masts, and she changed course to give the impression that she was heading for Murmansk.

The raider was helped on her way by a Do 26 of the Trans-Ocean Wing of the Luftwaffe and by weather ships disguised as fishing vessels, but the seas grew worse and her escorting U-boat began to ice up so that she had to return to her base.

Through blizzards and misty weather the *Atlantis* worked her way down the coast of Greenland, dodging the ships she sighted because she did not wish to draw attention to the fact that she was at large until she had reached her operational area. This, she learned on April 16, was to be the South Atlantic, while the *Orion* was assigned to the North Atlantic.

It was laid down by the SKL that as soon as the *Atlantis* had been sighted by the enemy or made her first sinking she would receive further orders, and in the same signal the SKL passed on information regarding British patrols and shipping which had been obtained from documents captured in Norway. By April 24–5 the *Atlantis* was in the area of the south-west trades and had crossed the equator; she had also redisguised herself, as there was no likelihood of a genuine

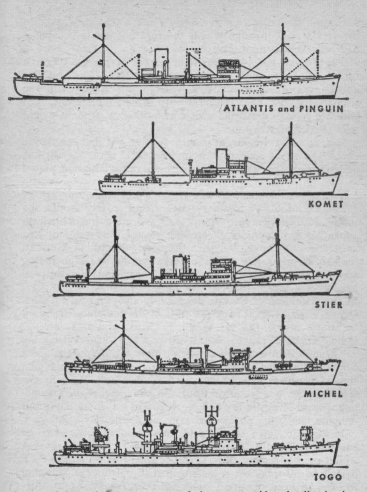

ATLANTIS and PINGUIN

KOMET

STIER

MICHEL

TOGO

A general idea of the appearance of the secret raiders in disguise is given by these sketches. The "Togo" is shown as a fighter-direction ship, to which she was converted after her unsuccessful attempt to break out from the Channel.

(The sketches are reproduced by courtesy of Dr. E. Groner Archiv fur Marine, Berlin)

Russian ship being in these waters. It had been originally intended to assume a Norwegian disguise, but "in view of the changed political circumstances," observed the ship's diary with reference to the German invasion of Norway, this was thought to be useless. A British disguise was also considered, but rejected, as the Germans did not have sufficient information about the paintwork, lights carried and general behaviour of British merchant vessels at sea in the South Atlantic. Accordingly the *Atlantis* became outwardly the Japanese *Kasii Maru*, of 8,400 tons, and steamed on southward.

The ship that now appeared as the *Kasii Maru* had begun life as the *Goldenfels* of the Hansa Line, a freighter of 7,860 gross tons. She was diesel-engined, which gave her a very great radius of action, and her cargo holds were packed with supplies of every kind; she had stowed on board 3,000 tons of oil, 1,200 tons of coal, 1,200 tons of fresh water and 400 tons of food. Concealed behind collapsible bulkheads which looked like part of her sides were six 5.9-inch guns, one 75-millimetre gun, six light anti-aircraft guns, and four torpedo tubes. This was the standard armament of almost all the raiders. The *Atlantis* also carried ninety-two mines, and a Heinkel 114 seaplane. Her crew consisted of nineteen officers (four to be sent away in charge of prizes) and 328 petty officers and men.

Her captain was Bernhard Rogge, an outstanding officer in the history of naval warfare. He was to keep to the sea in the *Atlantis* for 622 days, steaming 102,000 miles and sinking or capturing twenty-five ships. At the time of taking command of the *Atlantis* he was forty years old and had served in the German navy since 1915; comparatively early in his career he had specialised in the training of young officers and had commanded the German navy's two sail training ships, the *Gorch Fock* and the *Albert Leo Schlageter*.

On May 2 the *Atlantis*, being then on the fringes of the route from Capetown to Freetown, sighted what Rogge hoped to be her first victim, the Ellerman liner *City of Exeter*, but after consideration he decided not to attack—firstly, because he did not wish to embarrass himself at the outset of a cruise with prisoners from the British ship; and secondly, because he realised that the *City of Exeter* was sufficiently fast to delay her capture a long enough time to give the alarm. Accordingly there was no attack, and later on, in the log of another ship—the *City of Bagdad*, captured on July 11—Rogge found that the *City of Exeter* had in fact given the alarm, as her captain had considered the *Atlantis* to be suspicious.

After this disappointment, however, Rogge had only another day to wait before his first sinking, for on May 3 he sighted a grey-painted ship, carrying one gun aft, which he ordered to stop. The alarm was given below decks in the *Atlantis* by a siren, and the crew went to action stations.

Most of the members of the crew who had previously been allowed on deck had been small, dark men whose appearance, at a distance, would be in keeping with the ship's Japanese disguise. They wore scarves round their heads and sunglasses, and they had their shirt tails hanging out of their trousers. A few "passengers," including a "woman" with a pram, were allowed on the boatdeck, while officers on the bridge wore a minimum of merchant navy uniform. Everyone else was kept below.

Now, as Rogge ordered the strange ship to stop he hoisted the German flag, and when the enemy refused he opened fire. From a distance of about four kilometres the 5.9s of the *Atlantis* began to hit, first on the stern, then on the bridge, knocking out the wireless, and then amidships. The ship stopped and let off steam while the crew took to the boats, but not before the badly wounded wireless officer had given the alarm with the signal QQQ (meaning "I am being attacked by a disguised enemy merchant ship").[1] The damaged vessel was found to be British—the *Scientist*, 6,200 tons gross, bound from Durban to Liverpool with 2,500 tons of maize, 1,150 tons of chromium and 2,600 tons of wattle bark. She had been set on fire by the shells of the *Atlantis* and was now burning brightly in the falling twilight. The

[1] In addition to the QQQ alarm for an armed enemy merchantman and SSS for submarine attack RRR was used as an emergency call in the event of meeting an enemy surface warship.

fire could be seen for miles around, and to quench it quickly Rogge ordered the blazing ship to be torpedoed; the survivors were picked up. Only two members of the *Scientist's* crew lost their lives.

Rogge at once set himself to examine information derived from the *Scientist* and her survivors. He concluded that Allied merchant ships sailing by themselves had orders to keep as close to the coast as possible and to be fully blacked-out by night. He also observed what he had wanted to know before; the colour scheme for painting Allied merchant ships in these waters was: superstructure greyish-yellow, and hull grey or black.

After the *Scientist* had been sunk the *Atlantis* headed off on a course of 220° to lay mines off Cape Agulhas before the loss of the British ship became known. Prior to laying the mines she made a wide detour south of the Cape and then turned back to give the impression that she was coming from Australia. The weather was too good for minelaying, for Rogge realised that the wake of the German ship must have been visible for miles in the phosphorescent sea. Nevertheless the laying took place, though under conditions of some excitement, as stars down on the horizon were continually being mistaken for ships' lights. Fifty-five kilometres away the lighthouse at Cape Agulhas could be seen, at the southernmost tip of Africa.

It was now time for another disguise, and the raider became the Dutch steamer *Abbekerk*. As soon as the minefield had been laid Rogge's first concern was to get away as quickly as possible from an area in which he might be picked up by the reconnaissance planes of the South African Air Force. When he had done this he took up station along the route from Durban to Australia and ordered up his Heinkel. This plane gave trouble throughout her life, and on this occasion—her first attempted flight—her engine fell out. Rogge remembered that he had tried hard to get Arado 196's instead of the Heinkels when he was fitting out.

Finally, the plane was repaired and got in the air, and for days found nothing—the Durban-Australia route had been moved to the south. Rogge then went to a point which he believed to be the intersection of the routes between Durban and Batavia and Fremantle and Mauritius, and there, on June 10, they sighted the first ship that they had seen for five weeks.

This was the Norwegian *Tirrana*, of 7,230 tons, who made off with the *Atlantis* in chase, firing as hard as she could. Her first hit was only scored after seven salvos and then thirty-two more were necessary—150 rounds in all—before the Norwegian stopped. She was found to be on her way from Mombasa to the United Kingdom, via Suez, with a cargo of wheat, flour and wool. Five of her people had been killed by the *Atlantis'* shells.

A German crew was put on board, but it was found that the prize did not have sufficient fuel to enable her to be sailed back to Germany, and for six weeks she waited at an ocean rendezvous while the *Atlantis* tried to capture a loaded tanker. When Rogge had to give up hope of doing this he placed on board her the 126 prisoners he had taken and sent her to Italian Somaliland.

Once the *Tirrana* was out of sight with her prisoners, who might one day be liberated and tell what they had seen, the *Atlantis* was painted dark-brown all over. This it was hoped would make her resemble a Dutch or Norwegian ship under Allied control.

While looking for the tanker she could not find, the *Atlantis* picked up a message on June 19 from Radio Australia stating that the steamer *Niagara* of 13,000 tons, had been sunk by a mine off Auckland. Rogge knew that the only mines in those waters must have come from Ship 36, Commander Weyher's *Orion*. Having got as far as Auckland, via the Horn, she had presumably passed on into the Indian Ocean (since nothing had been heard to the contrary), and this meant that the *Atlantis, Orion* and Ship 33 (*Pinguin*) were now all working in the Indian Ocean. Up to a point it could be said that that vast sea was getting overcrowded, with three raiders in it at the same time. Rogge reduced speed to barely steerage way, and at five knots idled through the long swell where the routes from Sundra, Mauritius and the Cape met.

At last, on July 11, a ship came in sight. Rogge let her pass and then followed her, keeping just on the horizon. His reason for this delay was that there were internationally recognized periods in which the coastal stations were to listen with particular care for S O S messages on the 600-metre band, and he did not want to attack during one of these times.

At the proper time he increased speed and closed to attack. He waited until he was about two miles away, then dropped his disguise and opened fire.

His opponent at once sent out an S O S, adding that she was being shelled. An American vessel picked this up and asked who was shelling her, whereupon *Atlantis* made QRU —meaning "Nothing for you to worry about". The American then rejoined, telling the *Atlantis* to stop wirelessing, as it was clear that the QRU had not come from the same ship that had sent the S O S. *Atlantis* then signalled "Nothing happening," and by that time, with her fourth salvo, she had put out of action the wireless of the ship she was chasing. This ship then stopped; she was the British *City of Bagdad*, of 7,506 tons, with a cargo of 9,300 tons of steel, chemicals and machinery. The Germans got extra satisfaction from this capture as the *City of Bagdad* had been the German *Geierfels*, taken as a prize.

It was now clear to Rogge that the British authorities had ordered that ships attacked should get through an S O S at all costs—this was something that was not altogether unwelcome to the Germans, as many S O Ss were false alarms and added considerably to the general confusion of the situation.

The *City of Bagdad* was sunk, but on July 20, nine days later, by which time the British ship was overdue at Penang, a general warning was issued that a warship or U-boat was operating 500 miles off Dondra Head, the southernmost point of Ceylon. This was the first warning given, so that apparently the *Atlantis'* intervention in the exchange of signals between the *City of Bagdad* and the American ship had thrown the latter off the scent. Rogge, of course, did not wait to be sure of this, but headed away at once towards the south of the Straits of Malacca, where he picked up what he hoped would be the route towards South Africa. Here he cruised, heading west.

The *Atlantis* had only two days to wait, for on July 13 she came up with another British ship and opened fire. The British ship replied with a single gun, but the *Atlantis* was able to overwhelm her almost at once, and set her on fire, finally torpedoing her. She was the *Kemmendine*, of 7,769 tons, from Glasgow and the Cape of Rangoon with a small cargo of whiskey and beer. Clearly British commercial exports were getting fewer, and many ships were having to leave the United Kingdom empty, or almost empty, to pick up the cargoes abroad which were necessary for carrying on the war.

Up to this time Rogge had not used his wireless to communicate with Germany for fear that it might provide the British with a directional bearing, but now the SKL ordered him to get in touch with them in order to help in the briefing of other raiders.

What the SKL required was the location of the ship reporting, her state of operational readiness, details of her successes and any special experiences which she had had. It was considered that the danger of a directional bearing being taken in the middle of the ocean was negligible, but in any case the risk, such as it was, was taken in vain, for a signal then sent by the *Atlantis* and consisting of sixty groups did not get through to the station at Norddeich in Germany, and it was not until five months later that the *Atlantis* was able to get news of herself home.

After disposing of the *Kemmendine*, Rogge planned to cruise from south to north where four routes crossed—Malacca to East Africa, Australia to Aden, Sunda to Mombasa, and Durban to Mauritius and Colombo—but a well-protected convoy was reported in the neighbourhood, and the *Atlantis* moved on.

The German ship now had 339 prisoners on board living in the holds of a cargo vessel cruising along the Equator, but by this time the *Tirrana* had returned from her trip to Italian Somaliland, where she had left the first batch of prisoners, and Rogge decided to send her to German-occupied

47

France with the prisoners he had since taken, although, to enable the *Tirrana* to get home, would mean having to give up 450 tons of fuel.

While the prisoners were being transferred from the *Atlantis* by boat the raider was slowly moving ahead through fog and driving rain. Only one of her engines was working, the other being under repair. A ship suddenly appeared from out of the squall, and disappeared again. The *Atlantis* followed her, found her again and after four salvoes and six minutes of chase she surrendered. She was the Norwegian *Talleyrand*, of 6,731 tons, on her way from Sydney to England with 16,000 bales of wool, 22,686 sacks of wheat, 240 tons of teak, and 4,500 tons of steel. Her crew numbered thirty-six, all Norwegians and one of them a woman. The *Talleyrand* was armed with a single 4.7-inch gun, and as the *Tirrana* was similarly armed, the ammunition was transferred to her.

There was not enough oil in the *Talleyrand's* tanks for her to go back to France with the *Tirrana*, but what oil she had was transferred to the *Atlantis*, with a gain to the raider of an extra two months' endurance. The *Tirrana* sailed for St. Nazaire, her upper deck still carrying a cargo of motor cars.

During this time the *Atlantis* was continuously exercising her aircraft, which dropped dummy bombs and practised diving on the ship and tearing away her radio aerial with a trailing grapnel.

So far the *Atlantis* had sunk four ships of 28,205 tons, and captured one of 7,230 tons; by August 11 she was finished with her repairs, and was now in the *Pinguin's* area. Perhaps surprisingly, she remained there instead of moving out to the north or north-east of the Indian Ocean to produce a diversionary effect. Early on the morning of August 25, being 200 miles north of Rodriguez, she sighted a strange ship, clearly outlined against the brightening sky and steaming very slowly. The *Atlantis* opened fire and the ship stopped without an alarm signal being heard. She was the *King City*, of 4,744 tons, carrying 7,300 tons of coal from Cardiff to Singapore. The reason for her slow speed was found to be a defect in her boiler-room ventilation. This ship was scuttled.

As the *King City* had not used her wireless successfully there was no immediate reason why the *Atlantis* should leave the area in which she was operating, but in fact a few days later Rogge decided to head eastwards. On August 27 he intercepted an S O S from the British tanker *British Commander,* fairly near by, saying that she had been stopped by an unidentified vessel, and Rogge guessed this to be the *Pinguin.*

On September 9 the *Atlantis* picked up the *Athelking,* of 9,700 tons, on her way from Australia to East Africa, and attacked her. The British ship refused to stop and the *Atlantis* sent ninety-one shells after her before she hove to, her captain dead and her hull so badly damaged that it was impossible for the *Atlantis* to take on any of her oil. During this chase the wireless signals of another ship had been heard close at hand, and on the next day this other ship was sighted by the German's seaplane, heading away as fast as she could go, having picked up the *Athelking's* S O S. The seaplane went into action with bombs and machine-guns, putting the wireless out of action and driving the crew to take cover, so that the *Atlantis* was able to come up unseen, just as the native crew of the chased ship abandoned the engine room in confusion. The ship was the *Benarty,* of 5,800 tons, carrying wolfram, lead, teak, rice and leather. She was sunk by explosive charges.

In the waste-paper basket of the wrecked wireless room of the British ship various scraps of paper were found which made it possible for the Germans to read part of the new British merchant navy code which had, on August 19, replaced that taken in a ship attacked earlier.

After sinking the *Benarty* Rogge realised he would have to shift his cruising station once more. According to the war diary of the *Atlantis,*[1] Rogge felt that his sinkings and those of the *Pinguin* had compromised the whole of the Indian Ocean, and accordingly he headed south-east, taking care

[1] Throughout the book quotations from the war diaries of raiders are taken from the SKL records and appreciations of the respective cruises (see p. 180).

not to meet the *Pinguin* lest the two ships, both disguised as Allied vessels, might take each other for enemies.

On September 19 the *Atlantis* sighted a blacked-out ship. Rogge was anxious to capture her intact so that he could send his prisoners home, but she refused to stop, gave the alarm and was set on fire by the guns of the German raider. Her crew abandoned ship, and the vessel sank.

"The red-hot hull going down in a cloud of flames and steam presented an extraordinarily impressive spectacle," observes the raider's war diary. The ship was the French *Commissaire Ramel,* of 10,061 tons belonging to the Messageries Maritimes and the biggest ship that the *Atlantis* had sunk up to that time. Her crew were mostly Australian, with a few members of her original French complement; her cargo was steel, wheat, soap, leather and fruit.

Strictly speaking, this sinking had been done outside Rogge's area, but it would seem that throughout the cruise he never felt under any obligation to refrain from what was, in a way, poaching.

For a fortnight after this the *Atlantis* hove to, overhauling and redisguising. While this was going on Rogge learned that his prize, the *Tirrana,* had been lost within sight of home; not only could the ship have been fitted out as an armed merchant-cruiser herself, but with her went the mail, reports and requests from the *Atlantis*—the first mail the crew had been able to send home since sailing six months before, and reports which gave details of the experience of this new form of warfare as well as requests for supplies to be sent from Germany to the *Atlantis* by blockade runners. The loss of the *Tirrana* was heartbreaking and quite unnecessary. Lieutenant Waldmann, who had been in command of the prize, had called Norddeich repeatedly as he approached Spanish waters, but he received no reply. He did hear, however, that the British were making air attacks on the principal Biscay ports, as well as laying mines in their offing. Accordingly he tried to find a suitable small port in the south of France from which he could report and ask for orders. With this in mind he stopped a French fishing vessel and made her take him to Arcachon, whence he telephoned to Bordeaux, receiving instructions to make for the Gironde. On the way the *Tirrana* was torpedoed by the British submarine *Tuna*, capsized and sank within two minutes. Sixty prisoners, including women and children, lost their lives.

After receiving this news, Rogge took stock of his situation after six months at sea. He had steamed 32,000 miles, and he had used up 47.5 per cent of his fuel and 61 per cent of his provisions; this meant that he could keep the seas for seven months longer without reprovisioning.

On October 22, watching the Straits of Sunda, he stopped the Jugoslav steamer *Durmitor*, of 5,623 tons, and although Jugoslavia was at that time still neutral he put a prize crew on board and sent her off with prisoners to Italian Somaliland, with her cargo of 8,200 tons of unprocessed salt, which had been on its way from Spain to Japan. Her trip to the temporary safety of Italian East Africa was a horrible one. She was short of coal, so that her maximum speed was five knots, and, says the official German report, "there was a necessary disregard of humane considerations." The 313 prisoners lived on top of the salt in the holds, with very little water to drink, and none to wash with, and the ship was infested with vermin. To help move the vessel sails were set every night between the mainmast and the funnel, but were taken down in the daytime, because it was thought that the sight of a steamship crossing the Indian Ocean under sail would arouse curiosity in any passing Allied vessel.

What coal there was was very bad, and all the boilers but one leaked; the miserable prisoners tried to persuade the commander of the prize crew to make for a neutral port, but he refused. The prisoners in these shocking conditions also appear to have quarrelled amongst themselves, which aided the Germans in maintaining order. By the time that twenty-five days had passed since the *Durmitor's* parting from the *Atlantis*, the former had no more coal, food or water and was still not in sight of the coast of Somaliland; all the wood in the ship, including barrels, hatch covers and derrick beams, had been sawed into small bits with the only handsaw on board. A compound of ash, coal, sawdust, asphalt, paint, paraffin, and lubricating oil was used as fuel. To make things

51

worse, the ship was not able to enter Mogadishu, the nearest Italian port, as it had recently been bombarded from the sea by the British and was considered to be probably blockaded as well. Accordingly the ship beached herself at Warsheik, north of Mogadishu, where it was possible to lay hands on about four hundredweight of coal, and about a quarter of a ton of beans—but there was no water. However, this tiny quantity of coal sufficed to get the ship to Kismayu, where a few months later she was captured by the British.

For weeks after Rogge had taken the *Durmitor* he could hear her being called anxiously from Hong Kong, Singapore and Colombo.

On November 1 the *Atlantis* left the Straits of Sunda and headed into the Bay of Bengal. On the night of the 8th–9th she sighted a camouflaged tanker; she herself was disguised at this time as the British armed merchant-cruiser *Antenor,* and the tanker did not discover the ruse until the German boarding party was alongside. The tanker was the *Teddy,* of 6,750 tons, a Norwegian vessel carrying 10,000 tons of fuel oil and 500 tons of diesel oil from Abadan to Singapore. The prize crew took her away 500 miles to the southward to wait for a favourable time to replenish the tanks of the *Atlantis.*

Immediately after this, in the bright moonlight another tanker was sighted. The *Atlantis* again claimed to be H.M.S. *Antenor* and ordered the tanker to stop. This newcomer gave her name as *Ole Jacob* and did stop, but at the same time sent out a message saying that she was being held up, and giving her position.

A boarding party led by an English-speaking officer then took over the ship, which was found to be carrying 9,274 tons of aviation spirit from Singapore to Suez. The *Atlantis* sent out a radio message cancelling the *Ole Jacob's* alarm, and then the next morning sent her off to join the *Teddy.*

Having stopped the *Teddy* on the 9th, and the *Ole Jacob* on the 10th, a third prize came the way of the *Atlantis* on the 11th, when, in the morning, she sighted a Blue Funnel liner. On being challenged, the liner sent out an S O S which was picked up by a coastal station, but for some unexplained reason it was not passed on until the evening, after it had been coded—a process which entailed a further waste of time.

The *Atlantis* opened fire and her first salvo hit the liner, killing the captain and everyone else on the bridge. Because of this the secret papers on board were not destroyed, and fell into the hands of the boarding party. The ship was the *Automedon,* of 7,528 tons, on her way from Liverpool to Penang, Singapore and Shanghai. She was carrying aircraft, cars, machinery, textiles, cigarettes, provisions and mails. The *Atlantis* took on board fresh provisions, cigarettes, whisky, the mail and the crew of ninety-three men, together with three passengers, one of whom was a woman. The *Automedon* was then blown up, and on November 11 the *Atlantis'* score stood at thirteen ships of 93,805 tons.

All the oil that the *Atlantis* could stow was now taken from the *Teddy* for subsequent use, and the Norwegian ship then set on fire. Commenting on this, the SKL appreciation of the *Atlantis* cruise makes one of its very few criticisms of Rogge, describing the sinking as a mistake as long as there was any chance of getting the *Teddy* back to a German-held port, or passing on her oil to another ship. The quantity of oil concerned, the staff appreciation points out, would have made the *Orion* independent for the rest of her cruise.

The sinking was also a mistake from an immediate point of view, for the ship burned with a huge fire which could be seen for miles around—a sight, says the war diary of the *Atlantis,* "most impressive but utterly unwelcome."

Rogge's defence against these criticisms would appear to have been that he could not spare another prize crew, as the *Ole Jacob* had to be sent to Japan with urgent dispatches, including the secret documents found in the *Automedon.*

Although Japan was at that time still neutral, the *Ole Jacob* was able to use Japanese ports as though they had been her own; she exchanged her cargo of fuel oil with the Japanese for diesel oil and eventually made her way back to Bordeaux in July 1941.

Meanwhile, the *Atlantis* headed for the Far South, to the Kerguelen, replenishing on her way from another captured Norwegian tanker, the *Storstad,* taken by the *Pinguin.* She also met the latter ship for an exchange of information and ideas. When the *Atlantis* had exchanged fuel oil for diesel oil orders were received from the SKL for a new division of operational areas. After overhauling, the *Atlantis* was to enter the Arabian Sea; the *Pinguin* was to raid Australian waters to the eastward; Ship 45, the *Komet,* was to attack in West Australian waters; Ship 36, the *Orion,* was to go home, after an unhappy cruise; and Ship 41, the *Kormoran,* the first ship of the second wave of raiders, was to begin operations west of Freetown and then come round the Cape into the Indian Ocean.

On December 9 Rogge learned that he had been awarded the Knight's Cross of the Iron Cross and he began preparations for a long overhaul in remote Kerguelen, where nobody seemed to have been since the French gunboat *Bougainville* had called there in February 1939. Prospects for water and shelter appeared good, and on December 14 Rogge took his ship into Gazelle Bay. As he did so she ran aground on the steep-to rocks. His first attempts to get her off failed, and divers sent down reported holes in the forepeak and the forward compartments of the double bottom. Finally, after thirty hours of hard work, the ship was kedged off after listing her from side to side and running her engines full speed ahead and astern to try to shake her loose

The raider stayed twenty-six days in Gazelle Bay, an air reconnaissance having shown the island to be completely uninhabited. A regular watch was kept to seaward and a gunnery fire-control position was set up ashore, so that if necessary the ship's guns could fire over the mountains at an approaching enemy without the ship herself being seen.

Much work was done during these days; the ship was overhauled, repainted, her disguise changed and the damage suffered on grounding was repaired. Despite this every member of the crew was given a chance to go ashore—for the first time since March, nine months previously. Once landed, they hunted rabbits and duck, and collected sea-shells and Kerguelen cabbage. A pipeline half a mile long was rigged from a waterfall to the ship to supply drinking water, and

Christmas was celebrated with a great party at which every member of the crew received a present, most of them coming from a share-out of the booty taken in the *Automedon*.

Two weeks' uninterrupted diving was necessary to repair underwater damage; several yards had been torn off the central plate of the keel and the bottom of the ship dented over an area of about 100 square feet. The underwater oxy-acetylene cutter was out of commission, so that the damaged plates had to be drilled piece by piece and then pulled off by the ship's capstan, while a paravane spar was used to take the place of the missing part of the keel. It was typical of Rogge that he himself put on a diving suit and kept an eye on the operations, which were finally finished on January 11th, when the *Atlantis*, disguised as the Norwegian freighter *Tamesis*, set sail once more. As she got out into the open sea there were a few moments of concern, but it was soon clear that in average weather, at least, the damage the ship had received did not affect her seaworthiness. However Rogge knew that things might be different in really bad weather and accordingly asked if he might take his ship to Japan for dry-docking.

This request was refused by the SKL on the ground that it was politically inadvisable to use Japan as a base at that time, and Rogge was told either to operate in the South Atlantic or to come home to Germany, depending on the degree of seaworthiness of his ship; in any case, he was told, his stay in the South Atlantic would be short, and would be considered as a stage on the journey home.

However, before starting for the South Atlantic there was one more operation Rogge wanted to attempt in the Indian Ocean. In the secret papers taken from the *Automedon* there were details of the route being taken by Allied merchant shipping between the Mozambique Channel and Singapore, and on this route Rogge proposed to cruise.

On January 23 he flew off his plane on a reconnaissance flight which revealed a vessel about sixty miles away. As the *Atlantis* came up towards her she turned away. Following her, the raider was barely able to keep her in sight, with her funnel and masts just on the horizon.

Then came some delicate manœuvring. The position of the sun and the general visibility made it difficult to keep the enemy in sight. If all had gone well the *Atlantis* would have waited for an attack until she could see her opponent silhouetted against the evening sky, but this was not possible and in the dark the *Atlantis* unknowingly passed her prey.

As soon as it was light Rogge decided that, as they were nearing the Seychelles, he must attack without the refinements of a long stalk which would enable him to come right up to the enemy without arousing his suspicions. Accordingly the plane was flown off, and diving down out of the sun tore away the merchant ship's aerial and bombed and straffed her decks. The ship replied with an anti-aircraft gun. The *Atlantis* came up at full speed and at a range of about 8,500 yards opened fire. Just as she did so the merchant ship, having rigged a spare aerial, sent out the QQQ alarm, which was, however, not understood ashore in the Seychelles. After eight hits the ship—identified from her distress signals as the British S.S. *Mandasor*—was fiercely afire, and her crew of nineteen British and sixty-three Indians abandoned ship. As they did so the seaplane landed alongside the lifeboats; she damaged one of her floats, turned slowly over and sank. The *Atlantis* picked up her crew, as well as the survivors of the *Mandasor* (two Britons and four Indians lost their lives), who said that their ship had been carrying 2,000 tons of pig iron and 1,800 tons of tea from Calcutta to the United Kingdom.

Meanwhile Seychelles radio was vainly asking for a repetition of the *Mandasor's* QQQ. Although the radio station was unable to understand exactly what was going on, there was sufficient suspicion ashore for a signal to be sent to the steamer *Tantalus* warning her to change course. In view of the alarm having thus been given, Rogge decided to move against the tanker route from the Persian Gulf.

The next sighting report was on January 27, when he was informed from the look-out that the British liner *Queen Mary*, of 83,000 tons, was in sight. This was the biggest prize possible for a German commerce raider, but Rogge had to admit to himself there was nothing that he could do about it—first, because the *Queen Mary's* speed was so much greater than his own that she could easily escape, and second, because she was almost certainly steaming under a heavy escort which would be able to stand off and destroy the *Atlantis*. So the German ship turned away. In fact the *Queen Mary* was not in the neighbourhood at this time, and the ship seen by the *Atlantis* was probably a smaller three-funnel liner which would also have been fast enough to have a good chance of escape had the *Atlantis* attacked.

So Rogge went on to his tanker route, zig-zagging across it in great wide sweeps. The weather was ideal for air reconnaissance and he bitterly regretted the loss of his seaplane.

On January 31, by night, the *Atlantis* came up with the British ship *Speybank*, of 5,154 tons, and captured her before she could send any message. The ship was carrying manganese ore, carpets, tea and shellac from Cochin to New York. She had so much of value on board that Rogge sent her away with a prize crew and told her to rendezvous with him later, finally sending her home as a prize on March 21. The *Speybank*, on her return to Europe, was converted by the Germans to an auxiliary minelayer, under the name of *Doggerbank*, and was sunk, in error, by a U-boat in March 1943.

On the day after the *Speybank* was taken another ship was sighted, a Blue Funnel liner, advancing out of a squall. But the British ship *Troilus* was keeping an excellent look-out and saw the German. She turned away, reporting a suspicious ship. The *Atlantis* turned to follow her on a parallel course over the horizon, but the *Troilus* outsailed her and got clean away. The vital importance of a good look-out is clear, but it would seem that in most cases the German warships were able to do much better than the Allied merchant vessels.

At about this time the Germans learned that the British Admiralty had laid down that every ship's captain had the duty to send out warning signals in the event of his being attacked or sighting anything suspicious, even if by so doing

57

he endangered his ship or crew. At the same time, according to German intelligence sources, the need for better look-outs was being emphasised, routes were being moved into the shelter of coasts and aircraft escorts and auxiliary cruisers were becoming increasingly available.

On the night following the escape of the *Troilus* another attack in the dark was made. Fire was opened on a tanker, which hove to immediately. As she did not make any signals, shelling was stopped, but in the meantime the main steam pipe of the attacked ship had been damaged; this shut off all the lighting in the ship, and amidst the bursting of the shells, the darkness and the shrieks of escaping steam, panic broke out amongst the Chinese crew who flung themselves overboard.

The ship was the Norwegian tanker *Ketty Broevig*, of 7,031 tons, carrying 6,370 tons of fuel oil and 4,125 tons of diesel oil from Bahrein to Lourenco Marques. In the morning the damaged steam pipe was repaired, and with a prize crew on board the tanker was sent off to a rendezvous with her captor, which was to take place on February 18.

At this stage the SKL once more communicated with the *Atlantis*, ordering her to meet the supply ship *Tannenfels*. Rogge acknowledged this order and reported that he was ready "to make use of ability to remain at sea as long as possible."

He also asked for a meeting with the pocket battleship *Scheer*, which had been at sea since October 31, and with the *Kormoran;* the *Speybank* was to go home, while the *Ketty Broevig* was to help the *Pinguin* in minelaying operations off the coast of Australia.

Rogge met the *Tannenfels* and gave her what supplies he could spare, and also refuelled the Italian submarine *Perla*, which, like the *Tannenfels*, had left a Somali port on the approach of the British forces; at the same time, Rogge learned that another German supply ship, the *Uckermark*, had also left Kismayu and had headed for Diego Suarez, in Vichy-controlled Madagascar.

On February 11 there was a meeting between the *Atlantis*, *Tannenfels*, *Ketty Broevig* and *Speybank*, and the four ships lay peacefully together far out in the Indian Ocean; to join them there soon arrived the *Scheer*. This meeting between the pocket battleship, the armed merchant cruiser, and the three supply ships represented the biggest numerical concentration of German warships ever seen during World War II outside European waters.

The ships worked together from February 17 to 25, *Atlantis* searching to south and east, while the *Scheer* operated to the south-westward. All that the *Atlantis* found was a Japanese ship, and two Vichy-French submarines, the *Pegase* and *Monge*, escorted by the supply ship *Lot*. By February 23 Krancke, captain of the *Scheer*, and Rogge apparently came to the conclusion that the area in which they were operating was an unprofitable one. This, comments the SKL's appreciation of the operations of the ships, was unfortunate, as the *Scheer* and the *Atlantis* together "could have alarmed the whole of India," as well as led the enemy to believe that an elaborate diversion had been staged to relieve the pressure on Italian Somaliland. At this stage the SKL reflected on what they called the "acute lack of success of the auxiliary cruisers" due to the difficulties of re-equipping and refuelling.

On February 25, after the *Scheer* and *Atlantis* had separated to southward, they were to have met again, but all that Rogge found at the rendezvous was a prize belonging to the *Scheer*—the tanker *British Advocate*. The *Scheer* was steaming away from the Indian Ocean as fast as she could, after having sighted British aircraft and having learned that two British cruisers, the *Canberra* and *Leander*, had been seen to the east of Madagascar. After this, the *Scheer* went straight home to Germany, where she arrived on April 1.

The *Scheer* had a fairly adventurous war, both on the oceans and in home waters, and her career did not finally come to an end until she was sunk by bombing at Kiel on April 9, 1945. For some time after the war she lay on the bottom of a corner of the harbour, upside-down, with her dull-red bottom lying out of the water like a basking shark, but in the reconstruction of Kiel it was decided to fill in the dock where she lay with rubble, which was piled over and around the sunken ship, so that now she lies unseen and upside-down in the middle of dry land.

There was a final rendezvous of the *Atlantis*, the *Speybank*, the *Ketty Broevig* and the *British Advocate*, and then the ships went their respective ways. The *British Advocate* was sent back to Bordeaux, where she arrived safely on April 29; and the *Ketty Broevig*, together with another German fugitive, the *Coburg*, from Massowa, was picked up by the *Canberra* and *Leander* as the result of a clue let fall by the Italian authorities.

Then came the news that the *Pinguin* had been caught and sunk by the British cruiser *Cornwall*, not very far away, as distances go in the Indian Ocean. It was now necessary to refuel the *Perla* again, so that the *Atlantis* had to wait at her rendezvous while the *Speybank*, with a prize crew on board, acted as a scouting vessel until she left for Bordeaux. Meanwhile the *Atlantis* and the tanker *Nordmark* had been refuelling the *Perla* and three other Italian submarines on their way home from Somaliland to Europe—the *Archimede, Guiglielmotti* and *Ferraris*—giving them fuel oil, lubricating oil, water, rations and cigarettes. After this had been done, an understanding on identification was reached with the Italian naval authorities so that there was no danger of the submarines sinking any of the raiders or their auxiliaries.

On March 31 the *Atlantis* had been at sea a year and received a message of congratulations and good wishes from Raeder. She was now cruising off the Mozambique Channel without seeing anything, so that Rogge deplored even more the loss of his aircraft. However, one small piece of good fortune came his way on April 5, when he sighted the Vichy-French transport *Chenonceaux*, which he knew would soon report meeting him. He was anxious that he should be reported because he was leaving the Indian Ocean, and he hoped that the British would continue to believe him there.

As Rogge steamed away he reflected on what he had learned during his eleven months' stay in the Indian Ocean, and reflected, too, on what the British had learned and the measures they had taken to confound him.

First, there was the much greater use of diversive routing —as far as he could see all the traffic between the United Kingdom and Australia was now going via Panama—and there were many lesser changes which took Allied shipping out of his reach, but which meant at the same time that Allied merchant ships were taking longer on their journeys and using more fuel. Clearly British warships were being pinned down on convoy duties, but Rogge did not believe that any ships other than transports were being escorted. The growing suspicion and vigilance of Allied ships sailing alone made daylight attacks very difficult; in future, Rogge concluded, he would in most cases have to attack at night, without warning. Shots across the bows now meant that the ship attacked had time to send an alarm.

Hitherto it had been Rogge's practice to fire first with his 75-Millimetre gun which was mounted aft, or with a single 5.9, then to fire with a half-broadside of 5.9s, and only after that with all the guns which would bear. This routine would now take up too much time, and it was also clear that it would no longer be possible to chase an enemy which was out of range, for the time needed to get within range would enable the ship he was chasing to give the alarm. Rogge laid down new instructions for engaging the enemy, but he was careful to stipulate that there should be no more firing than was necessary to destroy the enemy wireless; after that had been done the enemy was to be given a chance to surrender.

Rogge noted that by now he had disposed of sixteen ships of 111,132 tons, at a cost to his enemies of only thirty-three persons killed as compared with 917 taken prisoner. He had used up 104 per cent of his original provision of oil, 167 per cent of his water and 65 per cent of his coal.

On April 8, rounding the Cape of Good Hope, he was once again in the South Atlantic. His first duty was to meet a whole series of supply ships. There was the *Alsterufer*, from Hamburg, and the *Dresden*, which had broken out of Santos, had been refuelling the *Scheer*, and now had little food left. In addition there was the *Nordmark*, which had also been attending the *Scheer* as well as U-boats, and the

Babitonga, which had been at Santos since September 3, 1939.

On April 17, at four o'clock in the morning, the *Atlantis* sighted the silhouette of a steamer in the moonlight; by first light the steamer had the appearance of a Bibby liner, and the *Atlantis* opened fire without warning at about 9,200 yards. The first salvo missed, but the second hit, knocking out the wireless room; altogether there were six hits.

Within a short time the ship was recognised as the *Zamzam,* of 8,299 tons, or the Egyptian merchant fleet, and therefore technically neutral. She had previously been the Bibby liner *Leicestershire,* and a kind of a floating trade fair called *British Exhibitor.* On board her were a crew of 107 and 202 passengers, who presented special complications, for 140 of them were Americans, including members of the British-American Ambulance Corps on their way to the Middle East. One hundred and fifty of the passengers were missionaries, and altogether on the passenger list there were seventy-seven women and thirty-two children. Rogge's most immediate problem was to save the passengers' lives, for, according to his war diary, the passengers were either still on board the sinking ship or were swimming about in the sea.

Everybody was picked up and put on board the *Dresden,* the only casualties being three people badly wounded. The cargo the *Zamzam,* it was discovered, consisted of lubricating oil, fertilisers, steel, radio sets, typewriters and cosmetics.

From April 19 to 25 the *Atlantis* and the *Kormoran* refuelled and replenished together from the *Alsterufer* and the *Nordmark,* and three eagerly awaited aircraft were taken on board the *Atlantis.* The replenishment was interrupted by the appearance at another rendezvous of the *Perla,* once again in need of supplies. When she had been attended to, the *Dresden,* with her prisoners on board, was sent by order of the SKL to St. Jean de Luz. One of the prisoners managed to bring with him a photograph of the *Atlantis* which he had taken and which after its appearance in an American magazine was to play an important part in the subsequent story of the raider.

Now Rogge found himself in an area from which he could

attack ships running between Freetown and Capetown, Trinidad and Fernando Noronha, as well as tankers bound from the West Indies to Freetown; for this purpose his ship was now disguised as the Dutch motor vessel *Brastigi*.

The new aircraft sighted their first ship on May 1, but she was lost when the *Atlantis* tried to intercept her. As Rogge had expected, the Arado planes proved much more useful than had the Heinkel, for they were smaller, which meant a shorter take-off, and they had a higher speed.

On May 14 the *Atlantis* came up with the *Rabaul*, of 5,618 tons, from the United Kingdom to Capetown with coal, and shelled her, so that she sank in flames. Four of her crew were killed and three wounded.

Despite another oiling from the *Babitonga*, Rogge decided to stop his engines to save fuel, and on May 17 lay drifting on the fringe of the route from Freetown to Capetown, as he had found it marked on a captured British chart.

The ability to drift without using any fuel, while at the same time being able to start up the engines again at once was an enormous advantage which diesel-engined raiders had over those driven by steam, for the latter had to keep their fires going all the time if there was any prospect of action.

Past midnight on the night of the 17th it was all quiet, for there was not even the noise of the engines. Two large ships, completely blacked-out, were seen coming through the fine night directly towards the *Atlantis*. Rogge ordered the engines started—slowly, to avoid showing sparks from the funnel. A moderate trade wind was blowing.

"There was a slight haze and a huge moon in its first quarter shed its light through broken clouds," says the war diary.

The two ships were clearly large warships. They "loomed higher and higher, and their bow waves were clearly visible. The leading ship was a battleship of the *Nelson* type, and with her was an old aircraft-carrier of the *Eagle* type," continues the war diary.

It seemed impossible to get away; but the moon was behind the British ships, and the *Atlantis* stood against a dark and hazy sector of the horizon. Slowly she increased speed, keeping her stern towards the enemy, and moved away, while the British ships passed at a distance of about 7,000 yards. An hour later they had disappeared over the horizon.

At exactly this moment one of the motor exhausts burned out. The *Atlantis* stopped, and then moved off slowly to the S.S.W., taking care not to follow on the reciprocal course of the British ships in case other units were following them.

On May 21 a Greek ship was attacked at night; on being shelled, she stopped and stated that she was under charter to Switzerland. Having verified this, Rogge let her go on condition that she did not use her wireless.

Two days later another ship was sighted at night; as she was burning lights she was taken for a neutral and was not attacked. On the next day a ship was sighted by Rogge's planes, trailed and then attacked by night. Searchlights were switched on, the 5.9s opened up, and the first salvo set the enemy on fire. Five more salvos were fired; the funnel and mast of the enemy collapsed and aircraft in crates on the ship's deck started to burn; soon the ship was enveloped in flames. Her crew lowered her boats, but their ship kept on turning around in circles, with her helm jammed, so that suddenly there was danger of her ramming the *Atlantis*. Rogge fired a torpedo to sink the ship, now brightly burning, but the gyro of the torpedo failed and it turned round and headed back towards the *Atlantis*, which, as her war diary points out, "was in an unenviable position, for there was the burning ship heading towards her at a speed of five knots, while the circling torpedo was coming nearer and nearer".

The torpedo just missed the bows of the *Atlantis*; a second torpedo from the raider missed its target, but a third hit the stern of the blazing ship and sank her. Then began the task of picking up survivors, which was difficult in the dark, as the boats had no lights. Rogge was finally successful, and the rescued British seamen stated that their ship had been the *Trafalgar*, of 4,530 tons, carrying 4,500 tons of coal and two aircraft. She had not had time to give the alarm.

Various arrangements were then made for trans-shipping prisoners to the *Babitonga*, which went off to meet a U-

64

boat supply tanker, the *Esso Hamburg,* and replenish from her and from the *Egerland.*

. At this stage the SKL ordered the *Atlantis* to continue to operate on the South American routes and the northern part of the Capetown-Freetown route until the end of June, when she was to meet the *Orion.*

After an engine-room overhaul and the assumption of another disguise the *Atlantis* set off on June 11; on June 16 she celebrated the fact that she had been at sea for 445 days, the time record set up by the *Wolf* in World War I. During this period she had sailed 71,411 miles.

The following day air reconnaissance sighted a ship on a S.S.E. course, and once more a night attack was made. The ship was very high in the water, and painted a light grey. The gunners of the *Atlantis* underestimated the range, and the attacked ship had time to transmit an RRR signal.

After thirty-nine rounds the *Atlantis* ceased fire, as the enemy had stopped and was lowering boats; Rogge closed to sink her with a torpedo, but once again his torpedoes played him false. Two missed and a third struck too far forward to do much damage, so that he had to sink the ship by gunfire. Twenty-nine survivors were picked up, five were known to have lost their lives, and seventeen were in a boat which could not be found; two months later this boat drifted ashore near Rio with nobody in it. The sunken ship was the *Tottenham,* of London, of 4,640 tons, bound from the United Kingdom to Alexandria via the Cape, carrying aircraft, aircraft spare parts, provisions, tractors and cars.

Having picked up all the survivors that she could find, the *Atlantis* hastened away from the scene of the sinking at full speed, heading south-westwards. For four days she cruised slowly along routes leading to Montevideo, Pernambuco, Freetown and Capetown, listening to a lively radio traffic.

News came suddenly of the loss of three of the *Atlantis'* supply ships. The *Esso Hamburg* and *Egerland* had been sunk at the beginning of June by the cruiser *London,* and the *Alstertor* had been scuttled off Finisterre after having been intercepted by aircraft and destroyers. The prisoners taken by the *Atlantis* were thus released and valuable mail fell into British hands, including the war diary of the *Pinguin*, and various codes, ciphers and other confidential documents which had been taken from British ships.

On June 22 a ship was sighted from the *Atlantis* at dawn. As the light improved she was seen to be a medium-sized armed vessel, towards which the *Atlantis* steered a collision course. Rogge opened fire at about 9,000 yards and the enemy made RRR, which the *Atlantis* successfully jammed. Then the British ship began zigzagging and, handled very skilfully, presented the smallest possible target to her enemy. After forty salvoes—190 rounds—had been fired by the Germans, only four hits had been made, and the forward 5.9 battery as well as No. 5 gun broke down, owing to a defect in the recoil mechanisms. The guns were cooled with sea-water and partly manhandled into position, while Rogge turned to bring the disengaged battery, on the other side of his ship, into action. As this was being done the enemy stopped, and lowered her boats. She was the *Balzac*, of 5,372 tons, from Rangoon to Liverpool with 4,200 tons of rice. Of her crew of forty-seven, three British and one Arab were killed. This was *Atlantis'* twenty-first victim, and her total score was now 139, 591 tons.

In the long running fight the *Balzac* had had plenty of time to have got her RRR through, and it was accordingly necessary for the *Atlantis* to disappear from the west side of the South Atlantic.

On June 27 the *Atlantis* was ordered by the SKL to meet the *Orion*, homeward bound from the western Indian Ocean, four days later and transfer to her enough fuel to keep her at sea until September. This was very desirable, as otherwise the *Orion* would have had to try to run the British blockade during the short summer nights. In turn, said the SKL, the *Atlantis* would refuel from the *Anneliese Essberger*, which would appear at a rendezvous during August. Once this had been done, Rogge could stay out until late autumn.

Keeping the raiders at sea through the summer was complicated by the sinking of the *Bismarck* and the rounding up of nine supply ships sent to sea for her replenishment and that of other raiders. In addition the British Admiralty had by this time received so much information about the ship from the survivors of the *Zamzam,* and from the prisoners of the *Trafalgar* and *Rabaul* freed when the *Alstertor* was sunk, that the SKL felt that the raider's activity in the Atlantic was henceforward compromised. Accordingly they were considering the advisability of sending her into the Pacific via the Indian Ocean, and then home round Cape Horn in time for Christmas.

Meanwhile, when Rogge met the *Orion* on July 1, he found that her problems were much more serious than he had previously realised. She urgently required 500 tons of fuel; without this, said her captain, Kurt Weyher, her engines would have to stop and she would have to drift about the ocean for six weeks or more, until the arrival of the *Anneliese Essberger.* Rogge refused Weyher's request, saying that if he did not do so the *Atlantis* in her turn would not have enough fuel to move into whatever new area she was sent by the SKL, and she also would have to wait for the *Anneliese Essberger.* Rogge pointed out that the *Orion* used as much fuel in one week as the *Atlantis* used in two months, because of the difference in consumption between the *Orion's* turbines and the diesels of the *Atlantis,* and that it was clearly more economical to use whatever fuel there was in the latter engines. In actual fact Rogge's calculations gave a somewhat exaggerated result; the amount of the proportion between fuel used by the *Atlantis* and that used by the *Orion* was probably 1 : 4 rather than 1 : 8, but, nevertheless, Rogge's main contention was clearly sound, and Rogge was in fact upheld by the SKL after an exchange of forceful signals. *Atlantis* was told to set off for the Pacific, while on the other side of the world the German tanker *Munsterland,* lying in Yokohama, was ordered to meet her in the Society Islands with a fresh consignment of fuel.

Rogge notes in his war diary that the attitude of his crew when he told them what was being further required of them —after a performance which no other crew has rivalled before or since—was "exemplary."

Off went the *Atlantis* via Gough Island and the Cape of Good Hope, into a hurricane which blew in the regions where the Flying Dutchman had met it, and blew nearly as strongly. Force 11 on the Beaufort Scale was reached and the ship hove to. When she was able to move once more she sailed for a month far from steamer routes, heading first south of Australia and then well to the east of New Zealand. To keep his crew busy, Rogge held a minute inspection of the ship, which lasted for days on end, and overhauled every single piece of the ship's equipment. By August 25 the *Atlantis* was back in an area in which ships might be sighted, but nothing happened until September 10, two hours after sunset. The raider was about half-way between New Zealand and the Society Islands when a ship came in sight, out of a squall, rather badly blacked-out—the first enemy ship that they had seen for eighty days. The enemy was heading away from the *Atlantis*, which chased at full speed, while the fleeing merchantman gave the QQQ alarm, from which she was discovered to be the *Silvaplana*, a Norwegian motor vessel of 4,793 tons. The *Atlantis* tried in vain to jam the alarm, and when the *Silvaplana* had stopped and Rogge put a prize crew on board he sent another signal purporting to come from the *Silvaplana* cancelling the QQQ. However, stations in Australia and at Raritonga were suspicious and asked for a confirmation in code, which Rogge was unable to give.

The *Atlantis*, accompanied by the *Silvaplana*, then went on to her rendezvous, arranged in the previous July with the *Munsterland*, and here she also found Ship 45, *Komet*, which had arrived in the Pacific via the north-east passage, sailing through the ice along the north coast of Siberia. Her commanding officer was a rear-admiral, Robert Eyssen, while Rogge was only a captain—a point which became of some importance when in the course of their discussions a difference of opinion emerged about the sharing of stores. Rogge, it is not surprising to find, had his own way, and the ships separated; the *Silvaplana* went straight to Bordeaux, after a very violent hurricane off Cape Horn, and the *Atlantis* headed north-eastward towards Pomotu Archipelago and then Pitcairn Island. On October 1 the ship had been at sea for eighteen months—as compared with the year originally planned for the duration of the voyage. As far as oil fuel was concerned she had enough to enable her to stay out until March 1942, but her engines were showing signs of wear, and Rogge believed that from this point of view alone a return to Germany by Christmas was essential.

There were now food shortages because there was little fresh food on board and the potatoes from the *Munsterland* were found to be unfit to eat. There was what was described as "a severe cut in the prisoners' rations," and the crew found themselves eating stew and little else four times a week; the food situation grew worse and this was another factor which influenced Rogge's decision to return home.

The ship sailed along what seemed a promising track marked on a chart taken from the *Silvaplana*, but nothing was seen, and the weather was too bad for flying. On October 9 the ship reached Vanavana, in the Pomotu group, and a large number of the crew were able to go ashore and enjoy surf bathing. This was the first time anybody had been on shore since Kerguelen, nine months previously.

The scene was one of South Sea romance, with palm trees, friendly natives, blazing sun and white beaches, but it was very soon necessary to move on. For a while the *Atlantis* waited about 100 miles north-east of Pitcairn, under the lee of Henderson Island, sending out her seaplane without result.

Then on October 18 Rogge gave the order to sail for home; they were to go via Cape Horn, and on November 13 were to rendezvous with *U 68* 500 miles south of St. Helena, refuel her, and then go on to do the same service for *U 126* north of Ascension Island.

On the way to the first rendezvous there were two celebrations, for on October 31 the ship had been at sea 600 days, and on November 8 she had circumnavigated the globe.

On November 13 came the meeting with *U 68;* the *Atlantis* changed her disguise and careened herself in mid-ocean, flooding tanks so that she listed first to one side and then to the other while her waterline was painted. Three days later she headed for her rendezvous with *U 126* off Ascension, another stage on the journey home. A ship, apparently on

69

its way to Capetown, was sighted from the air, and the *Atlantis* chased her for a whole day, only to see at nightfall that she sailed with all lights on, and therefore was probably a neutral. Accordingly, pursuit was given up. On November 21 air reconnaissance reported another ship, but as the plane landed on the water she was overset, and it was not possible to find again the ship which had been seen.

On the next day *U 126* appeared, and was secured to the *Atlantis,* who took down her port main engine to replace a damaged piston. The commander of the U-boat, Lieutenant Bauer, came on board with members of his crew and Rogge at once offered them the submariners' dream—hot baths all round. Peacefully the two German warships drifted on, until the look-out in the *Atlantis* reported a heavy British cruiser of the *London* class in sight. The submarine cut her line and the hose through which she was refuelling and crash-dived, leaving her captain and part of her crew still in the *Atlantis.* Rogge swung his ship on one engine in such a way that her hull might hide the U-boat from a sea-plane catapulted from the British cruiser; but he was too late. The seaplane signalled SSS at once, and then circled over the water, where there heaved slowly a great patch of oil—oil which had been in the hose, cut when *U 126* dived.

Rogge knew that the enemy ship, with eight 8-inch guns, was vastly more powerful than the *Atlantis,* and that even had the *Atlantis'* engines been in full working order the enemy was about fourteen knots faster. The only hope that he had was to lure the British cruiser nearer, within range of the German guns and torpedoes.

The British cruiser was the *Devonshire* (Captain R. D. Oliver), which opened fire at extreme range. The first two salvoes fell short; the *Atlantis* stopped and gave the RRR alarm, saying that she was the British ship *Polyphemus.* The *Devonshire* suspected a trap, for her seaplane had reported that there might be a U-boat with the strange ship. An additional reason for suspicion was that the *Atlantis* was transmitting "RRR—RRR" in groups of three letters, whereas orders had recently been issued, with a contingency like this in mind, that Allied ships should henceforward send the

RRR signal in groups of four letters—"RRRR . . . RRRR . . . RRRR." The *Devonshire's* captain remembered how when the *Cornwall* had sunk the *Pinguin* she had closed to within range of the German's guns and been badly hit. Accordingly Captain Oliver decided to remain out of range, while his plane circled the *Atlantis* and while he called up the C.-in-C. South Atlantic to make sure that the ship in sight could not possibly be the *Polyphemus*.

Both the plane and cruiser kept on challenging, making NNJ, to which the *Atlantis* in her role as *Polyphemus* replied:

"What do you want now?"

The plane circled round again and reported that the ship under observation had the wrong shaped stern for the *Polyphemus*—curved instead of straight.

An hour went by. Rogge still had a slight hope that *U 126* might be able to get into position and attack, as the *Devonshire* steamed rapidly backwards and forwards at a distance of about 17,000 yards, well out of range, but the first lieutenant of the submarine, who had taken command of the boat when his captain had gone for his bath, believed that the *Devonshire* would close the *Atlantis* and accordingly stayed near the latter ship to have a better chance of using his torpedoes.

The *Devonshire* came round again, with flags flying at her fore and main, and one after another three 8-inch salvoes crashed down around the *Atlantis*—the C.-in-C. at Freetown had reported that the strange ship could not possibly be the *Polyphemus*.

The first salvo was short, a shell from the second hit forward, and with the third a shell hit the hatch of the aircraft storage space and set the aircraft and her spares on fire. The ship's intercommunication system broke down and she made smoke, but all that she could do under its cover was to launch boats and rafts and prepare to scuttle herself. Altogether she was hit eight times, and two of her men were killed; the rest abandoned ship. Rogge was the last to leave, and at 09.58 her magazine exploded and the ship sank in two minutes.

Now the whole crew of the *Atlantis* were in the water. Because of the report from the seaplane that there was almost certainly a submarine in the neighbourhood, the *Devonshire* made off. Nobody in the British navy had ever forgotten that in September 1914 when the cruiser *Aboukir* was torpedoed and sunk by a German submarine her two sister ships that were with her stopped to pick up survivors and were both sunk in their turn by the submarine.

Rogge started to get his crew together; with whistle blasts he collected them, and set the boats to collecting wreckage, bits of which were lashed together for use by men who had not been able to find place in the boats or on the rafts. A light trade wind was blowing and it was sunny and warm, with no heavy swell. There were numerous sharks, but they kept at a respectful distance as Rogge started a roll call amongst his men; altogether there were seven missing. As this was going on the U-boat surfaced, her captain went back on board and began to deal with the problem of the survivors, who were, of course, far too numerous to be taken on board his boat. He divided the survivors into three groups—one group was taken below in the submarine; one group, with their life-jackets inflated, were placed on the deck of the submarine, ready to swim for it if the submarine had to dive; and the third group, in boats and on rafts, were taken in tow. The tow lasted thirty-eight hours, with so many breaks of the lines that soon there were not enough left, as a course was steered by *U 126* for Pernambuco; the night was cold, and the men, clad only in shorts, suffered very much. The three groups—those below, those on deck and those in the water—changed places regularly, and the cook of *U 126* excelled himself, managing to serve hot meals to everyone on both days.

Meanwhile, Dönitz, at U-boat headquarters in France, was organising a rescue; three submarines and the supply ship *Python* were ordered to pick up survivors, and this was done on the night of November 23-4. The *Python* went on with her business of replenishing U-boats, and on December 1 was south of St. Helena, with her submarines on the surface, when another three-funnelled British cruiser appeared

—a sister ship of the *Devonshire*. The submarines dived—
U 68 with some difficulty, as she had been loading torpedoes
and her torpedo hatches were open; the other submarine,
UA, also dived and attacked the enemy, which was the
Dorsetshire. The submarine fired five torpedoes, and all
missed, so that the captain of the *Python* knew that there
was nothing to do except to scuttle his ship. As the *Python*
capsized and sank, the submarines resurfaced and began to
pick up the survivors, including most of the men from the
Atlantis. Altogether there were now 414 men in the sea;
each submarine took on board 100 men; the rest were placed
in ten lifeboats and taken in tow.

Learning of this, Dönitz began to organise yet another
rescue from his headquarters in Brittany.

Eight submarines—four German and four Italian—went
down to the South Atlantic to seek the survivors, and all were
picked up, though 360 men were on tow in open boats for
ten days, and sixty on tow for twenty days.

This extraordinary rescue operation gave the Germans one
special, unexpected dividend, for *U 124,* on her way to take
part in it, met the British cruiser *Dunedin* and sank her off
St. Paul's Rocks.

All the rescue submarines were back at St. Nazaire between
December 23 and 29, and by January 1, 1942, the survivors
of the *Atlantis* were gathered together in Berlin to be fêted.
Rogge received from Hitler the Oak Leaves to the Knight's
Cross of the Iron Cross.

The *Atlantis* had been at sea from March 31, 1940, to November 21, 1941, and she had sunk or captured twenty-two
ships of 145,697 tons; she was at sea 622 days and had
sailed 102,000 miles.

Back in Berlin, before taking up in April a new appointment as Chief of Staff, Officers' Training and Education—his
old specialisation—at Kiel, Rogge wrote a long report on his
cruise and set down some important lessons and principles.

First, he wrote, it was the duty of a raider to keep the
enemy occupied for as long a period of time as possible, rather
than simply to sink ships. Once it became known that a raider
was operating in an area it forced the enemy to sail his ships

in convoy, with a waste of time, tonnage and escorting vessels. It followed from this that the best tactics to use was to appear just long enough in one area to make the enemy take to convoys, and then leave that area, to reappear as quickly as possible in another part of the world, attack shipping there and start the whole process all over again.

In short the raider captain's most effective weapon against enemy trade was the actual existence of his ship, so long as the enemy was kept aware of it by being dealt an occasional blow.

Considering the situation which would arise when a raider's usefulness was finally over, Rogge came to an important point of global strategy when he put forward the idea that rather than scuttle his ship, or take it to a neutral port for internment, the raider captain's duty would be to take his crew ashore and "wage war on land against enemy colonial possessions, protectorates, mandated territories or dominions"—this was the course which had been followed by the captain of the *Königsberg* in World War I.

Rogge then went on to discuss the selection of crews. For these voyages he insisted that it was necessary to take only men who had learned a trade in civil life. Unskilled men became too bored and too demoralised.

The choice of doctors, he said, was of great importance; apart from medical duties, the two in the *Atlantis*—Drs. Reil and Sprung—had rendered the most valuable service as welfare officers, since members of the crew with worries or grievances were much more willing to confide in them rather than in the executive officers.

It would seem that early in the cruise the ship's catchphrase taken from a popular song became: *"Das kann doch einen Seemann nicht erschüttern"* ("But that can't shake a sailor"), and it remained a standby joke in all kinds of emergencies until the bitter end.

Rumours, said Rogge, had to be watched with the greatest care, and their circulation stopped at once.

When promotions or other good news for members of the crew reached the ship through official channels it was the custom to pass it on to its recipient on a "Good News" form specially designed on board. There was a ship's newspaper based on the radio reports of the DNB (the German official news agency) and there were frequent performances of amateur theatricals. The making of models went on just as it always does on board any ship in any navy or merchant service which is away from home for a long time.

Food was always the same for everyone, officers and men alike, and Rogge laid it down that when there were luxuries available from prizes, et cetera, they were to be issued to all ranks "like water."

Courses by more or less qualified officers and ratings were given in mathematics, history, English, political economy and typewriting. Discussion groups were held on Sunday morning, but apart from that Sunday was kept, as far as possible, as a day of rest. A good store of gramophone records of quality had been laid in before the ship sailed—with gratifying results according to Rogge. The case of the band was different, he said, since it numbered no accomplished players. However, sing-songs were frequent, especially on deck in the evenings in tropical waters.

There was a careful censorship of outgoing mail, not only from the point of view of security but also from the personal point of view, so that "small bitternesses" might not be sent home, reaching families or friends months after the grievances had been forgotten.

To help break the monotony a scheme of "leave on board" was devised by which members of the crew had, in batches of twelve, eight days off. They lived in the isolation hospital —which was never needed, since the ship was kept free from disease—read, sunbathed, wrote poetry or fiction, played games and had nothing to do with the ship's life except at meal times, or when action stations were sounded. Officers and petty officers had the same privilege, but were able to spend their spare time in their cabins. Altogether during the cruise almost everyone on board had two spells of this leave.

In April 1942 Rogge took up his appointment at Kiel. A year later he was made Director of Officers' Training and Education, and at the end of the war he was a vice-admiral, second in command of the German fleet.

The record of Rogge and the *Atlantis* speaks for itself; he was a skilful, humane and tenacious officer with a ship and crew worthy of him.

II
Orion • SHIP 36

FROM THE *Atlantis*, the most successful of all German raiders, we turn to the *Orion*, Ship 36, the unfortunate. we met with the *Atlantis*, drifting in the South Atlantic with no fuel on board, waiting for an oiler. In addition to this question of fuel there was an even greater problem which served to make the lives 'of her officers and crew nearly unbearable during a cruise which lasted from April 6, 1940, to August 23, 1941; that was the state of her engines. The *Orion* was a single-screw ship of 7,021 tons, formerly the *Kurmark* of the Hamburg-Amerika Line (Hapag), built by Blohm and Voss at Hamburg in 1930, and engined with half the propelling plant of the liner *New York*. This ship of 22,000 tons had been built just after the First World War at a time when it was expected that the passenger liner of the future would be a medium-sized vessel of slowish speed. With the end of the 'twenties, the Norddeutscher Lloyd, then Hapag's great rival, the Cunard Line, the French Line and the Italians were all building very large and very fast ships. The best that Hapag could do to meet this competition, beyond making plans for a very large ship (about 65,000 tons) that was never built, was to reconstruct the *New York* and her three sister ships, taking out their old engines, putting new and more powerful machinery into them, and making them longer. It was half of the old engines from the *New York* that were installed in the *Orion*, and they were to give a heartbreaking amount of trouble.

The fact that a ship with engines in this condition should have been sent out to cruise the seas for over a year probably provides an answer to one of the biggest problems raised by the German conduct of cruiser warfare: since the armed merchantmen were such successful raiders, at least in the first two years of the war, why were there not more of them? From the example of the *Orion* it would seem that almost anything in any way suitable was used and that ships suitable for the work of armed merchant raiders were very few.

The *Orion,* it will be recalled, had made her way out of the Baltic with the *Atlantis* in March 1940, having similarly been delayed on her trials by bad weather. Her captain was Commander Kurt Weyher, thirty-nine years old, who, like Rogge, had specialised in the training of officers. On April 1, 1940, just as he was about to set out on his cruise, he was promoted to captain.

The armament of the *Orion,* concealed like that of the *Atlantis,* was much the same—six 5.9-inch guns, one 75-millimetre, and two 37-millimetre anti-aircraft guns. She carried six torpedo tubes and 228 mines. Her seaplane was an Arado 196, to be replaced in Japan by a Nakajima 90-11. In her hull was stowed 4,100 tons of oil fuel.

Her first disguise was as the Dutch *Beemsterdijk.* When he sailed Weyher was told that he would have to do without the U-boat escort which it had been intended to give the ship, but no one said why this was so, and it was only after they had sailed that Weyher and his crew heard, on the radio, of the opening of the Norwegian campaign for which the escorting U-boat, together with all other German warships, was urgently needed. It was the hope of the SKL that the *Atlantis* and the *Orion* would serve to draw British warships and especially aircraft carriers away from Norwegian waters.

On April 10, steaming north, the *Orion* picked up a message in clear which showed that the *Beemsterdijk,* whom she was supposed to be, was in fact in the West Indies. As this news could clearly have been picked up by British ships as well, it was decided to re-disguise the ship at once—this time as the Russian vessel *Soviet,* a transformation which had an additional advantage, since it was unlikely that a Dutch ship would find herself as far north as the position reached at that time by *Orion*.

The raider's first cruising area was to be the eastern half of the Indian Ocean, but on April 16 she was ordered to wait in the North Atlantic to make the Allies believe that a pocket battleship was at large, and only to go on to the Indian Ocean after her first success had drawn attention to her presence at sea.

Weyher decided that the best area in which to work would be the junction of the routes from New York to Gibraltar and from the English Channel to Panama. On April 17 he passed an armed passenger steamer going fast on the opposite course at a distance of about 4,000 yards. Because of the difficulty of accommodating a large number of prisoners, he let the ship go, and held on. On the 24th the German armed merchant raiders secured their first success of the war. At 0517 an armed steamer was sighted on a converging course. The *Orion* let her pass astern, and then slowly, to avoid frightening her, turned and followed. The German fired a warning shot from the 75-millimetre gun, and signalled to her to stop and not to use her wireless. The ship at once sent out an RRR message with her position and her name, *Haxby*. After six minutes' shelling the ship started to list and lowered her boats. Her captain and twenty-three men were rescued by the *Orion,* but seventeen men lost their lives. She was a British ship of 5,207 tons in ballast from Glasgow to Corpus Christi, Texas. The *Orion* headed off to the south-east, and on that night passed another ship. In its study of the cruise the SKL comments that the *Orion's* war diary does not say why an attack was not made.

The next task was to disguise the ship again, for a Russian vessel would have no reason to be so far south. Accordingly, the *Orion* now became the Greek *Rocos*. The time had now come to make the world believe that there was a German pocket battleship at large in the Atlantic, and Weyher began to radio a broken message: ". . . by pocket battlesh . . ."

On May 1 he crossed the equator, and then topped up his fuel supply from the tanker *Winnetou*, which had been sent to meet him from the neutral port of Las Palmas. He took on board 1,720 tons and then sent the tanker off again to meet him in the South Pacific.

On May 21 Weyher rounded Cape Horn and headed across the Pacific for New Zealand. He did not steer a Great Circle course, but took advantage of the Peruvian current. New orders from the SKL laid down that he was to operate from mid-June until the end of September off the coast of Australia and New Zealand, meet a supply ship in the Japanese-owned Caroline Islands, and then go on to the Indian Ocean and the Atlantic.

The *Orion* arrived in Hauraki Gulf, off Auckland, on June 13. It was a fine clear night, horrible for minelaying because the visibility by the light of a moon in the first quarter was about twelve miles. Two hundred and twenty-eight mines were laid, one of which was to sink the liner *Niagara*, of 13,415 tons, while others disposed of the *Port Bowen*, of 8,267 tons, and *Baltavia* of 1,739 tons.

From Auckland, *Orion* turned east to her rendezvous in the Society Islands with the *Winnetou;* on the way an American ship was seen but was not spoken to. Plane reconnaissances became impossible for the time being on June 17, when the Arado capsized in the swell alongside the ship. As she was being hauled inboard she had her wings smashed. Repairs took seventeen days, and before they were over the *Orion* had been in action.

On the night of the next day lights were sighted and followed until dawn, when the strange ship was ordered to stop; nothing happened and fire was opened. The ship did not stop, but neither did she give the alarm. Finally a whole 5.9 salvo was dropped just short of her and then she hove to—she was the Norwegian motor vessel *Tropic Sea*, of 5,781 tons, carrying 8,100 tons of Australian wheat from Sydney to the United States.

This ship was taken along for a while with a prize crew on board and then sent home, together with fifty-five prisoners. When nearly in sight of her destination the *Tropic Sea* was stopped by the British submarine *Truant* and scuttled herself. The *Truant* managed to pick up the prisoners from the *Haxby*, a nearby Sunderland flying-boat picked up some of the Norwegians, and the rest of the Norwegians, together with the German prize crew, got ashore in Spain. The officer in charge of the prize crew, Lieutenant Steinkraus, afterwards crossed Russia by the Trans-Siberian Railway and in Japan joined the *Ole Jakob* as captain.

The *Orion* met the *Winnetou* again, but bad weather interfered with refuelling, as the raider was rolling badly, being very light in the water since she had disposed of her mines.

Now the *Orion* spent fruitless days on the trade routes; in beautiful weather, under a heavenly sky, she beat up and down, trying all routes that it was possible to cover: Tahiti to the Straits of Magellan; Wellington and Auckland to Sydney; Tonga and Suva to Yokohama; Wellington to Vancouver; Sydney to San Francisco; and though she steamed on she found nothing, and it gradually became clear that all these routes had been moved since the sinking of the *Niagara* had showed that there was an enemy raider in the neighbourhood. Most of the scouting on this part of the cruise was done by the *Winnetou,* as the plane was much handicapped by the heavy swell. Finally, on August 7, the *Orion* filled her tanks for two months more in the Coral Sea and set out for the waters between Australia, New Zealand and New Caledonia.

Off Brisbane, on August 10, she sighted smoke from a ship going in the opposite direction; she turned and followed out of sight, postponing attack until it would be nearer nightfall and too late for the shore-based planes of the R.A.A.F. to intervene. When, finally, the time came to close, the ship to be attacked was easily identified by her clipper bow as the *Triona*, of 4,400 tons, a steamer engaged in the phosphate trade. Fifteen minutes after the *Orion* had come in sight the *Triona* suddenly altered course through 180° and hurried off in the direction from which she had come.

Weyher notes in his war diary that he did not follow because he was not fast enough to catch the *Triona* before dark. In addition he thought that his presence in these waters was still unknown, as the *Triona* had not given the alarm but had presumably altered course just as a precautionary measure.

By seven minutes to seven that evening the *Triona* had run into a rain squall, and the *Orion* headed for a position closer to Brisbane, after which her captain proposed to take a look at the route from that place to Noumea, in New Caledonia.

For two days he was off Noumea, noting that the coastwise lights were extinguished but that street lights were still on, and were of value for purposes of navigation.

A large part of August 14 was spent looking for the Arado, as she had been forced on the sea through a defect in her fuel pump, which had meant that she used too much petrol. After five hours the missing plane was picked up and reported that there were three ships in Noumea, one alongside the pier. Weyher adjusted his disguise on this day, cutting down two derrick masts and rigging another mast aft. This was done because British reports of the *Widder* (Ship 21) being at large had been picked up, and as the *Widder* and *Orion* were sister ships it was decided that the most conspicuous features of the latter's appearance should be changed. Two days later the *Orion*, heading south, sighted smoke, which proved to be from a ship heading for Noumea at ten and a half knots. It was getting dusk and there was not much time for an interception before Noumea was reached. Steaming on through the tropic darkness, the steamer set lights; a little later *Orion* did the same, and then, by lamp, signalled her to stop and not to use her wireless. After one warning shot the ship stopped, and proved to be the French *Notou*, of 2,489 tons, with 3,602 tons of coal from Newcastle, N.S.W.; she was sunk and the *Orion* left for the Tasman Sea.

A signal was received from SKL ordering her to refuel once more in the Pacific and then come home via the Indian Ocean. Weyher was further told that the *Komet* (Ship 45) was in Far Eastern waters via the "Northern Seaway." The *Pinguin* (Ship 33) was to enter the Indian Ocean in September, and moving through Australian waters, was to reach the Antarctic in December. News was also given of the orders for the *Atlantis*.

On August 20, while the *Orion* was between Cook Strait, which separates the two islands of New Zealand, and Sydney, a steamer suddenly appeared a little forward of her beam, out of a rain squall. *Orion* altered course to come between the ship and New Zealand waters, which offered the nearest shelter, and at 1737 ordered her to stop. This she refused to do, and sent out a warning signal saying that she was the

Turakina. *Orion* opened fire on a forward bearing; the sea was heavy enough to make gunnery difficult. The *Turakina* replied with her stern gun, but within a few minutes she had been hit four times—forward, on her bridge, between the bridge and the funnel, and half-way up the foremast, and fire broke out amidships. Meanwhile, her stern gun was still in action, each round missing the *Orion* by a narrow margin, and only when the *Turakina* had been hit twice more did the gun's rate of fire slacken. After seven hits, as darkness fell, the *Turakina* slowed down and firing ceased. For a few minutes the two ships lay together while *Orion's* crew watched the *Turakina* burn. Then as she settled down, the *Turakina* opened fire once more, and the *Orion* finished her off, first with gunfire and then with torpedoes. There was no explosion, but the ship sank slowly on an even keel, burning fiercely, the flames reflecting in the waters of the night and mounting high up into the sky—a torch which could be seen for miles away.

Orion received no damage, except that the false sides of the ship, behind which the guns were concealed, had been damaged by blast.

The *Turakina's* survivors were swimming around in the sea, which was too high to permit the use of lifeboats by the *Orion* to pick them up; accordingly the Germans lowered rubber dinghies into the water, which went around fishing out everyone that could be found. In all twenty-one were saved, seven of whom were wounded, out of a crew of fifty-seven. The sunken vessel was a ship of 8,706 tons, carrying 4,000 tons of lead, 1,500 tons of grain, 7,000 tons of wool, as well as fruit and piece goods.

In the *Orion* the radio operator heard *Turakina's* RRR message being repeated by Brisbane, and all next day there was lively wireless traffic between ships and planes. Weyher decided to move on towards the south-west edge of Australia, although bad weather was forecast there, as the *Kreuzerkriegskarte* (Cruiser Warfare Map) showed that there were an average of fifty ships a month to be expected passing through the area.

Cape Leeuwin was reached, and the raider began to search the routes between Capetown and the South Australian ports, and those from Aden and Colombo, but nothing happened. The anticipated bad weather fully materialised, and soon the *Orion* was rolling up to 34° to either side, so that even if an enemy had been sighted gunnery would have been very difficult. However, mines were laid off Albany. Some dummies were left floating around to draw attention to the presence of the field and so cause delays to shipping while the area was swept.

When 130 miles from shore they were sighted by a Lockheed Hudson of the R.A.A.F.; the crew had already been sent below as a precaution and the only people on deck were a few men in civilian clothes. While the Hudson circled round twice and then went away, the *Orion* held on her course as though nothing was happening, and in the wireless room could be heard the signals of at least six aircraft presumably searching from Busselton. It was clear that the searchers were approaching the *Orion,* but before they reached her night fell, and although the engines of the planes could be heard they were not seen, and under cover of rain, bad weather and the dark, the *Orion* altered course.

Next morning, when they were 350 miles south-west of Cape Leeuwin, the air search could be heard still going on, but nothing more was seen, and the *Orion* headed through bad weather towards a rendezvous with the *Pinguin*.

On September 9 it was learned that exactly one month hence the supply ship *Regensburg* would be at Ailinglap, in the Marshall Islands. Sorting out these arrangements necessitated a lengthy signal being sent to Tokio, and in case the enemy had taken a direction-finding bearing on it *Orion* continued westward to give the impression that she was really on her way to the Cape of Good Hope. As soon as the exchange of messages was completed she turned round and went back into the Tasman Sea. Nothing was seen, and a trip to the Kermadec Islands also produced no result. On October 10 the *Regensburg* was met at Ailinglap, and the two ships then went on together to Lamutrik to meet the *Komet*, the *Regensburg* going ahead as a scout. On the way, very early in the morning of October 14, the lights of a ship were sighted, and the *Orion* turned towards them. In order that he might pretend to be a long way away Weyher ordered the lights of his ship to shine only dimly, and then, to give the impression of a gradual approach, they were slowly brightened. For an hour the silent chase went on in the dark, the pursued ship apparently quite unwitting of what was happening, until the *Orion* morsed her to stop and then fired two warning shots.

The ship was the *Ringwood* of 7,302 tons, a Norwegian in ballast from Shanghai to Ocean Island, where she was to load phosphates for Bermuda or Halifax via Panama. The *Ringwood's* equipment was found to be in excellent state and much of it, together with some stores, was put on board the *Orion* before the Germans scuttled their prize.

On the next morning another ship was sighted, apparently of about six or seven thousand tons. The *Orion* turned to chase, but found that owing to the state of her engines and her foul bottom she could only make twelve and a half knots. The unknown ship carried unidentifiable neutrality markings, and accordingly was permitted to draw away and disappeared.

On October 18 the *Komet* was met at Lamutrik.

After talking over the situation Weyher and Eyssen, the captain of the latter ship, decided that the two ships should work together, for the time being, against the route between New Zealand and Panama. The idea was also discussed of an attack on the rich phosphate and copra island of Nauru, but no decision was reached.

Eyssen was considerably the senior of the two officers, but from what follows it does not appear that he in fact commanded both ships when they were working together.

With the two raiders was the tanker *Kulmerland,* which had come to Lamutrik to replenish them, and the three ships sailed together, keeping in line abreast as far as possible from each other without an enemy ship being able to pass between them unseen. In this way they covered a front of between ninety and one hundred miles. By night, the ships moved closer together to keep within visual touch.

On the way south the *Orion* stopped the American ship *City of Elwood,* and on November 3 Eyssen commented in his war diary that it was not "a very cheerful beginning" and went on to say:

"But the fact that it is known that a German auxiliary cruiser is operating here will cause added anxiety, and our real operations area is far enough away."

This area was reached four days later, at the junction of the routes between the Cook Straits and Panama and Auckland and Panama—a spot more than 400 miles away from the nearest air base. They searched the area for four days, found nothing and moved 300 miles southward. Again they had no luck, and moved south again. Finally, on November 24, the two captains decided that there was nothing useful to be done in these waters, and that the proper thing to do was to attack Nauru, a place too far away from any British base for enemy forces to interfere with the German attack. On the next day, as they headed north, they found a tiny New Zealand coaster, the *Holmwood,* of 546 tons, taking sheep and wool from Chatham Island to Lyttelton. The possible use of this ship as an auxiliary minelayer was discussed, but as her maximum speed was only eight to nine knots it was decided to scuttle her, after taking on board her sheep and her twenty-nine passengers and crew.

On November 27, at three in the morning, a big ship was sighted, blacked out. The raiders switched on their search-lights and fired warning shots. The attacked ship signalled: "RRR *Rangitane* attacked," adding her position. After being shelled she stopped. This was the largest passenger ship sunk by any of the German surface raiders during the war—she was of 16,712 tons, and carried 303 passengers and crew (thirty-six of whom were women). Only three men lost their lives. Some of the prisoners were sent to the *Kulmerland,* which now had thirty-nine women and five children on board.

The ship was bound from Auckland to Panama and Liverpool and had on board 14,000 tons of butter and frozen meat. It soon became clear that her RRR message had got through, and Wellington and Awarua were heard repeating it, while the New Zealand Naval Board sent out a warning to all ships to keep at least 200 miles away from the area where the attack had taken place. The *Rangitane* was scuttled and the raiders went on. On the evening of the same day a plane was sighted, although the ships were now 450 miles from the nearest air base. The plane flew past the raiders at a distance of about ten miles, but apparently did not see anything, as she remained within sight for about twenty minutes without sending any signals.

It had originally been planned that the two ships should pass through the Coral Sea on the way to Nauru, but as the sinking of the *Rangitane* had become known it was thought likely that no ships worth attacking would be found there.

Plans were now made for the attack on Nauru, which Eyssen believed would prevent an entire year's output of phosphates from the island reaching its market—between 700,000 and 800,000 tons.

According to the war diary of the *Orion* it was decided to start the attack with an air reconnaissance; if this were not possible, then the *Komet* was to approach the island to see what ships were in the neighbourhood. In the meantime a difference of opinion had developed between the two German captains relating to the treatment of the prisoners. Eyssen was anxious to land all his prisoners, except regular soldiers and some volunteers for the R.A.F. who had been taken from the *Rangitane,* on some remote island whence they could be rescued within reasonable time. Weyher, on the other hand, wished to land only coloured members of ships' crews, because the officers and men of the merchant navy which were held captive would be of great value to the British if they were able to return to duty. Moreover, all the prisoners had had a chance to learn many details about the German ships which would be much better kept secret.

Meanwhile, a landing party of 187 men, under the *Komet's* second-in-command, was made ready, but before it could go ashore there was smoke on the horizon and for eight hours *Orion* and *Komet* tore after a ship whose traces they could hardly see. Finally, having been caught and shelled, the ship, after sending her RRR, stopped, with three of her crew killed. She was the *Triona,* which had avoided the *Orion* four months before, and aboard her were 1,112 tons of food and piece goods on their way from Melbourne and Newcastle, N.S.W., to Nauru and Ocean Island. Amongst the sixty-eight prisoners taken were six women and one child.

86

The *Triona* was sunk by torpedo—a measure criticised afterwards by the SKL as being a waste of torpedoes—and the two German ships turned back to the attack on Nauru.

On December 7 weather was too bad for air reconnaissance, and the *Komet* led the way in. Two ships were seen waiting off shore to load; presumably the loading was being delayed by the heavy swell running, which made it impossible for the landing party from the raiders to get ashore. As the Germans waited another ship came in sight; it was shelled at once and stopped without being able to give the alarm, and was scuttled after her crew had been taken off. She was the Norwegian *Vinni,* of 5,181 tons, bound in ballast for Nauru, where she was to load phosphates for Dunedin.

The swell continued the next day, and it was decided that rather than land the German ships should confine themselves to sinking the freighters lying off the island. The attack was made at first light, the two ships coming from north and south, and three vessels were sunk immediately. They were the New Zealand *Komata,* of 3,900 tons, sunk by the *Komet,* and the British *Triadic,* of 6,378 tons, and *Triaster,* of 6,032 tons, sunk by the *Orion.* All these ships were in ballast, and 166 prisoners were taken, there having been no casualties. Altogether the raid on the island had resulted in five ships of 26,000 tons being sunk.

On learning of the raid, the SKL sent its congratulations and added that the operation of two ships together had led to great success. It will be recalled that the SKL a few weeks afterwards was to criticise Krancke of the *Scheer* and Rogge of the *Atlantis* for not combining to work together in the Indian Ocean.

There were now in the hands of the Germans 675 prisoners, of whom fifty-two were women and eight children, and some of these were landed on Emirau Island. Both the German captains stuck to their original points of views as to who should be set ashore, Eyssen landing everybody except regular soldiers and the R.A.F. volunteers, while Weyher only landed coloured prisoners; all prisoners were rescued by the British shortly after being set ashore.

In the meantime the *Komet* withdrew for the time being,

while the *Orion* waited for one more day in case a landing at Nauru was possible, and then went slowly to Lamutrik, where she arrived on New Year's Eve. It was decided that the *Orion* should undergo as thorough a self-refit as possible, after 268 days at sea, while waiting for more fuel from Japan. The refit was to take place at Maug, 800 miles to northward, for by that time it was feared that both Ailinglap and Lamutrik had been compromised as secret bases, since the prisoners from the *Komet* and *Orion* had now been released. It was accordingly decided to move on to Maug, but the promised tanker, the *Ermland*, had not yet arrived, and it was necessary to wait for her. The *Ermland* had 183 white prisoners on board and she had to be kept out of the way while the *Orion* was re-disguised. In addition to fuel the tanker had a Nakajima seaplane—a 90–11—which was a better machine than the Arado, having a very low landing speed (about fifty m.p.h.). The *Ermland* handed over her oil, and went off to Bordeaux, where she arrived on April 13, after having collected the *Scheer's* prisoners from the *Nordmark*. The *Ole Jacob* was also present. This large-scale movement of ships shows again the complicated and widespread organisation that was required to keep the raiders at sea. So, too, does the fact that already the *Orion* had been serviced by eight different ships.

By February 2 Weyher was ready to sail again from Maug, this time for the Indian Ocean, passing to the east and the south of New Zealand and Australia. Moving down through the Coral Sea, she passed between Bougainville and Villa Levalla, in the Solomons.

On February 16 the *Ole Jacob* reported sighting a Sunderland, which called up Port Moresby, the nearest Australian base, in a code which could not be read. There was a coded reply, followed by Port Moresby calling a ship which the Germans believed to be the flotilla leader *Stuart*. It was now essential to get out of the closed Coral Sea as quickly as possible, and also for the *Orion* and the *Ole Jacob* to separate. The two ships moved along south of the Solomon Islands and parallel to their axis. On the next day the Sunderland appeared again. This time she went away without making a signal, but later in the day, when a ship was sighted, Weyher decided to leave her alone for fear that she might send an alarm which would bring the Sunderland back to the spot.

On February 20 *Orion* ran into a hurricane, which did much damage as the great, crazed seas swept her deck. The raider refuelled from the *Ole Jacob* on the 25th, and then went through more bad weather, but after that there was nothing but a long dull trip right up into the middle of the Indian Ocean, during which nothing happened. After refuelling at a meeting-place called Hermann in Area S—Siberia—in the Indian Ocean, the *Orion* held on westward towards Madagascar. On May 18, as soon as it was sufficiently light the raider flew off the Arado, which made a routine patrol and then, a quarter of an hour before she was due back, reported a British heavy cruiser only about forty-five miles from the *Orion*, adding the enemy's course and speed and the information that the aircraft had probably not been seen. The *Orion* swung away from the enemy at full speed, but two hours later smoke was sighted over the horizon at a distance of about twenty-six miles. For half an hour the smoke followed; then it disappeared, and the relieved Weyher calculated that before he had received the aircraft's warning he had been steering a collision course with the British cruiser. It was another example of the value of scouting aircraft; the two planes carried by the *Orion* between them made eighty-five flights.

The war diary of the ship assumed that the cruiser had been escorting troops on their way to Iraq, to put down Rashid Ali's rebellion, but in fact the British ship was either the *Cornwall* or the *Glasgow,* which had shortly before left Mauritius to look for raiders. It was the *Cornwall* that had, ten days previously, sunk the *Pinguin,* and this sinking, plus her narrow escape was a very good reason for the *Orion* to leave the Indian Ocean, and orders to do this shortly afterwards reached Weyher from the SKL.

On May 27 the raider's Nakajima plane was lost while taking off when the ship was near the coast of Madagascar. The Cape of Good Hope was passed in very bad weather, with the wind gusting up to Force 12 on the Beaufort Scale, a very high sea and south-westerly swell.

In Area Andalusia, north of Tristan da Cunha the *Orion*

met the *Atlantis* on July 1, as has already been related, and oiled for the last time from the *Anneliese Essberger*.

More bad weather was met with; the ship rolled shockingly, despite the fact that 750 tons of water were taken on board as ballast, and the plates on the ship's side which were used to conceal the guns were torn away.

Oil, as almost always, was Weyher's preoccupation, and he learned from the SKL that the *Egerland,* on her way to supply him, and the *Lothringen,* which had been sent to take her place, had both fallen into British hands. There was now nothing for the *Orion* to do but come home, and she started back on July 21. At this time the Axis ships which had taken refuge in Brazilian ports were ordered to break out, as it was feared that they were about to be seized under American pressure. The SKL remarked, in their appreciation of the *Orion's* cruise, that the break-out of these ships caused confusion among British patrols, which helped to permit the *Orion* to safely pass between Africa and Brazil. But before that happened, on July 29, seven and a half months since her last success (off Nauru), the *Orion* met a merchant ship. All that afternoon the raider kept her just in sight, and began a run in towards her in the twilight. She approached to within torpedo range and then fired three torpedoes. Nothing happened, so the *Orion* opened fire. The attacked ship immediately signalled: "RRR *Chaucer* gunned torpedoed," gave her position and turned away into the darkness. The *Chaucer* was making a lot of smoke and the visibility was bad, while, to make matters worse, the German guns' crew were blinded by the flashes of their own weapons. Weyher altered course to bring the disengaged broadside into action. The *Chaucer* returned fire; there were several near misses and the *Orion* was slightly damaged by splinters. The *Orion* fired three more torpedoes, and they, like so many German torpedoes of early wartime pattern, failed to explode. Immediately after this, however, the enemy stopped, and the *Orion* checked fire. She switched on a searchlight, and it could be seen that the *Chaucer* was lowering her boats and was sinking. All forty-eight members of her crew were picked up, and Weyher then fired four more torpedoes at her. None of these exploded, and finally, after having expended ten torpedoes in vain, the *Orion* sank the *Chaucer* by gunfire. The sunken ship had been of 5,792 tons, in ballast from Middlesbrough to Buenos Aires.

On August 6 another ship was sighted at one o'clock in the morning, by bright moonlight, but it was not possible to get close enough to attack. Early in the afternoon of the same day the raider's plane saw a ship about forty miles distant, but Weyher decided not to take action because the visibility was so good that the ship would certainly be able to give the alarm long before he, with his deplorable engines, would be able to come up with her.

On August 15 *Orion* blossomed out again in a new disguise —as the Spanish *Contramestre Casado;* she was now off the coast of Spain and on the last lap of her journey. She was picked up first by a U-boat escort, then by aircraft, and finally by destroyers and minesweepers to the Gironde, where she arrived on August 23. She had been at sea for 510 days, during which she had steamed 112,337 miles and sunk twelve and a half ships of 80,279 tons. The half ship is her share in sinking the *Rangitane* together with the *Komet.*

There was no question of a ship with such unreliable engines being sent out on the high seas again; her armament and various items of special equipment were taken from her and used for the ships of the second wave of raiders that were then fitting out. Finally, under the name of *Hektor,* she was sunk by bombs off Swinemünde on May 4, 1945.

As for Weyher, his wartime journeys were by no means over, for he was sent first to the staff of Naval Group Command South and then to the Black Sea as Senior Officer of 10th Local Escort Division—a scratch force of small converted merchant vessels—after which he served as Naval Officer in Charge, Crete, and then, in the same position, in the East Frisian Islands until the end of the war.

III
Widder • SHIP 21

In CONTRAST to the first two of the disguised German raiders, which roamed all over the waters of the globe, the third to sail, the *Widder*, spent her entire operational life in the Central Atlantic, where she was able to sink ten ships of 58,645 tons between May 6 and October 31, 1940.

The *Widder*—the word means Ram—was a sister ship of the long-suffering *Orion*, and was originally the *Neumark* of the Hamburg-Amerika line. Her armament and equipment were similar to that of the *Orion*, and so, in the early stages at least, was her capacity for giving trouble to her own crew. Her conversion to a raider was completed by November 30, 1939, but such difficulties arose during her trials that she was not ready to sail until May 6 of the following year.

By that time the nights were far shorter than desirable for an unobserved escape into the Atlantic around the north of Scotland and Iceland. However, most of the Norwegian coast was in German hands, so that it was possible to give the new raider much better cover and reconnaissance than had been provided for the *Atlantis* and the *Orion*. Operations were still going on around Narvik, but it was realised that the naval effort the Allies were having to make in support of their troops there would be furnished, in part, at the expense of the patrols guarding the way into the Atlantic.

The operational area assigned to the *Widder* was a zone in the North Atlantic lying south of 40° north and west of 30° west, roughly half-way between the West Indies and Dakar, but separated from the West Indies and the coast of South America by the boundary of the Pan-American neutrality zone, which the *Widder's* captain, Helmuth von

Ruckteschell, captain in the Naval Reserve, was under strict orders not to violate.

Leaving the Elbe on May 6, the *Widder* was at once attacked by a British submarine, but she was able to avoid the two torpedoes fired at her. Another submarine was sighted the next day. On the night of the 8th–9th the *Widder* left Bergen, with all available officers and men hard at work disguising the ship as the Swedish freighter *Narvik*. Steaming up the Norwegian coast in the spring twilight of the Arctic, and sheltering where possible in the daylight, the *Widder*, on May 13, sighted a strange vessel coming out of a rain squall. Action stations were sounded, and the raider turned away, followed by the mysterious vessel, which was at first thought to be a British destroyer but was later recognised as a submarine of the *Clyde* class (she was, in fact, the *Clyde* herself), which followed her for half an hour on the surface at full speed, the two ships exchanging fire as they went. Finally the submarine gave up the chase, and the *Widder* retired to the shelter of the Norwegian coast.

On the next day the raider was out again, favourable reports on ice and enemy activity having been received from the trawler *Vinnen*, sent ahead for scouting purposes. The *Widder* refuelled from the *Nordmark*, and then was soon up against the ice barrier, suffering some damage as she worked her way along its very edge westwards. There was thick weather and rain, but, having dodged an icebreaker on its way to Jan Mayen, by May 21 the raider had Cape Farewell abeam and was heading due south for a rendezvous with the supply ship *Königsberg*. The *Widder* was early at the rendezvous and had to wait for four days, drifting with her engines stopped to save fuel. Finally the supply ship arrived and Ruckteschell took on board enough fuel for four months. The *Königsberg* was sent into Vigo, but on her way she was intercepted by a French cruiser and scuttled herself, with the loss of a valuable cargo of rubber and copper.

By June 8 the *Widder* was on the route between Trinidad and the Azores, and wished to fly off her seaplane. This had to be delayed owing to the plane's faulty engine, and in the meantime the *Widder* was steaming at eight knots, with her engine room at four hours' notice for thirteen and a half knots for reasons of fuel economy. It was also calculated that keeping the ship in readiness for full speed of 14.8 knots would cost at least three tons of oil per day more than would otherwise be used.

After steering slowly towards Panama for three days, Ruckteschell, according to his war diary, turned back on reaching the edge of the neutrality zone and patrolled some distance from it. On the morning June 13, at 0935, his lookouts reported smoke, and he ordered steam for thirteen knots.

Half an hour later the smoke was seen to be from an armed tanker bound for Trinidad (and therefore in ballast). Ruckteschell opened fire at just over 6,000 yards and hit with the third salvo. The crew of the tanker abandoned ship, and Ruckteschell finished her off with a torpedo. She was the *British Petrol*, of 6,891 tons. Two members of the crew lost their lives in the shelling, and the rest were picked up by the *Widder*. The tanker had not been heard to send out an SOS, and it was discovered that her aerial had been shot away before she could do so.

For ten days the *Widder* criss-crossed the sea slowly between the Azores and Trinidad. On the moonlight night of June 17–18 she saw a big freighter heading for Bermuda or the United States, but she did not challenge it because it was thought that the ship was American. The raider's plane, after a four-hour flight on June 24, broke down, this time for good, and henceforward Ruckteschell was without air reconnaissance. There was another mishap on the next day, and the ship had to remain stopped for six hours while the engine-room complement dealt with salt in the intake valves. This was particularly annoying, for at this very time the SKL signalled the news that the Norwegian steamer *Sticklestad* was in the neighbourhood on her way from Casablanca to Fort de France, in Martinique.

Just as repairs were finished a ship was sighted which it was thought might be the *Sticklestad*, and the *Widder* manœuvred to let her pass about four miles astern. A warning shot was fired, and the ship stopped. The boarding party, to its surprise, found that she was not the *Sticklestad* but another Norwegian, the *Krossfonn*, of 9,323 tons, a tanker in ballast also from Casablanca to Fort de France.

The *Widder* went on looking for the *Sticklestad*, but although the Norwegian signals could be heard the ship could not be found. In the meantime the *Krossfonn* was sent into Brest, which was newly in German hands; she was the first prize to be brought to that port. In order that her appearance might not attract suspicion on the way, her tanks were flooded with water, as a tanker in ballast going towards Europe would be a very extraordinary phenomenon.

By now it was clear that the raider's plane would never fly again, and Ruckteschell ordered that its petrol and 200 fifty-kilogramme bombs should be thrown overboard. The *Widder* went on along the edge of the neutrality zone. On July 7 she stopped the Spanish ship *Motomar*, with iron, manufactured goods and agricultural machinery from New York to Rio. Her papers were in order and she was released. Three days later, on the same course, smoke was sighted, and half an hour later a medium-sized loaded merchant ship was seen, holding on her course towards the *Widder*, which opened fire. The first salvo straddled and six more were fired before the crew of the merchant ship took to their boats, but the ship did not give the alarm, as the first salvo had shot away her wireless aerial. The *Widder* came closer, and some members of the merchant ship's crew tried to man the 4-inch gun which she carried aft, but the *Widder* was within light automatic range and, sweeping the decks of the enemy, prevented the gun from being brought into action.

This ship was the British *Davisian*, of 6,433 tons, with 4,000 tons of coal and 2,000 tons of chemicals and briquettes from Cardiff to Barbados, Grenada and Trinidad. Her crew of fifty, six of them wounded, were brought on board, as were some fresh provisions—potatoes, tinned food and tobacco—before the ship was torpedoed. Giving evidence at the trial of Ruckteschell for war crimes in May 1947 Captain John H. Jolly, who had been second officer of the *Davisian* when she was sunk, said that the raider had continued firing on the British ship for eight minutes after she had signalled that she was obeying instructions. As a result of the shelling three men were killed. Ruckteschell, surveying his prisoners from his ship, commented that they were "Englishmen, not Scots, insolent and noisy."

There were now 100 prisoners on board, and the sick bay of the raider was nearly full.

Three days later another medium-sized freighter was sighted; fire was opened, checked and then opened again when the ship began to send an SOS. By this time the *Widder* was close enough to hit the freighter's bridge with her 37-millimetre gun and explode the enemy's ready-use ammunition, so that the freighter caught fire. She was the British *King John*, of 5,228 tons, in ballast from London to Vancouver with fifty-nine people on board, including survivors of the Panamanian steamer *Santa Marguerita*, which had been torpedoed by a U-boat. In his war diary Ruckteschell refers to these unfortunates as "Yugoslavs, Portuguese, Maltese and Spaniards . . . dirty and lousy people."

The problem of accommodation for prisoners was solved drastically by putting everybody but the captain and chief engineer of the *King John* and the seven wounded men into boats and telling them to make for the Lesser Antilles, some 240 miles distant. The *King John* was then sunk. the Germans noting with satisfaction that the SOS which she had sent out made an error in her position of 150 miles. Further to confuse the enemy as to his position and intentions, Ruckteschell steamed northwards as long as the boats were in sight, and then, when they had disappeared, altered course almost due east.

On July 13 the *Widder* asked for supplies, which she was told would be ready in a fortnight, to be brought to a rendezvous by the tanker *Rekum*, which was then at Teneriffe; the *Widder* was now redisguised as the Spanish *El Neptuno*.

On July 18 the French cruiser *Jeanne d'Arc* reported the arrival of forty-one men from the *King John* and *Davisian* at Anguilla. The stories which they told provided the British Admiralty with the first detailed eye-witness accounts of any one of the German raiders.

The Admiralty warned the cruisers *Dorsetshire* and *Can-*

berra, together with the armed merchant-cruisers *Alcantara, Pretoria Castle, Asturias* and *Bulolo,* and the sloop *Milford,* but they were unable to find the raider.

While the *Widder* was being sought, she was drifting in the Atlantic or cruising dead slow while repairs were being made to her engines and her disguise once again altered. On July 24 a tanker was sighted, in ballast, but Ruckteschell let her pass as the *Widder* was now within fifty miles of her rendezvous with the *Rekum,* and he did not wish to attract British attention to this area. When the *Rekum* arrived she proved a great disappointment, as she had brought no fresh food.

On August 1 the *Widder* had to forego another possible prize; smoke was sighted on the horizon, but Ruckteschell decided not to give chase, as he had been warned by the SKL that the British had taken a directional bearing from a recent short signal of his, and warned Allied shipping of the presence of a raider in the neighbourhood, though by some mischance the raider's position was miscalculated by about 500 miles.

Yet another tanker was sighted on August 4 heading for Trinidad, and therefore in ballast. All day long the *Widder* followed her just over the horizon, then at night she closed to within about 2,500 yards and opened fire without warning. Thirty rounds were fired into the tanker at top speed; nine shells were seen to hit, while the ship stopped and her crew could be seen getting into boats, which disappeared into the night. Nine days later they were picked up by the British tanker *Cymbeline.* The ship attacked was the Norwegian tanker *Beaulieu,* of 6,114 tons, on her way from the Azores to Amba; four of her crew lost their lives, including the captain.

Ruckteschell first tried to sink the abandoned ship with a torpedo, but the torpedo ran around in circles, and she had to be destroyed by explosive charges. As soon as she was plainly sinking the *Widder* steamed away towards the Azores at thirteen knots. Within a short distance of the islands, on August 8 and at midday, she sighted a medium-sized ship steering south. The *Widder* followed, trying to get into

97

position to attack later in the day from out of the setting sun. This was not possible, so that Ruckteschell waited until nightfall and then, at moonrise, managed to come around behind his target, silhouetted in the moonlight. Once more he attacked without warning at very short range—3,500 yards. Out of forty rounds five or six hit the enemy and she began to burn forward. Then, closing to within 2,000 yards, Ruckteschell opened up with his light anti-aircraft guns, firing on the bridge and the merchant ship's gun. Two boats got away with thirty-four people on board, the entire ship's company, and were all picked up by the raider, while the ship was finished off by a torpedo and further shelling. She had been the Dutch *Oostplein,* of 5,095 tons, carrying 5,850 tons of coal and coke from Cardiff and Hull to Buenos Aires.

Commenting on these sinkings, Ruckteschell wrote in his war diary: "Two night attacks have succeeded, but the week has cost us 314 tons of oil fuel, twice as much as usual . . . we have now got enough for about twelve weeks."

Two days later, as the *Widder* was idling northward, a three-masted barque was sighted at a great distance—about 30,000 yards. On approaching, she was seen to be under full sail and flying Finnish colours. The *Widder* fired two warning shots, and the sailing ship backed her mainmast and stopped. She was the *Killoran,* of 1,817 tons, with 2,500 tons of maize and 500 tons of sugar from Buenos Aires to Las Palmas. Finland at that time was neutral—later she was to join the war on the German side—but the ship was blown up and her crew taken aboard the *Widder,* who now held 116 prisoners of thirteen different nationalities, amongst them six captains.

The raider held on northward. On August 11 she stopped in a flat calm, but, says Ruckteschell in his war diary, "In flat weather it was difficult to watch the horizon, so I went at five knots south-west to get into a somewhat windier area," where she lay drifting on the Trinidad-Azores route. The engine-room personnel had now been working uninterruptedly since the beginning of April. Ruckteschell began training his deck people to help them, and managed to let twelve to fourteen men at a time from the engine room have leave on board.

Remarking on his various difficulties with the *Widder's* propelling machinery, Ruckteschell observed in the war diary that: "A steamship for this purpose (raiding) is and remains a foolishness." This was the same conclusion as that to which Weyher had come very soon, as the result of his experiences with the *Orion*. Steam had to be kept up all the time; if a boiler were shut down it took twelve hours to get it going again, and if the additional boiler was not used the ship's highest speed was thirteen knots. Even this, Ruckteschell commented, was hard to hold in warm water.

By moonlight, on August 16, a ship was seen at about 13,000 yards' distance, but Ruckteschell allowed her to pass "with heavy heart," as he said in the war diary, where he entered the reason for his act—there was too much moon for him to get close enough to sink the enemy without the alarm being given.

However, when he reflected on this decision later in the war diary, Ruckteschell blamed himself for not having remained in the vicinity of the enemy ship until moonset and then seen what might have been done. On this day he also received orders to refuel again from the *Rekum* at the end of September; meanwhile, until September 8, he cruised slowly southward.

After five days a medium-sized freighter was sighted. Ruckteschell resolved on the same form of attack in the dark, without warning, that had been successful in the cases of the *Beaulieu* and the *Oostplein,* and he retired to wait over the horizon. It was not pitch dark until eight o'clock, but moonrise came eighteen minutes later, which meant that there were just eighteen minutes in which to overpower the enemy.

The raider and the freighter came together on opposite courses. At eight minutes past eight *Widder* opened fire at 2,500 yards. The enemy's gun was hit and her ammunition set on fire. By searchlight the Germans read her name— *Anglo-Saxon,* a ship of 5,594 tons. *Widder* fired a torpedo, and the heavily laden ship sank with an explosion. The smoke from this blew over the *Widder,* so that the Germans could smell coal dust in the air and recorded in the war diary the presumption that the sunken ship was carrying a cargo of coal. Two lights were seen in the water after the explosion, presumably from boats; one morsed briefly and then there was nothing more. Ruckteschell did not look for survivors—an omission which was to cost him dearly after the war was over—giving the pretext in the war diary that the boats were "only 800 miles from the Canaries" and "the wind was favourable."

At Ruckteschell's trial Able Seaman R. G. Tapscott of the *Anglo-Saxon* said that the raider fired on the two life-boats as they moved away from the ship. One boat after seventy days at sea reached the Bahamas. Two of the eight people in her survived. The radio operator had died, and the other men, after ten days, had jumped overboard.

On August 26 Ruckteschell moved his cruising area a little to the east, so that ships steaming north or south on normal routes would be to westward. This was done because of the later moonrise, for although the new position was bad for observation around sunset, for a long time after that the evening sky was lighter than the sea.

At midday on the same day two ships were sighted, one a medium-sized freighter and the other a tanker on the way to Trinidad. The *Widder* manœuvred to attack the latter, but found her too fast. Ruckteschell gave up the chase, but by the time that he headed for the other ship she was almost out of sight and was fast enough to get away. Thus both attacks failed.

Ruckteschell now decided that he had been in this area long enough, for the survivors of the *Anglo-Saxon* might have reached safety and given a warning. Accordingly he headed to the northern edge of his zone of operations in the hope of finding fully laden ships heading eastwards from America. On the morning of September 2 a ship was sighted making about twelve knots. She was another tanker in ballast, and was not seen until she was just abeam of the *Widder.* This meant that if the raider turned towards her suddenly she would almost certainly become suspicious and send out an alarm; accordingly Ruckteschell let her pass out of sight and then followed on what he presumed would be her course towards Trinidad. Six hours afterwards the enemy came in sight on the bearing expected, but the *Widder* hung back until all her boilers were ready. Since the day on which two ships had been missed for lack of speed Ruckteschell had kept fires in all his boilers despite the extra cost in fuel. Now he was able to work up to fourteen knots and continued the chase across the sea by starlight. At 20.14 the shadow of the ship which he was stalking could be seen, a starshell was fired by the *Widder* and her guns opened up at about 2,600 yards. After the first salvo a boiler blew up aboard the merchantman and she was unable to use her gun, as her whole after-part was covered in steam.

Fire was checked and then reopened when it was heard that the enemy was trying to send an SOS. The enemy's bridge was taken as target and was soon ablaze; firing then once again ceased. Steaming around the burning ship, the Germans could read her name—*Cymbeline* of Liverpool, of 6,317 tons. She was then torpedoed and sank. Four hours were spent searching for survivors, of whom twenty-six were picked up—leaving ten men, including the captain, missing.

The survivors of the *Cymbeline* said that their captain had seen the *Widder* that morning and had wirelessed a warning of a suspicious ship, a warning which had not been heard by the Germans.

After this Ruckteschell made more changes in the ship's appearance, altering masts and derrick booms and covering all the white paintwork with an indefinite brownish colour, so that the ship would not show up in the moonlight. At the same time he painted his ship grey, presumably to give her the look of a British auxiliary cruiser.

The time was coming to refuel again, but before that happened Ruckteschell decided to appear somewhere as remote from the refuelling rendezvous as possible, so that attention might be attracted away from his meeting-place with the *Rekum*. Accordingly he went to the south-east end of his area across the route from Trinidad to Freetown.

Each night as he steamed on his way he hauled off his

course for an hour, as soon as it was dark, to throw off a possible shadower.

"If the English ships did that," Ruckteschell observed in the war diary, "I could practically never catch another one of them."

September 7 and 8 were spent fighting with engine trouble, and in tropical rain squalls the port engine failed completely. The rain stopped, but dark clouds still obscured the moon. Lights were seen coming nearer—one an ordinary steaming light, the other illuminating a flag which could not be distinguished. At 19.39 the *Widder* fired a starshell and morsed an order to stop. The strange ship obeyed and proved to be ·Greek—the *Antonios Chandris,* of 5,866 tons, carrying 6,616 tons of coal from Cardiff to Buenos Aires. Various stores and some meat were taken on board and the ship blown up. Her crew were put in their boats, which Ruckteschell described as "well found," adding that they would have "no shortage of water, as it was raining."

Finally the day came for the meeting with the tanker—not the *Rekum* but the *Eurofeld*—and Ruckteschell thankfully stopped his engines, now capable of only five knots. His long trip to the south had cost him 500 tons of oil and brought him only one ship.

By September 16 refuelling was complete, and the *Eurofeld* made off at top speed, followed by the *Widder,* at the last gasp of her engines. The *Rekum* now appeared and was given mails, the war diary and reports to take back to Germany, while the *Widder* started repairs once again.

In fact repairs were now almost continuous, there being nothing but an endless series of breakdowns, partial or complete. On September 26 the raider's top speed was eight knots, not even enough to overtake a slow collier which was sighted and which had to be avoided.

Next day, when the engines had once again stopped completely at six in the morning, a ship was sighted heading straight for the raider.

There was no possibility of avoiding her, and the Germans went to action stations. The gunlayers made their way to their own weapons over the decks disguised one as the cook and the others as merchant seamen. They then prowled, apparently aimlessly, around their weapons, while the ship hoisted the Norwegian flag and two black balls signifying "not under control." The ship came closer, and then, as she passed across the *Widder's* bow, she was seen to be the Vichy French ship *Capitaine Lemerle*.

On September 28 the engines worked for nine hours and once more came to a dead stop; six days' continuous work got them to a state in which they were able to make five knots, and Ruckteschell realised that there was nothing to be done but go home, if that were possible.

He announced this intention to his crew on October 7 as the *Widder* worked up to seven knots, accompanied by strange noises and shakings from the engines; on the 10th he had more good news to broadcast through the ship—the *Rekum* had got home with the private mail and with despatches. At least, reflected the captain, the SKL would know what they had been doing, even if they never did get home.

Slowly they worked north-eastward towards France. Various ships passed them on an opposite course, but there could be no possibility of the raider chasing anything when her top speed was 6.25 knots.

One splendid opportunity was lost near home when a big Blue Funnel liner was identified on the horizon, but the disappointment was soon set aside by the arrival of the escorting planes and submarines which picked them up and took them to Brest, which they reached on October 31, having sunk 10 ships of 58,645 tons.

Guns and equipment from the ship were removed and installed in new raiders; Ruckteschell, after some months, received a new command—Ship 28, the *Michel*, which he held for nearly two years. He was the only one of the raider captains put on trial as a war criminal, and he was finally sentenced to ten years' inprisonment in 1947. He died in prison. He had been found guilty of failing to secure the safety of the crews of the *Anglo-Saxon* and *Beaulieu* and of continuing to fire on the *Davisian* after the captain of that ship had signified that she was being abandoned. He was found not guilty of various other charges.

The *Widder* survived the war and became the British freighter *Ulysses*, but afterwards was sold back to Germany and renamed *Eichenheim*.

IV
Thor • SHIP 10

IT WAS never the duty of a German armed raider to fight actions with Allied warships. A single comparatively small gun could, as will be seen later, put a raider out of action or even sink her. Therefore any ship likely to do serious damage to a raider's unarmoured sides had to be avoided whenever possible.

But one of the raiders, Ship 10—the *Thor*—in her career was forced to fight three British armed merchant-cruisers, and she put two of them out of action and sank the third— a very remarkable performance, which was due as much to skill as to good fortune.

The *Thor* was one of the smallest of the raiders, being of 3,144 tons (about the size of a large cross-channel steamer); she was built by the Deutsche Werft, Hamburg, in 1938, as the banana boat *Santa Cruz* for the Oldenburg-Portuguesische Line.

The SKL had always considered ships for the transport of bananas and other fruit as the ideal vessels to act as armed merchant raiders, and had always looked with favour on their construction from the earliest days of the rebuilding of the German navy. At one stage, under the Weimar Republic, it was alleged that the German navy was giving clandestine financial assistance to various banana plantations, so that these plantations would order ships which would be suitable for use as raiders by Germany in the event of war.

The advantages which the banana boats possessed were

two: they were fast compared with the average merchant ship, and they were small. The importance of presenting a small target will be seen from the *Thor's* experience of engaging British armed merchant-cruisers of equivalent armament and about six times the size.

The *Thor* was designed for seventeen knots. Her engines were oil-fired steam turbines, which seem to have behaved excellently, thus showing that Ruckteschell was wrong when he said that it was foolish to use a steam-engined ship as a raider. The maximum radius of action of the *Thor* was 40,000 miles at ten knots. Her armament was much the same as that of the other raiders—six 5.9-inch guns, one 60-millimetre to simulate the small gun carried at the stern of all Allied defensively equipped merchant ships, two 37-millimetre and four 20-millimetre light anti-aircraft guns, together with four torpedo tubes.

Her captain was Otto Kähler, who, when he took command in October 1939, was forty-five years old. He had joined the German navy in 1914, and, like Rogge of the *Atlantis,* had commanded both the German navy's sail training ships.

The *Thor* sailed from Kiel on June 6, 1940. The business of passing a raider out into the ocean was becoming a large-scale operation, partly because there was almost no darkness in the high latitudes and also because the Allied warships taking part in the fighting around Narvik were likely to be across the route of the raider. When the *Thor* sailed she had an escort of destroyers, aircraft and minesweepers, as well as a *sperrbrecher,* a converted merchant ship with a very heavy anti-aircraft armament and special minesweeping equipment generally used for the escort of coastwise convoys.

The first disguise assumed by the new raider was Russian —as the steamship *Orsk* of Odessa.

Very bad weather, of course, was the best possible thing to aid the *Thor's* escape into the Atlantic, and this was enjoyed to the full; the ship appears to have travelled constantly in a thick fog, with a good deal of snow. This fog had its disadvantage, as the German ship felt her way along the southern edge of the icepack, but its cover enabled her to emerge into the open ocean on June 16. Twice she was obliged to avoid enemy vessels—three ships on June 20, and one on June 23, south-west of the Azores. The latter was suspected of being a British armed merchant-cruiser, and the first three were passed, presumably because it was not desired to draw attention to the *Thor's* presence at sea until she was nearer her operational area in the South Atlantic.

Past the Azores, the ship took on another disguise: this time she was the Yugoslav *Vir* of Split, on her way from Liverpool via Horta to Pernambuco and Santos.

Writing in the war diary, Kähler said, on June 28, that as stores were consumed it was possible for him to begin to make a space forward for prisoners which he might take, but that this would have been impossible if he had not had his mineroom free, as in that case he could not have accommodated any prisoners until the mines had been laid.

To this the SKL added comment afterwards that if mines had been carried out it would have been necessary to wait until they had been laid off the Cape of Good Hope or a similar remote spot.

As it was, the *Thor* began operations on July 1, when she stopped the Dutch *Kertosono* with a single warning shot, and without the alarm being given. The prize was of 9,289 tons, on her way from New Orleans to Curaçao and Freetown with petrol, asphalt, wood and agricultural machinery consigned to British ports. Her crew numbered fifty-six, and there were nine passengers, including four women and a baby. The *Kertosono* was a fine ship, and Kähler decided to send her with a prize crew to Lorient, where she arrived safely twelve days later.

A week later, just south of the equator, another ship was seen, on the port bow, which turned away to eastward. A two-hour chase then followed, until finally the *Thor,* from about 8,000 yards, opened fire with a full broadside. There was a hit with the third salvo and the attacked ship did not succeed in using her 4-inch stern gun or her wireless, according to the raider's war diary.

A prize crew was sent over, which reported:

"English steamer *Delambre,* of 7,032 tons, under charter

106

by British Admiralty with cotton, hides, cotton seed from Rio de Janeiro to Freetown and Liverpool. Forty-four man crew, one passenger, all English."

The ship was scuttled, her people being brought on board the raider. The British captain said that he had had the same misfortune in the last war, having been taken prisoner by the *Möwe*.

On the morning July 9 another ship was stopped by shots across her bows; this was the Belgian ship *Bruges,* of 4,983 tons, a former German vessel, captured in 1914, now carrying 6,746 tons of wheat from Necochea and Mar del Plata to St. Vincent and Freetown. This ship was also scuttled and her crew of forty-four taken on board. *Thor* was now carrying ninety prisoners, accommodated in a space made for them by throwing overboard empty packing cases.

Five days later yet another ship was taken. At last light the British *Gracefield* was stopped off Trinidad; she was a ship of 4,631 tons, taking 7,430 tons of wheat and bran from Montevideo to Freetown and London. There was a high sea running which made boat-work difficult in the dark, and Kähler did not wish to use his searchlight for fear of attracting attention, but all members of the crew of thirty-six were brought safely on board. Two torpedoes were fired to sink the British ship, but one ran around in circles and Kähler had to use his guns.

The *Thor* continued on her course, more or less parallel to the coast of Brazil, and two days later she found a ship, on the latitude of Rio de Janeiro, heading for the River Plate. Coming up from behind a smoke-cloud, *Thor* attacked at once without warning, as Kähler had seen that the ship carried two guns aft and, in his own words, "wished to nip any resistance in the bud."

The enemy was straddled by the third salvo, then hit aft and set on fire. At this moment she began to send RRR, and a man ran aft to the guns. Fire was reopened, and there were two more hits; the RRR message stopped and the fire spread. As the ship slowed down her crew began to abandon her, and a boarding party from the *Thor* set off. Demolition charges were exploded in her hull; she turned right over and floated upside down, so that she had to be finished off with more 5.9-inch shells. She had been the *Wendover*, a British ship of 5,489 tons, carrying 7,250 tons of coal to Buenos Aires. Two out of forty members of her crew were killed—one was the wireless operator, and two more died of wounds on board the *Thor*, and were buried at sea by the Germans with full military honours, their bodies covered by the British flag.

On the afternoon of the next day there was yet another success, the Dutch *Tela* being stopped with a shot across her bows. She was a 3,777-ton ship with 5,451 tons of grain from Rosario to the United Kingdom via Freetown. The crew of thirty-three were taken on board and the ship sunk.

The *Thor* had now within seventeen days sunk six ships of 35,201 tons, and had on board 194 prisoners, so that, as the war diary commented, "the little ship is beginning to get crowded".

On board the *Tela* were found details of "Route 271", on which the last four ships had been met. Accordingly it seemed promising to keep on the same course, but for the next ten days nothing was seen, despite the use of the Arado for reconnaissance.

However, on July 28, at nine o'clock on a morning of good visibility, with a gentle breeze blowing, masts came in sight. From a distance of 28,000 yards it was clear that it was a big ship, either a cargo vessel or an armed merchant-cruiser. Her speed of sixteen knots suggested the former, and Kähler turned to investigate.

At 1001 the siren went in the German ship for action stations. The *Thor* turned to course 230 at seventeen knots and the other ship followed her round. The Germans saw she was a ship of about 14,000 tons, with tall upperworks, and her behaviour and appearance left them in no doubt that she was a British armed merchant-cruiser.

In view of his general orders to avoid any engagement with an enemy warship Kähler turned away and made off at full speed, with the British ship following at about 20,000 yards. The chase lasted until past noon. As the pursuer, which was the *Alcantara*, a former Royal Mail liner of 22,209 tons, began to come up closer astern she sent a long message in cypher.

It was clear that she was the faster ship, and Kähler decided that all he could do was to try to damage her enough to reduce her speed, so that he could escape.

At 1257 *Thor* dropped her disguise and reduced speed to fifteen knots. The seventeen knots she had been making caused so much vibration that gun crews and range-finders were hampered in their work.

One minute later the raider turned at right angles across the *Alcantara's* bows, hoisted the German flag and opened fire with her four-gun broadside at 14,000 yards. The *Alcantara* replied at once; *Thor's* third salvo straddled her and she turned away slightly, so that her starboard broadside would bear. The Germans had the sun behind them, while the British gunners were obliged to fire into it.

From the bridge of the *Thor* it was possible to see two hits on *Alcantara*—one between the bridge and the funnel, which produced a lot of steam, and one aft. The raider's second salvo cut the fire-control cable of No. 4 gun on the port side of the British ship and killed one rating. With the next salvo the *Alcantara* was hit on the water-line at the fore end of the engine-room on the starboard side; this caused a reduction in speed.

The British ship replied with three or four guns, firing independently and not altogether in a broadside. The British gunnery appeared good; Kähler noted in his report that hits in the water left behind "a poisonous green colour" on the surface, while their splashes were smaller than those of the German shells. The German shells which fell short in water burst on impact, throwing up columns of water heavily specked with black which drenched the British gun crews. In the British ship the noise of the action was so great that it was impossible to hear the orders given. Eight minutes after opening fire Kähler altered course and increased speed; the *Alcantara* changed course, too, a little, and the ships were steaming in opposite directions.

Kähler found that he could no longer reach full speed, on account of condenser trouble, almost immediately his ship was hit for the first time, on the starboard side of the upper deck, abeam of No. 1 hold. The British shell passed straight through the ship without exploding, but it tore away electric cables on the upper mess deck, extinguishing lights and stopping the ammunition hoists for the forward guns.

There was a certain amount of smoke, but no fire started, and the damage had been quickly repaired, when another shell burst on the starboard side of the boat deck. Splinters on the boat deck, and on the deck below, killed three men and wounded four, while the starboard torpedo tubes were temporarily out of action.

The *Thor* was still steering south, and now seemed to be steaming a little faster than the enemy. Accordingly Kähler turned slightly to bring his ship dead ahead of the British vessel so that she might present a smaller target. Fire was kept up by the *Thor*, with one, two or three guns, despite the difficulties in spotting caused by the German's own smoke and by the fact that the fire-control position on her bridge was masked by her own funnel.

Enemy shells were falling near, but at 1321 *Thor* had to cease fire, as the target was by now completely hidden in smoke. Accordingly Kähler turned to starboard to bring his ship out from behind the smoke and opened fire once more; no hits could be observed through the smoke.

Then, as the smoke cleared away, the *Alcantara* was seen to be stopped, although still firing with four guns. It was then 1329.

Kähler in his report says that he would like to have gone back to finish the enemy off, but that he had to keep in mind the fact that a single lucky shot might put him out of action for good; in addition, other British ships might soon arrive on the scene. Accordingly at 1335 he decided to break off the action and steamed away under cover of smoke. During the action he had fired 284 of his 5.9-inch shells. Later on, when Raeder received Kähler's report he specifically approved his having broken off the action.

The *Thor* buried her dead and began repairs, as well as a change of disguise, since it was realised that the *Alcantara* would certainly have radioed her description.

The *Thor, Pinguin* and *Widder* were now all more or less in the same area, but it was clear that the British Admiralty would not know which ship was which, nor, probably, whether there were in fact two ships at large or three.

As for the *Alcantara,* she went back to her base with a collision mat on her side and two feet of water over her tank tops.

By July 30 *Thor* had reached the latitude of Tristan da Cunha and slowed down to five knots for boiler cleaning and the completion of repairs. After twelve days' work Kähler reported to Berlin that he planned to operate on the route between the River Plate and the Cape of Good Hope, and then go on to a meeting with the *Rekum* that had already been arranged by Berlin. Here, in addition to replenishing his ship, he would be able to get rid of his prisoners and take on board more officers and men for duty as prize crews.

The Germans had by now found out that the most recent British anti-raider measures included the provision of spare aerials in merchant ships and the order that the RRR signal should be sent at once on suspicion, even at the risk of mistakes, which could be rectified afterwards. Merchant ships were warned that any ship approaching them was to be treated as suspicious. One of the effects of these orders developed on August 12 when the *Thor* listened with appreciation to five solid hours of transmission by Allied merchant ships of false alarms. The *Rekum* was met on August 25th, but Kähler found that the tanker was unable to accept his prisoners, and he decided to head back to Brazilian waters, steaming in long zig-zags. On September 8 the Yugoslav ship *Federico Glavic* was stopped, but as Yugoslavia at that time was neutral, and the ship had no British goods on board, she was released in accordance with orders.

By September 12 *Thor* was about 700 miles east of Pernambuco and she continued north until the 26th, when at nine o'clock in the morning her spotting plane saw a ship which an hour later was stopped with two shots across the bows. She was the Norwegian whaling factory ship *Kosmos,* of 17,801 tons, with a crew of eighty-nine, carrying 17,662 tons of whale oil from Walvis Bay to Curaçao. This

111

was an extraordinarily valuable prize, but the ship was short of fuel and Kähler did not believe there was any chance of getting her home with her wonderful cargo. She was also extremely conspicuous with two funnels side by side right aft so that there was no possibility of disguising her. For that reason her value as a depot ship would be compromised. In addition she was a slow ship, and the Allies would be on the look-out for her within a few days, as soon as she failed to arrive on schedule at Curaçao.

For these reasons the ship was sunk, to the annoyance of the SKL, which pointed out that it was proving much easier to get ships into French ports than had been expected, as the case of the *Kertosono* had shown. In any event, said the SKL, with so valuable a ship and cargo a risk would have been justified under any circumstances.

Just north of the equator, the *Thor* lay for twelve days having another boiler-clean. This had just been finished on October 8 when a big ship was sighted on a course which showed that she was on the way from Europe to America. The *Thor* gave chase and, opening fire at 9,000 yards, scored a hit at once. The Germans then checked fire, but the enemy ship continued to use her wireless. Fire was therefore re-opened, while the signals of alarm were successfully jammed. One hundred and seventy-five rounds were fired and four hits were scored. The ship was then torpedoed, but although her whole side from below the water-line to her upper deck amidships was torn open she did not sink until thirty-five more rounds had been fired. She was the British refrigerator ship *Natia*, of 8,715 tons, in ballast from London to Buenos Aires. Of her crew of eighty-five, one man was killed and one was wounded, and the *Thor* now had 368 prisoners on board.

It was urgent, wrote Kähler, that this question of prisoners should be solved. In addition to this difficulty he almost always had to deal with the problem of fuel. His ship could operate for four to four and a half months without refueling, but if she was to have full operational freedom she needed to replenish every two to three months.

An apparently insignificant shortage which threatened a

112

great deal of trouble was caused by the continual breaking of boiler gauges, but the SKL came quickly to the rescue. New gauges were ordered on September 22 and were delivered by the *Rio Grande,* which had broken out of Rio Grande do Sul on November 9.

The *Rio Grande* and the *Thor* were together from November 9 until November 16, and Kähler at last got rid of his prisoners. Before they were put on board the *Rio Grande* the prison ship was disguised as the *Belgrano,* a vessel known to be in German waters. This was to give the impression that the ship was working from Europe, but the prisoners were not, in fact, deceived.

The *Thor* steamed south once more, heading for the Cape of Good Hope–River Plate route. On November 24 she received news from SKL of enemy dispositions in the South Atlantic.

In the Freetown area the battleship *Resolution* had been reported on November 22.

In the area from West Africa to the Cape were eight cruisers—*Canberra, Devonshire, Shropshire, Dorsetshire, Cornwall, Delhi, Vindictive* and *Dragon.*

On the east coast of South America were the *Enterprise* and *Hawkins.*

The strong concentration in the South Atlantic showed the difficulties lying ahead. Meanwhile, from November 28 to December 2, the *Thor* was watching the River Plate, hoping to find the ships which she believed were leaving Montevideo; after the latter date she cruised along the Plate–Freetown route.

On December 4 the German radio announced that twenty-two Germans had been removed by the British armed merchant-cruiser *Carnarvon Castle* from a Brazilian vessel—presumably the *Rio Grande.*

Kähler in his war diary says that he assumed that the *Carnarvon Castle* had taken the place of the damaged *Alcantara* and that she would be patrolling the routes running northeast from the Plate (that is to say, those to the United Kingdom). Accordingly Kähler decided to remain south of the Plate.

On the very next morning, at 0531, a very large steamer suddenly appeared from out of the fog at about four miles' distance. She was clearly a British armed merchant-cruiser, and probably the *Carnarvon Castle*. Kähler hoped to slip back into the fog, but the British ship turned towards him.

Action stations were sounded at 0533 and the German captain ordered full speed. At first the *Thor* began to draw away, but the British ship gradually began to overhaul her, signalling by searchlight as she did so:

SC—Show your Identity.
K—Stop at once.

Thor held on, with her three after guns—the only ones that could bear—ready for use. Kähler still hoped to shake off the enemy in the thick weather.

At 0701 the *Carnarvon Castle* (for it was she) opened fire, and a minute later *Thor* replied, hoisting the German ensign. The range was about 13,000 yards and the enemy lay on the port quarter. *Carnarvon Castle* was now southward of the *Thor,* which began to work round to the north and the east, so that the British gunners would have the early morning sun in their eyes, as well as the smoke-screen which the Germans were already laying.

The British were firing irregularly with four 6-inch guns—two forward, one just forward of the mainmast and one at the stern—as well as from two smaller guns on the boat deck, aft of the funnel. By 0721 the *Carnarvon Castle* was following the *Thor* northward. Ten minutes later the raider was heading east and then south-east, so that the two ships were circling round each other. At 0730 *Thor* fired two torpedoes, but both missed just as the sun broke through the clouds. The range was now about 8,000 yards, falling to 7,000 and *Thor* was firing salvoes every six seconds. She scored five certain hits, three of which burst with a bright red flame, one of them forward of the bridge and two aft. The *Carnarvon Castle* was maintaining her speed, and kept on firing in the same irregular fashion, turning east to keep all guns on her broadside bearing. Changes of course had opened the range, and the

114

British shells were falling wide, their bursts turning the water bright green, as had done the shells of the *Alcantara*.

When the action had been in progress for an hour Kähler had to consider the possibility of his ship running out of ammunition; moreover, some of his guns were so hot from constant firing that they jammed on their mountings. Then suddenly, to Kähler's complete surprise, at 0802 the *Carnarvon Castle* turned north and disappeared at reduced speed, having failed to make a single hit.

By the end of the action the *Carnarvon Castle* had been hit repeatedly. She was on fire amidships, the A.A. magazine was flooded and only forty rounds of ammunition remained. A direct hit had started a cordite fire at No. 4 6-inch gun on the starboard side, another shell cut the exhaust from the main engine and a fire started in the funnel. Forty per cent of her exposed personnel were casualties.

As she steamed away the British vessel had a list to port; she had been hit in the funnel, on the promenade deck amidships, on the bridge and twice in the hull just above the water-line. She received emergency repairs in Montevideo, the patches put on her hull being made from plates salved from the wreck of the *Admiral Graf Spee,* which had been scuttled after the action of December 1939.

Kähler looked about his ship; seventy per cent of his ammunition had been used up, and some of the guns had fired as many as 115 rounds. Perhaps the hardest-pressed men in the ship, however, had been the engine-room complement working in a temperature of 140°.

The SKL sent a well-deserved message of congratulation, with the slightest hint that perhaps *Thor* might try not to do this sort of thing again, for it was clear that she had not only been skilfully handled, but also very lucky.

Fuel and ammunition were needed at once, and by December 21 the *Thor* was in the South Atlantic rendezvous area, where one after another there arrived the *Scheer, Eurofeld, Nordmark, Duquesa* and *Storstad,* the first friendly ships seen for five months.

The *Scheer* was the last to arrive, on Christmas morning,

and the pocket battleship and the armed merchant-cruiser greeted each other with cheers.

While replenishment was going on, Kähler and the captain of the *Scheer* discussed future operations in the middle of a series of Christmas parties held in the various ships.

At first the two commanding officers considered the possibility of their ships working together, but the twenty-six-knot pocket battleship would have been gravely handicapped by having to keep her speed down to that of the seventeen-knot *Thor;* at the same time the *Thor* was too slow to act as a scout for the *Scheer*.

As far as can be gathered from his war diary, Kähler felt that if he remained in the *Scheer's* company all that he could do would be to act as a tender and prison ship, and he succeeded in convincing Krancke, the captain of the pocket battleship, that this would be a great waste of a valuable ship.

Finally, it was decided that the two ships should stay in the South Atlantic until the end of January, operating separately —the *Scheer* keeping to the north of 30°, and the *Thor* to the south.

The two ships parted, after a present from the *Scheer* to the *Thor* of seven tons of meat and 62,000 eggs taken from the *Duquesa*. This ship, when taken by the *Scheer*, had had on board 3,500 tons of frozen meat and fifteen million eggs. Since then she had been used as a floating larder by the Germans, towed slowly around the South Atlantic by the *Nordmark*, as she had no more fuel. Finally, after replenishing the *Pinguin* a little later, she was scuttled.

January 1, 1941, was marked by a broadcast speech by Hitler, but the whole month passed uneventfully, and at its end the ship came north, crossing the equator on February 1. From February 14 to February 28 she was replenishing from the *Eurofeld* and *Alsterufer*, taking on board one thousand rounds of 5.9-inch ammunition, as well as torpedoes, which had to be transferred from one ship to the other lashed to rubber dinghies; all the replenishment operations were carried on in unfavourable weather with a heavy swell. However, by February 28 the *Thor* was ready to operate independently until the middle of May.

On March 3 Kähler had orders to meet ten whale catchers, which had been taken by the *Pinguin* in the Antarctic and were being sent home after refuelling from the *Spicheren* (which was the *Widder's* prize *Krossfonn* renamed). On March 5 refuelling of the whale catchers began, the little ships being brought alongside in pairs, and serious damage to the *Thor's* port boiler was repaired, 466 of this boiler's tubes having been burned through out of a total of 936. After this, Kähler took up a position west and south-west of the Cape Verde Islands, where he stayed from March 16 to March 20. At that time U-boats were working to the east of the islands and it was thought that this would drive unescorted Allied merchantmen to the westward, where they might be caught by the *Thor*.

However, things did not work out this way. Not until March 21 was anything sighted, and then the ship seen, thought to be on her way from New York to the Cape, was quickly lost, and the *Thor* could not find her again, as further search would have meant entering the area in which the U-boats were operating. There was, of course, no way by which the U-boat commanders could tell that the *Thor* was not, as she pretended to be, an Allied or neutral merchant ship.

Four days later, however, at seven o'clock in the morning, a cloud of smoke was once more seen on the horizon. There followed masts and a steamer could be seen zig-zagging and headed southwards. The *Thor* hoisted the Yugoslav flag and the crew went to action stations. At 0750 the ship turned away and was seen to be a big freighter with a gun aft; she made smoke and headed northward at high speed. As she seemed as though she might get away, the German flag was hoisted and fire was opened at 10,000 yards.

The ship being chased was heard by *Thor* to wireless:

"*Britannia* RRR 7° 24′ north 24° 30′ west gunned." This, of course, the German operator tried to jam, but the British ship's transmitter was very powerful and soon Sierra Leone radio could be heard repeating the alarm.

The *Britannia* was returning the raider's fire with her single gun, and kept on northward until, after *Thor* had fired 159 rounds, she appeared to stop. Kähler checked fire and as the raider came up she heard a signal to the *Britannia* which showed that a British warship was just over 100 miles away and coming at full speed to the rescue. As the *Thor* approached the stationary ship a man was seen in the water, hanging on to a tiny raft. He was picked up by the Germans and said that he had fallen overboard from the *Britannia* during the chase.

The 500 people on board the *Britannia*—200 crew and 300 passengers, including twelve women—took to the boats, and when they were out of the line of fire Kähler started shelling the abandoned ship, and she sank after having been hit sixteen times on the water-line.

The last signs of the *Britannia,* a ship of 8,799 tons, visible to the crew of the *Thor* were the boats on the water and a column of smoke and flame a thousand feet high as she sank.

Kähler decided to leave the *Britannia's* passengers and crew in their boats, because with a British warship approaching he had no time in which to pick them up. He steamed away with regret, for he did not want to leave at liberty anyone who had seen his ship.

In his report to the SKL on the cruise Kähler was at some pains to excuse himself for having sunk a passenger ship, adopting two contradictory lines of argument—first, that he could not tell that she was a passenger ship; and second, that she was not a passenger ship but a transport.

On the afternoon of the same day as that on which she had sunk the *Britannia* the *Thor* stopped the Swedish motor vessel *Trolleholm,* of 5,047 tons, under charter to the British Admiralty and carrying coal from Newcastle to Port Said. She was sunk by demolition charges after her crew had been taken off.

At midnight on March 29-30 a ship was sighted fully lit; assuming that she was therefore an American, Kähler avoided her and his ship was not seen.

The next ship the *Thor* met was reported early in the morning of April 4. In his war diary Kähler wrote:

"0615. Ten minutes after sunrise sighted heavy smoke on misty south-west horizon, through which masts and a funnel could be seen.

118

"We had been in this area since March 30 boiler cleaning and had so far seen nothing.

"The great quantity of smoke from this ship showed that she was a coal burner. I decided to close her to have a good look.

"At 0621 action stations. Ship was now distant 210 hecto-metres and kept on her course. I took her to be a neutral. I hoisted the Greek flag."

The ships were now heading towards each other at a high combined rate of speed. *Thor* moved over to get the sun behind her, and the other ship began to flash a lamp signal. At 0645 *Thor* hoisted the German flag and fired a shot across the bows of the oncoming ship.

"Just at this moment we could see two guns on her fore-castle, and this was clearly the third English armed merchant-cruiser to get in our way," continues Kähler, "and I opened fire at 0646 with our entire battery."

The enemy, the British armed merchant-cruiser *Voltaire*, of 13,245 tons, answered with two guns, and the size of their green bursts showed the German that they were probably 6-inch.

"We hit with our first salvo," Kähler goes on, "and within three minutes of our opening fire at 92 hectometres (about 9,200 yards) the enemy was heavily on fire amidships and from time to time she was completely covered in flames.

"She was firing irregularly with single guns. Her shells mostly fell short, bursting green and then white.

"My aerial was shot away. The only hit in the action.

"Smoke obscured the range and I turned to starboard. We were firing a salvo every six seconds at a range of 71 hecto-metres.

"At 0700 the enemy turned directly at me. I thought that he might be going to use torpedoes, so I turned away and then back. The enemy began to circle round, covered in smoke, but we could see our shells bursting with a light-coloured flash and his guns answering.

"At 0715 I tried to torpedo him. It was now clear that the enemy's steering gear had broken down and that he was steaming in circles. He was now completely covered in flames from

119

the bridge to the mainmast. Flashes from fore and aft showed that his guns were still firing.

"Three out of four of my guns on the engaged broadside were out of action, owing to a breakdown of the training gear, after it had become overheated. I turned around to engage the enemy with my other broadside. We hit him again and again with three guns, but his fore and aft guns kept on firing.

"I was having to head to north and the wind was blowing my smoke down on the enemy.

"0741 my last three guns broke down for the same reason as the others. I had to cease fire—at 59 hectometres—and manœuvre for a torpedo hit.

"The enemy also ceased fire and showed a white flag on the forecastle. I came to within 30–40 hectometres, but could come no further because of the danger of explosions. All the enemy's boats were shot away or on fire, and I began to pick up those of his crew already in the water. The burning ship listed to port, still steaming slowly in a circle."

The *Voltaire* sank at 0835 under a huge cloud of smoke and a pall of oil over the water. The action had lasted fifty-five minutes, during which the *Thor* had fired 724 rounds—more than half her total supply of ammunition. Her wireless was out of action, but she stayed at the scene of the action until 1300 picking up survivors. There were 197 of these, including the captain and nineteen officers.

After the action the wireless was repaired, the look of the *Thor's* masts altered, and she was disguised as a Russian, since she was once more coming into northerly waters, where a Russian ship might be sighted.

She refuelled on April 12–13 from the tanker *Ill*, to whom she transferred 170 of her prisoners, leaving fifty-seven from the *Voltaire* still on board, and steamed on towards home. On April 16 she made her last capture—the Swedish ship *Sir Ernest Cassel*, of 7,739 tons, in ballast. The ship was old and she was scuttled as soon as the crew had been taken on board.

On April 18 *Thor* turned east-north-east towards the coast of France, and five days later, in drizzling rain, she was met by an escort of two planes and three destroyers. She made her way through the Channel and via Cherbourg, Le Havre and the Hook, laying up in the daytime and steaming by night, and arrived in Hamburg on April 30, after a voyage of 329 days, during which she had steamed 57,532 miles and sunk twelve ships of 96,547 tons.

Kähler's next appointment was to the Department for Merchant Shipping in the OKM (Oberkommando der Marine), first as head of a section and then of the department.

In February 1944, having been promoted to rear-admiral, he was appointed N.O.I.C. Britanny, where he was taken prisoner by the Americans after the Allied landings, and sent as a prisoner of war to the United States.

The *Thor* and the *Komet* were the only two German merchant raiders to attempt two cruises. *Thor's* second cruise and her eventual fate is described later in this book (pp. 180-183).

V

Pinguin • SHIP 33

THE *Pinguin* was the first of the armed merchant raiders to be sunk, but no one did as much damage as she except the *Atlantis*, and nobody sank or captured as many ships. Altogether she disposed of twenty-eight vessels of 136,551 tons from the time she sailed from Germany on June 22, 1940, until she was sunk by H.M.S. *Cornwall* on May 8 of the following year.

Pinguin was a motorship of 7,766 tons—that is to say, almost the identical size as the *Atlantis, Orion* and *Widder*, with a speed of eighteen knots, and had a similar armament, which had been taken from the obsolete battleship *Schlesien*.

The raider had formerly been the *Kandelfels* of the Hansa Line and was commanded by Captain Felix Krüder, an officer forty-three years old who had joined the navy in 1915 and had been promoted from the lower deck. Like Rogge

121

and Weyher, he had served in the Inspectorate of Officers' Training and Education, and when war broke out was serving in the OKM.

His new command finished her trials on June 9 and received orders to operate in the Indian Ocean, off the Australian coast, and from December to March in the Antarctic, when the Allied whaling fleets, mostly Norwegian, would be busy. If for any reason the raider had to leave these zones of operation she was to go to the South Atlantic or the Pacific. The 300 mines which she carried were to be laid off Australia and on the west coast of India, between Karachi and Dondra Head.

The ship's first disguise as she steamed under escort through the Great Belt was as the Russian *Petschura*, and in ideally bad weather she continued up the Norwegian coast as if she were bound for Murmansk. The sea was too heavy for her escorting vessels to keep up, but it also proved too bad for submarines to do so either, for one which surfaced and began to follow her soon had to dive because of the weather, and the *Pinguin* was able to continue unmolested. Krüder noted in his war diary that if, as a result of this meeting, the British now thought that a raider was out, that would be all to the good once the *Pinguin* was actually at large, past the Denmark Straits.

But the weather, having been good from the point of view of escape, now improved and was therefore unfavourable. It was midsummer night and there was just a little dusk and no darkness to hide the ship. Krüder proposed to disappear into the fog banks which he hoped to find in the neighbourhood of Jan Mayen, and there wait for the misty weather which was needed for his break-out through the Denmark Straits. But there was hardly even a cloud in the sky; visibility was phenomenal and the peak of Beerenberg on Jan Mayen, 8,000 feet high, could be seen fifty miles away. Accordingly Krüder headed even further north to the southern edge of the pack ice, and waited there for a suitable opportunity for his break-out.

Weather reports permitted the hope that conditions might get worse in four days, with rain, which would be ideal, for

Krüder was worried about the risk of a full-speed dash along the edge of the ice pack in thick fog.

It is not clear what had become at this time of the German weather ships, disguised as trawlers, which usually proved invaluable on occasions such as these.

Waiting for the warm air which he wanted to move north towards Iceland and produce his rain and mist, Krüder noted in the war diary that, for an escape, suitable weather was more important than the moon or the time of year.

Conditions were at last favourable on July 1, and on one engine, at nine knots, *Pinguin* headed south. She waited for a few days to see if any unescorted ships might be found on the route between the United Kingdom and Canada, but had no luck.

At this moment of the war conditions were extraordinarily favourable for raiders in the Atlantic, as the French armistice meant the withdrawal of the French navy from its co-operation in the work of patrolling the seas, and at the same time British warships had also to be diverted from patrol work until the attitude of the French navy itself was clear. Thus the Germans noted that Force H, based on Gibraltar, was occupied with Oran, while the *Hermes, Australia, Dorsetshire* and *Cornwall,* they were told, had gone to Dakar. Further ships could be presumed to be near other French West African ports.

While the *Pinguin* was on her way south a fast passenger steamer of the Anchor Line had to be avoided, as there was no chance of overtaking her. On several occasions, also, Krüder turned away from neutral ships, which might have signalled his presence.

On July 10 the *Pinguin* was disguised as the Greek steamer *Kassos,* and on the 17th she met the German submarine *UA,* for whom she had brought out stores, fuel and torpedoes. The trade winds blew very hard, so that the process of transferring all this material took seven days because the submarine could not come alongside lest the sea throw her against the *Pinguin* and seriously damage her. Accordingly all the stores had to be ferried across from the *Pinguin* to the submarine by flotation bags. In all, eleven torpedoes and seventy tons of diesel oil were thus transferred, and the *Pinguin* then set off, towing the *UA* until the latitude of Freetown was reached, when the tow was cast off.

This was the first time that a submarine had been refuelled at sea by a raider, and Dönitz sent a message of his appreciation. It had been hoped that the *UA*'s planned operations off Freetown would draw away British patrol craft which might have been looking for *Pinguin*. In fact this did not happen, because, within two days of reaching her patrol area, the submarine had to go back to Germany for repairs to her machinery.

On July 31 the *Pinguin* was near Ascension Island and that morning, in clear weather, sighted a ship on the port bow and on a parallel course. This ship, on seeing the *Pinguin*, turned away, slightly as first, and then very sharply, at the same time giving the QQQ alarm. Krüder tried unsuccessfully to jam this, and at 1055, after a chase lasting two hours, he opened fire. The other ship hoisted the British flag and manned her stern gun. Closing to within about two and a half miles, the *Pinguin* scored several hits, which started a fire near the bridge as the crew left the ship in three boats.

The boarding party found four dead men on the deck of the ship, which was the British vessel *Domingo de Larrinaga*, of 5,358 tons, on her way from Bahia Blanca to Newcastle with 7,500 tons of grain.

The thirty-two survivors from this ship were taken on board the *Pinguin* (four of them were wounded) and the ship sunk by torpedo, after demolition charges had failed to do their work.

In his war diary Krüder remarked that he was not worried by the fact that the British ship's signals might have got through, as the British already knew that the *Thor* and *Widder* were in the area, and the appearance of a third ship would add to the uncertainty.

After this the *Pinguin* continued southward, passing the Japanese *Hawaii Maru* on the way, and then turned east to pass the Cape of Good Hope, where the raider in squally weather met a ship steaming very slowly so far from the ordinary trade routes that she was taken for a warship. As

124

she approached it was seen that she was a large merchant vessel; because of the bad weather a successful torpedo attack seemed unlikely, and Krüder let her pass.

On August 19 the ship's war diary comments on the fact that the British had now changed their merchant navy code, saying:

"Up to now we have had an almost complete picture of wireless traffic between ships, which was very helpful in judging the situation in the South Atlantic. But this state of affairs has now ended, a fact that is the more regrettable because such a picture would have been of great help when the ship entered the new operations area east of the Cape of Good Hope. It is to be hoped that the B-service will soon succeed in breaking the new code and letting us know."

In fact it did not require the B-service to break the code; this was done by the *Pinguin's* own communications officer, Lieutenant Brunke.

Because of recent reports of German raiders in this area, Krüder felt that the enemy could no longer be surprised by the laying of mines off Cape St. Francis. Accordingly, he decided not to do this, a decision afterwards approved by the SKL, and the *Pinguin* steamed north-eastwards towards the southern tip of Madagascar. On her way she took care to keep outside the 100-fathom line, as it was possible that the *Atlantis* had already laid mines in this area.

On August 26 the raider's seaplane was sent out, wearing British markings, and at 1250 she sighted a tanker which was carrying no sign of nationality. The seaplane flew low and dropped a message, pretending to be from the British senior naval officer in the area, ordering the tanker to alter course and maintain wireless silence, on account of the proximity of a German raider. The tanker obeyed. She and the *Pinguin* were now heading directly for each other, but by 1700 she was not yet in sight from the raider. The German plane was sent off once more to look for her. She could not be found, and a little later scraps of signals which were intercepted showed that she was not following instructions, but was trying to escape. Krüder decided that despite the nearness of the coast it was worth the risk of trying to find her again, and he ordered the plane away to tear down the tanker's aerial and remain by her.

In the war diary he wrote:

"I appreciated what I was asking of the aircraft and its crew when I sent it out just before dark with the order to land in the dark, in a swell alongside an unknown, possibly enemy steamer, and keep in contact with her until the ship arrived, but it was the only way to make sure of the tanker by night."

At 1748 the plane found the tanker again, tore away the aerial and dropped the order "Stop at once" (in English), at the same time opening fire with cannon and machine-guns on the bridge and across the tanker's bows. The tanker stopped at once, and the plane landed and, taxi-ing towards her, morsed in English:

"Remain stopping [sic] here. Cruiser *Cumberland* will go with you," and followed this with:

"Show your lights."

At 1826, guided by the lights, the *Pinguin* came in sight, and the aircraft radioed:

"We are both lying stopped here. Hi Hi."

By 1920 there was a prize crew aboard the tanker, which was the Norwegian *Filefjell*, of 7,616 tons, with 10,000 tons of petrol and 500 tons of oil from the Persian Gulf to Capetown under charter from the British government. She was unarmed.

While all this had been going on, the *Pinguin* picked up a signal from a merchant ship called *Bernes* saying that she was being stopped by a passenger ship. This had nothing to do with the *Pinguin*, but Krüder guessed that the "passenger ship" was in fact a British armed merchant-cruiser. Later the *Bernes* cancelled her signal and said that she was continuing on her voyage. It was clear that incidents of this sort would serve to heighten the uncertainty of the actual situation as far as the British were concerned.

The *Filefjell* had not been disposed of, and the *Pinguin* was still lying close by, when at three o'clock on the following morning a blacked-out ship came into sight. The *Filefjell* was told to stay where she was, and the *Pinguin* set out to intercept the newcomer; a half-hour's chase showed that she was also a tanker. At 0418 she was signalled to stop and did so, radioing at the same time:

"QQQ 29° 37' south 45° 50' east. Stopped by unknown vessel *British Commander*."

The *Pinguin* opened fire, and the *British Commander* radioed again:

"Now vessel shelling us."

This signal was repeated by Walvis Bay, and this repetition was in turn picked up in Germany via Portishead, and the SKL realised at last that the *Pinguin* was at work.

The *British Commander* was hit several times, and her crew abandoned ship, although the radio operator stuck to his work, repeating his news and his position until the last moment. The tanker was now finished off with shells and a torpedo; she had been a ship of 6,901 tons in ballast from Falmouth to Abadan, via Capetown. The shelling seems to have caused the tanker's transmitter to work intermittently. The Germans were misled into thinking that an operator was still at work and this was reported. It is now quite clear that Captain Thornton was the last to leave his ship.

Five minutes after the end of the *British Commander* another ship came in sight, a vessel with a raked stem and cruiser stern, steaming at about fourteen knots and obviously in ballast.

The *Pinguin* fired a warning shot, the ship stopped and hoisted the Norwegian flag; her crew was taken on board and the ship was at once scuttled. She was the *Morviken*, of 5,008 tons, from Capetown to Calcutta.

An hour later the prize crew in the *Filefjell* signalled the approach of yet another freighter, which within a short time was in sight from the *Pinguin*. The prospect of taking four ships in about six hours was tempting, but Krüder decided not to chase the newly-arrived vessel on account of the alarm which had been given by the *British Commander*. It will thus be seen that the determination of the captain and radio operator of that ship in sticking under fire to their posts had yielded an immediate reward.

The *Atlantis* was in the neighbourhood at this time, and

Rogge was worried to hear the *British Commander's* signal, as he had only recently sunk the *King City* nearby.

Krüder now took all the fresh provisions he could find from the *Filefjell* and sank her—an action for which he was afterwards criticised by the SKL, as the Norwegian prize would have been very welcome at home.

Later on, one of Krüder's officers, Lieutenant Hemmer, said that his captain regretted his decision after the *Filefjell* sunk, but that at the time he had thought that a prize would be merely a great nuisance.

The radio stir made by the *Filefjell* and the *British Commander* had, it was very soon learned, brought British forces into the vicinity.

On the morning of August 28 an aircraft was heard radioing from so close at hand that it was impossible to take a bearing. The war diary noted: "Sunderland or aircraft from cruiser or armed merchant-cruiser very near."

Krüder took what comfort he could from the fact that he was now 200 miles away from the last reported position of the *British Commander* and that, in addition, the visibility was only about ten miles. On the next day, from prudence, Krüder refrained from attacking a large Blue Funnel liner, clearly recognisable by the shape of her masts and funnel, as he felt he had been too long in that area. There was also the chance that the liner might prove to be an armed merchant-cruiser. In the war diary that night Krüder stated his conclusion that henceforward enemy ships would try at any cost to get off an RRR or QQQ message, even at the risk of the lives of their crews, and that this made even more important the successful snatching away of enemy aerials by the *Pinguin's* seaplane.

At the same time, Krüder remarked, orders intercepted for Allied ships to stay outside the 100-fathom line in this area meant that minelaying would serve little purpose, for it would be very difficult to get close enough to the coast to lay mines in such a position that the ships would have to enter the minefield on their way in or out of port.

Talking with the captain of the *Morviken*, Krüder discovered that the Norwegian had first taken him for a ship of the Wilhemsen Line, and became suspicious only when he saw that the ship was flying the Greek flag, since, as he said: "The Greeks have few good ships, and those good ships are not here in the East."

Acting on this hint, Krüder then redisguised his ship as the Wilhelmsen liner *Trafalgar* and remained in the same area; for this he was afterwards reproved by the SKL, which pointed out that this was only supposed to be his approach area. Accordingly he should have left it as soon as he had sunk the *British Commander,* since his presence was embarrassing the *Atlantis;* the two ships were within 100 miles of each other.

On September 5 the seaplane was lost, the engine-bed being broken in the heavy swell—much the same kind of accident as had occurred to the *Atlantis'* Heinkel, and an additional indication of the unsuitability of the He 114 for this kind of work. This, for the time being, put an end to the hopes of any more "aerial snatching."

On September 10 Krüder decided to make one more sweep in the direction of Madagascar and then leave for Australian waters; on the same day he picked up the radio repercussions of the attack on the *Benarty* by the *Atlantis.*

At dawn, two days later, the *Pinguin* sighted smoke. After just over an hour's steaming she ordered the enemy ship to stop and then opened fire. The enemy, however, turned her stern to the *Pinguin* and opened fire herself, scoring one hit, although the shell did not explode. The *Pinguin* hit her in return several times, her wireless was put out of action, and she was soon on fire everywhere, as what was left of her crew watched from the boats. This vessel was the *Benavon,* of 5,872 tons, a British ship carrying hemp and rubber from Manila and Singapore to London. Her captain and several officers had been killed and there were only twenty-eight survivors out of a crew of forty-nine. Her armament had been one 4-inch and one 3-inch anti-aircraft gun. She was sunk by gunfire, and on September 15 Krüder reported to the SKL that he was on his way to Australian waters.

He steered a course which he hoped was that followed by Allied ships on their way to and from Australia, and on the morning of September 16 he met and stopped without a shot and without an alarm the Norwegian *Nordvard,* of 4,111 tons, with 7,187 tons of wheat from Australia to Port Elizabeth.

Krüder decided to send the new prize home, with his prisoners, now numbering about 200, although this meant a sacrifice of 270 tons of diesel oil, 100 tons of water and provisions for 200 men for sixty days.

As the *Pinguin* approached Australia Krüder kept away from the coast until he decided on his minelaying plans. There was an important difficulty. As soon as a port was known to be mined, all the ports on the coast would be swept, so that it would be necessary to use mines which would not become active until forty-eight hours after laying. In that way Krüder would have time to mine one port and then move on and mine another, before the first batch of mines was discovered.

This process could be carried on even more satisfactorily if two minelayers were employed, and accordingly Krüder decided to keep his next suitable prize for use as an auxiliary minelayer.

The most suitable area in which to begin laying, he considered, was off Newcastle, N.S.W., and in the shallow water between that place and Sydney.

By September 27 it was at last calm enough to bring the spare aircraft up from the lower hangar and to assemble it. In the meantime the ship was sailing north-eastwards in the direction of Java, and on October 7 a ship came in sight, on a course which showed that she was coming from the Straits of Sunda to the south coast of Australia. The ship stopped in reply to a flag signal and a warning shot. She was unarmed and did not attempt to use her wireless.

This ship was the *Storstad,* a Norwegian tanker, which we have already met before serving as a tender to other raiders. She was of 8,998 tons, and when captured was carrying 12,000 tons of diesel oil and 500 tons of coal from British North Borneo to Melbourne and Adelaide. That night *Pinguin* topped up her own tanks with 1,200 tons of oil, and Krüder decided that the new prize, which he renamed *Passat* (trade wind in German), should be his auxiliary minelayer. Accordingly the

Passat transferred her Norwegian crew to the raider and loaded 100 mines, after which the two ships headed towards Australia. Krüder's plan was that the *Pinguin* should mine Sydney, Newcastle and Hobart, while the *Passat* attended to Banks Strait and the east and west ends of the Bass Strait, between Tasmania and the Australian mainland.

By the time the *Pinguin* was off Perth she had done a distance, since leaving Germany, equivalent to the circumnavigation of the globe—an event celebrated with the issue of a glass of rum to all hands. On October 28, having sailed southabout around Australia, the *Pinguin* was ready to lay between Newcastle and Sydney.

The night was dark and cloudy; searchlights could be seen and coastwise lights were as in peace-time. Water began to get through the mine ports aft, and the ship was trimmed by the head to bring her stern higher. Forty mines were laid and the ship went on down the coast to lay forty more off Hobart.

This laying also took place quite peacefully, despite searchlights on both sides of the D'Entrecasteaux Channel, and on November 5 Krüder tried to catch a passing tanker. She proved to be too fast to be taken at once, and as darkness was coming on Krüder decided to let her go, rather than compromise the minelaying, which he continued on the next night in Spencer Gulf, on the approaches to Adelaide.

The *Passat* had also been busy; it had been hard work getting the ship ready for her new task, stowing the mines, arranging demolition charges in case the worst happened, and briefing the crew on their behaviour if the ship were stopped or flown over. However, despite the difficulties of working an unfamiliar ship, all went well, and on November 8 the Germans received the first news of a success, when the Australian radio announced that a British freighter had been mined and sunk at the east end of the Bass Strait. On the same day the American merchant ship *City of Rayville* was also mined and sunk at the same place. This was the first United States ship to be sunk in the war. The *Passat* joined the *Pinguin* on November 15, and both ships were congratulated, according to the war diary of the SKL, on "the planning, preparation and execution of an exemplary opera-

131

tion." At the same time Raeder awarded the ships five Iron Crosses, First Class, and fifty Second Class.

There was now a lull of three weeks before it was time to attack the Antarctic whaling fleets. The *Pinguin's* engines, which had now been running uninterruptedly for five months, were overhauled. Krüder decided that instead of sending the *Passat* up the west coast of India minelaying, he would take her with him southward as a scout. Both ships were equipped with an ultra-short-wave radio called "Hagenuk Gear," which had a range of about 100 miles but which could not be picked up at a greater distance, so that the two ships together could easily cover an area seventy miles broad.

While repairs were going on with both engines stopped, on November 17 in the evening, smoke was sighted. Krüder started first one engine, which gave him ten and a half knots, and then, as soon as possible, the other one and followed the ship in the growing darkness, only to lose her and then find her again at midnight, when she stopped at Krüder's order and lay in the beam of his searchlight. She was the *Nowshera,* a British ship of 7,920 tons, carrying 4,000 tons of zinc ore, 3,000 tons of wheat and 2,000 tons of wool from Adelaide to Durban and the United Kingdom. Unhappily for Krüder's prisoners she had a large crew, numbering 113, mostly Indians, who had to be fitted somehow into the already terribly overcrowded holds of the German ships.

The captured ship was fitted with a Japanese 4-inch gun, and had some protection consisting of sandbags and steel plates on the bridge, wireless cabin and engine-room skylight. She had not succeeded in getting signals through, but her codes and secret papers had been destroyed.

Eight hours' hard work followed, as stores were taken out of the *Nowshera*—mostly rice for the Indian prisoners—and the ship was scuttled. On the next day the overhaul of the raider's engines continued. Smoke was sighted again on the 20th; both engines were started, but the one recently overhauled was kept at reduced speed, so that it might be properly run in. For a while Krüder followed the foe on a parallel course to make out which way she was going. In a little while it became clear that she was heading towards the southern

132

part of Australia. When the enemy's masts and funnel were just over the horizon she turned away from the raider at full helm and at about twelve knots' speed. The chase would be long, especially as the newly repaired engine had to be treated gently, so that there would be plenty of time for the pursued ship to give the alarm. The only way to avoid that seemed to be by a night attack. However, as the morning advanced, the sea went down and Krüder decided that he would be able to use the seaplane to snatch the enemy's aerial, and if that failed, to bomb him. The *Pinguin* followed the plane at her best possible speed. Ten minutes after she had taken off, the seaplane was over the ship, now seen to be British, swooping down and then pulling out of her dive with the aerial trailing behind, caught in the grapnel. The British ship opened fire with a machine-gun and hit the plane in one of her floats; the plane, however, flew on to drop a message on the enemy's bridge in a bag to which were attached long streamers.

"Stop your engines immediately. Do not use wireless. In case of disobedience or any resistance you will be bombed or shelled."

The enemy kept on, while the seaplane dropped an unarmed bomb and then an armed one alongside. As the British merchant ship turned away she made smoke and, presumably with a spare aerial, gave warning that she was being attacked from the air, adding her position and name—*Maimoa*.

The plane was temporarily baffled and flew back to the *Pinguin* to report, while the *Maimoa* added to her distress signals details of her course and speed. This latter was eleven knots—information which conveyed to Krüder the fact that he would be within range two hours later.

At 1530 the plane said that she must land. There could be no question of stopping the chase to pick her up, but Krüder dropped a cutter, with provisions, signal lamps, etc., to remain with the seaplane in case it was not possible to come back to her until the next day.

Half an hour after this, *Storstad*, which appears to have reassumed her original name on completion of her minelaying mission, reported that there was another ship in sight at a distance of about 18,000 yards. Krüder kept on after the

Maimoa and came up with her at 1645. After two 5.9 salvoes she stopped and her crew of eighty-seven were taken on board the raider. By 1915 the *Maimoa* had been scuttled, and Krüder went back to pick up the seaplane and the cutter. This was successfully done, despite the dark.

The *Maimoa* had been a refrigerator ship of 10,123 tons, carrying 5,000 tons of frozen meat, 1,500 tons of butter and lard, 17,000 boxes of eggs, 1,500 tons of grain and 100 tons of piece goods from Fremantle via Durban to the United Kingdom.

Early next morning the *Storstad* came up again with the sighting report that she made the previous day, saying that the ship she had seen was also heading for Africa at eleven knots, apparently suspecting nothing.

The *Pinguin* headed to intercept and by ten o'clock that night did so. The raider switched on her searchlight, fired a warning shot and morsed the enemy to stop. The ship made RRR and the *Pinguin* opened fire, at the same time jamming the signal, which suddenly was repeated very strongly by someone nearby. The *Pinguin* kept up her fire, and the enemy was hit in the wireless cabin, in the funnel, on the upper deck and in the steam steering gear. She stopped and her crew scrambled into their boats. Sixty men (out of eighty-nine) and one woman were rescued. Another boat, which drifted away in the darkness and could not be found, was afterwards picked up by an Australian warship.

The *Pinguin's* boarding party reported that the newly won prize was the *Port Brisbane*, of 8,739 tons, with 5,000 tons of frozen meat, butter and cheese, and 3,000 tons of wool, lead and piece goods from Adelaide via Durban to the United Kingdom. One of the ship's officers had been killed. The boarding party added that the ship was armed with two 6-inch and one 3-inch anti-aircraft guns.

The *Port Brisbane*, though scuttled, did not sink fast enough and had to be finished off with a torpedo just before midnight, whereupon the *Pinguin* left the area at full speed.

At last the order came to move on to the Antarctic in the region of the Bouvet Archipelago. On November 24 Krüder was told that his ship was to search for the whaling fleets from east to west in the area and report again between the middle and end of January, with a view to moving to the west coast of India by February 1 for minelaying and commerce raiding.

As a tailpiece to the raider's operations in Australian waters the Australian government information service issued at this time a list of sixteen ships overdue and presumed lost by enemy action. "A proud list of glorious success in the war against commerce," was the somewhat fulsome comment in the war diary of the SKL.

A further overhaul of the *Pinguin* was finished on the 28th, and she was painted black all over. The raider was now in reasonably good condition except for the marine growth on her bottom, which, it was calculated, reduced her full speed by at least one knot.

On November 30, while steaming west before turning south, Krüder received a sighting report from the *Storstad* at 1130. The situation gave promise of a long chase, and Krüder, altering course towards the newly sighted ship, sent the *Storstad* out of the way with orders to meet him at a rendezvous to the south-west in three days' time. Six hours after the *Storstad's* signal had been sent the *Pinguin* herself could see smoke. Krüder kept out of sight and on a parallel course waiting for dark. If the ship which he was following showed no lights she would be certainly an enemy, and Krüder planned to come in at once and attack without warning, shelling her at least until her wireless was put out of action. In fact the ship did not set lights and when it was dark Krüder approached her stealthily. By 2230 he was within a mile of her on her starboard quarter; suddenly the enemy turned hard to port and headed away. Krüder opened fire at once; the first salvo hit the wireless cabin and the steering gear. The ship was thus at a single blow speechless, out of control and on fire, and her crew abandoned her as the flames lit up the night sky and were reflected in the water.

She was the *Port Wellington*, sister ship of the *Port Brisbane*, of 8,301 tons, with 4,400 tons of frozen meat, cheese, eggs and butter, 1,750 tons of steel and 1,200 tons of wheat and wool from Adelaide for the United Kingdom via Durban. Her armament had been two 6-inch and one 3-inch anti-aircraft guns. On board her was a crew of eighty-two men, together with seven women passengers.

Krüder saw the British ship burn with some regret, for he would have been glad of some of her valuable stores. However, salvage was not possible and the *Port Wellington* was scuttled.

The *Pinguin* had now sunk eleven ships and had on board 405 prisoners. The prospects were poor of sending them to Germany in a prize. It was unlikely that a suitable motor ship could be found, and any other kind of vessel would probably not have sufficient fuel, for the ships encountered on the Africa–Australia run were mostly big coal burners.

Accordingly Krüder decided to send his prisoners home in the *Storstad,* which sailed off to rendezvous Andalusia in the South Atlantic, topping up the *Atlantis* on the way. At Andalusia she gave 6,500 tons of her 10,000 tons of diesel oil to the tanker *Nordmark* and she herself reached the Gironde safely on February 4.

Finally all was ready for the attempt to carry the war into the Antarctic. As the ship steamed south the weather began to get cold and on December 17 the first iceberg was sighted. Thus the *Pinguin* during her cruise had sailed both the Arctic and the Antarctic oceans.

On December 18 the SKL signalled: "Anglo-Norwegian whaling area this year is in a zone of about 200 miles around South Georgia. Those taking part are *Harpon, Thorshammer, Pelagos, Vesfiord, Ole Wegger* and probably two or three more. All under English charter."

The next day the *Pinguin* ended her run south, turned north-west towards Bouvet Island, and began a west to east search. Many icebergs were sighted, and many of the *Pinguin's* namesakes as well, but only a few whales.

On the day before Christmas Eve *Pinguin's* wireless operator heard for the first time the radio-telephone intercommunication traffic between members of the whaling fleet. On the same night Krüder learned from Berlin that he had been awarded the Knight's Cross of the Iron Cross.

The seaplane was flown off on Boxing Day at noon, and two hours later signalled that she was making a forced landing. She was picked up three hours later after a full-speed dash by the *Pinguin* on a radio directional bearing. The plane reported having seen nothing, but on the next day Norwegian whalers were heard to the westward, and mention was made of the presence of the *Pelagos* and *Ole Wegger*.

As the *Pinguin's* war diary says, the ship had sailed through icebergs and along the edge of the pack ice without seeing anything from south of Madagascar to south of Freetown, virtually the whole breadth of Africa. Now whale-catchers could be heard exchanging bearings with their factory ships, but Krüder needed to haul out to the north-west to get a clearer radio picture, from which it was learned that a tanker was about to visit the whalers, bringing fuel and taking away whale oil. On December 29 there was heavy snow, and the German look-outs had a hard time finding a channel through the icefield. The whalers' R/T was now coming in loud and clear to the westward. This R/T was of great value in locating the whaling fleets, but it also presented difficulties, because by its use a catcher might give an alarm which would enable the factory ship to make her escape.

On the next day the *Pinguin* lay stopped amongst the icebergs listening to whale-catchers complaining to each other of the presence of fog and the absence of whales. On New Year's Eve the *Pinguin* began to work round to the north of the fleets, getting between them and the open sea. The *Ole Wegger* reported that she and her six catchers were fairly well under the lee of the ice, while *Pelagos* and her seven catchers were exposed to the bad weather. The two fleets exchanged New Year greetings, and one remarked to the other that nothing had been heard of the tanker. The uninhibited use of R/T showed that the whalers felt themselves in complete safety as far as the risks of war were concerned.

As the whalers were clearly waiting in their present positions for the tanker, Krüder decided to wait for her, too, as an addition to his bag, and so the *Pinguin* lay still, listening "with almost paternal interest," as the war diary puts it, to the two groups as they eagerly caught whales.

At about noon on January 3 the managers of the *Ole Wegger* and the *Pelagos* were heard in conversation, discussing the fact that the tanker was now fourteen days overdue and that the *Pelagos* was almost out of oil. *Ole Wegger,* on the other hand, still had 600 tons of fuel oil, but her whale-oil tanks were almost full and she would not be able to deal with many more whales.

The two managers decided to wireless the tanker company for news, while *Ole Wegger* was to give some of her fuel to the *Pelagos,* at the same time filling her whale-oil tanks from that ship, so that, with her tanks full, she would be ready to go home.

The address of the company owning the missing tanker, Krüder heard, was in New York, and therefore he presumed that the tanker would be American. In order to avoid the international complications of an attack on the whaling fleets in which an American ship might be involved, Krüder decided to attack almost at once, preferably while the two factory ships were exchanging oil. The *Pinguin* then intercepted the tanker company's reply saying that their ship would be delayed a fortnight, but not giving any definite time of arrival. Krüder listened on, waiting to hear when the two big ships were meeting. The R/T suffered from snow interference but at ten o'clock on the morning of January 6, the Germans heard that the *Thorshammer* was about 400 miles south-west of the *Ole Wegger*. Then, just before the R/T closed down, one of the *Ole Wegger's* catchers asked if he could send mail by the *Solglimt* as he wanted to write one more letter. From this it was deduced that the tanker expected would be the Norwegian whale-oil transport *Solglimt,* of 12,000 tons, and it was presumed that she would start by visiting the *Thorshammer,* then the *Ole Wegger,* and finally the *Pelagos*.

The *Pinguin* began to close the *Ole Wegger* on the 6th. There came a heavy snowstorm and the Norwegians were heard discussing the unprecedented weather, which, they said, was so thick that they were losing whales they had already captured and marked with flags prior to towing them to the factory ships. Other voices were heard talking the same language far away in the Weddell Sea. At last the weather improved and the *Solglimt* could be heard getting nearer; Krüder waited. He decided that he would attack when the two big ships were alongside each other and therefore unmanoeuvrable, that he would attack out of what dusk there was in the midsummer night of the Antarctic, and that he would come up to the enemy on the side on which the whale-catchers were not lying. On the 13th the *Solglimt* and *Ole Wegger* were at last alongside each other. Krüder approached slowly on a westerly bearing, and late at night saw the lights of the two ships together. Then a snow squall shut out all visibility. It cleared suddenly, to show Krüder that he was right on top of his prey.

"The ships lay side by side in the light of innumerable lamps on their decks," said the war diary. "There were many whales alongside. I ordered the ships not to use wireless or R/T. I did not fire a gun in order not to alarm the catchers, but sent out two boats with prize crews."

The *Pinguin* stopped at this moment, the engine room reporting that one motor was out of action, a cylinder cover having cracked. Repairs were started at once, as the prize crews flashed the message:

"Ships in our hands."

The *Ole Wegger* was of 12,201 tons, and had on board 7,000 tons of whale oil and 5,500 tons of fuel. Her crew numbered 190 and she had stores for ten weeks. The *Solglimt* was almost the same size (12,246 tons), with 4,000 tons of whale oil, 4,000 tons of fuel oil and a crew of sixty men, with accommodation, if necessary, for about 300 more. In the neighbourhood were four whale-catchers, each of 300 tons, which were also captured. Three others escaped, for the *Pinguin* had no hope of catching those whom she had not taken by surprise on account of her engine breakdown. It was feared that the escaped catchers would give the alarm to the *Thorshammer,* but, in the meantime, Krüder sent a signal telling them to get on with their whaling and adding that the German Reich would pay them for their whales. There now re-

139

mained the other factory ship, the *Pelagos*, to be dealt with. Krüder left his two prizes and steamed away from the *Pelagos*, to confuse the Norwegians already captured, who were watching. Once out of sight, he turned back and headed for the *Pelagos*, listening the while as she talked to her catchers, and as she called, in vain, the *Solglimt* and *Ole Wegger*.

In the growing dusk, at 2209, lights were sighted, but between them and the *Pinguin* lay an icefield, around which the raider had to feel her way, passing as she did so one of the catchers flagging a whale. Krüder expected the alarm to be given, but nothing happened. The white lights of the factory ship grew closer, and it was seen that she was hard at work, with five catchers alongside.

The *Pinguin* came up at full speed to within 200 yards of the Norwegian ships just as eight bells sounded for midnight. Morse signals were made, the boats with the prize crews were lowered and the ships were in German hands within a few minutes. One catcher was boarded and at once used to round up the others, while the captain of the *Pelagos* was told to order his remaining boats back. The new prize was again a ship of 12,000 tons, with 9,500 tons of whale oil and 800 tons of fuel; her crew numbered 210 and she had provisions for ten weeks. Her seven catchers were boats of 250–300 tons, admirable for use as anti-submarine craft if they could ever be got to Europe.

This two-day operation against the whaling fleets was the most successful performance of any German raider at any time during the war. There had been taken 36,000 tons of ships, plus eleven whale-catchers, over 20,000 tons of whale oil and about 10,000 tons of oil fuel.

Krüder hoped that he might still be able to take the *Thorshammer*, but nothing more was heard from her, and he had to presume that the catchers from the *Ole Wegger* had given the alarm.

Now Krüder had to make plans for the prizes which he had secured. The *Pelagos* was to go home as soon as she had topped up from the *Solglimt*. The *Ole Wegger* was very conspicuously a factory ship, with little chance of getting through the blockade unobserved, and accordingly she gave her oil back to the *Solglimt* so that that ship might go to a German-held port with the catchers.

A thick fog handicapped the execution of these plans, while the ships lay together under cover of the ice, with dead whales alongside acting as fenders. Krüder was anxious to communicate with the SKL, but that meant going some distance away in order to deceive the enemy direction finders. Accordingly he waited until he got rid of his fourteen prizes. The *Pelagos* and *Solglimt* now had enough fuel to steam from the Antarctic to the Arctic and return to Germany via Greenland if they wished to do so. The disposal of the *Ole Wegger* and the catchers would be more difficult, and Krüder considered laying them up at Kerguelen until it was more convenient to send them home.

Finally, the SKL ordered Krüder to bring the *Ole Wegger* and the catchers to meet the *Nordmark* in the Andalusia area, after which the *Pinguin* was to return to the Indian Ocean.

In the meantime the *Pinguin* had been down to the edge of the pack ice and in brilliant sunshine had a splendid view of the Polar continent.

The meeting at Point Ursula in Area Andalusia took place, the *Nordmark* still towing the *Duquesa,* who was now reduced to burning her own decks and derrick booms in order to keep her refrigerating plant going. The prizes were sent home, except for one of the catchers, *Pol IX,* which was converted into an auxiliary minelayer and renamed *Adjutant,* and then the *Pinguin* left, too, taking with her from the *Duquesa* 1,200 cases of eggs, twenty-three and a half cows, 410 sheep and seventeen sacks of oxtails. On February 18, the *Alstertor* arrived at Ursula with mails from home, and Krüder sent back to Germany the last of his war diaries before leaving for Kerguelen, where he stayed from March 12 to March 25.

Torpedoes, stores, coal and an aircraft which had been received from the *Alstertor* had to be properly assembled and stowed, the holds had to be cleaned out, a dreadful mass of detritus—coal-dust, rotten vegetables and sacking—

having gradually formed during the eight months' cruise, while apart from the usual overhauls and repairs divers were sent down to examine the rudder and screw. At the same time the ship's side was cleaned again down to ten feet below the water-line. Before leaving the island Krüder arranged to send home the *Ole Wegger* and the catchers and then sailed for rendezvous Siberia, where he was met by the *Ole Jacob*. Krüder had been originally told to meet the *Ketty Broevig*, of whom much had been hoped both as a tanker and a minelayer, since, as Krüder had showed with the *Storstad*, a tanker would be the last vessel to be suspected of minelaying, but the *Ketty Broevig* had scuttled herself to avoid capture. The *Ole Jacob* was at the rendezvous instead.

Krüder appreciated that things were becoming difficult for raiders—the sinking of the *Ketty Broevig* and of other supply ships was one indication; more important was the fact that there were no longer any independent sailings in the vicinity of British bases, and Krüder felt that what he called "free cruising" was no longer worth while, since ships nearing ports or focal points were protected, while ships on the high seas kept so far from the ordinary routes that the question of finding them became, more than ever, a matter of good fortune.

The *Adjutant*, the former whale-catcher, might be able to help him as a scout, but the British now seemed to have air reconnaissance and radio direction finding almost everywhere. Krüder believed that the RAF's flying boats were now operating from Mauritius, the Seychelles, Diego Garcia and other bases, while there appeared now to be more cruisers available in the Indian Ocean. Therefore Krüder thought that the only prospect of success under these circumstances was to make a quick raid on an area, pick up a few prizes and then leave immediately. In this way Allied trade in the waters attacked would be disrupted, and cruisers attracted to them from areas which the *Pinguin* might subsequently raid.

It was in accordance with these ideas that Krüder chose the northern part of the Abadan to the Cape route as an operations area, but in addition he wanted to pick up another tanker to replace the *Ketty Broevig* as an auxiliary minelayer. He started by searching south of the Seychelles and found nothing, although the *Adjutant* and the *Pinguin* were together sweeping an area 150 miles wide. Working further north, however, the *Adjutant* reported a ship in the morning of April 24. The vessel seen was about 6,000–8,000 tons and making about eleven knots. The *Adjutant*, having reported to the *Pinguin*, retired to leave the bigger ship's field of fire free, but ten hours later the *Pinguin* still had not come up to the scene, as she had been having trouble getting her seaplane on board. The *Adjutant* shadowed as best she could and at five-fifteen the next morning the *Pinguin* finally arrived, dashing by the little whale-catcher at full-speed, and firing on the stranger, whose aerial was at once shot away. After three salvoes fire was checked and the crew of the ship, seventy men, taken on board the raider.

This ship was the *Empire Light,* of 6,800 tons, from Madras to Durban with ore and hides. Her rudder had been put out of action when she was shelled, and there was nothing for it but to scuttle her.

After this the co-operation between the two ships and the *Pinguin's* seaplane continued, and on the evening of April 28 the seaplane sighted a ship for which the *Pinguin* headed. After a five-hour chase another ship came up, and towards this newcomer the *Pinguin* steered. The chase lasted all night, but at first light *Pinguin* opened fire, destroying the ship's radio and steering gear from a range of 5,000 yards. With an auxiliary wireless the ship began to make distress signals, but they were very faint and Krüder did not believe that they would get through. The ship, which finally stopped and was abandoned, proved to be the *Clan Buchanan,* of 7,880 tons, with army and air force equipment from the United States to Madras, as well as mail. Once again the *Pinguin's* gunnery had been a little too good, and the *Clan Buchanan* also had to be scuttled because her steering gear had been damaged.

She had had 110 people on board and all these were saved;

secret papers were found floating on the water in a container which had failed to sink, and these included cyphers, the war diary of the British cruiser *Hawkins* and details of the ships which had been mined off Newcastle, N.S.W., on the *Pinguin's* minefield.

On the same day the *Adjutant* glimpsed for a few moments another ship, and the Germans looked for her all day in continuing squalls of rain, without success. The *Adjutant* was sent off to Point Violet in rendezvous area Siberia, while Krüder decided to go nearer to the entrance of the Persian Gulf in the search for the tanker which was to become a minelayer. On May 7 she found a tanker, the *British Emperor,* but there was no question of taking her as a prize, for she continued sending out her distress messages although in flames until she sank.

"For the first time one of the many raider reports wirelessed by attacked merchant vessels at imminent peril to themselves was to bring the retribution for which they called," [1] comments Captain S. W. Roskill, R.N., the author of *The War at Sea,* the official British history.

The message from the *British Emperor* was picked up by the cruiser *Cornwall* (Captain P. C. W. Manwaring), which headed at once towards what she considered to be the most promising place in which to look for the raider. With the help of her seaplane she found the *Pinguin* disguised as the *Norwegian Tamerlane,* and Captain Manwaring suffered from the same doubts as did Captain Oliver later, when he was in sight of the *Atlantis,* not knowing for sure whether the suspicious ship was friendly.

The confusion was increased by the *Pinguin* sending her own raider reports, claiming to come from the *Tamerlane.* All day long the *Cornwall* and her seaplane between them kept in touch with the *Pinguin;* and when the *Cornwall,* at five-fifteen in the afternoon, came right down on top of the raider, Krüder knew that there was nothing for it but to fight.

Captain Roskil thus describes the subsequent action and its repercussion:

[1] Op. cit., vol. I, p. 384.

"The raider realised that the game was up, discarded her disguise, and opened a rapid and accurate fire with her 5.9-inch guns, one round of which hit the cruiser and put her steering gear out of action temporarily. After a short delay the *Cornwall's* gunfire became accurate and at 5.26 the raider blew up. Twenty-two British or Indian prisoners and sixty German survivors were rescued. The methods employed by the *Cornwall* in shadowing, trying to identify and closing the raider were the subject of some adverse Admiralty comment. The action certainly emphasised the skill with which such enemy ships disguised their identity, the serious dilemma in which the captain of a ship was placed while trying to pierce the disguise, and the danger of approaching such a ship—which must possess the tactical advantage of surprise—too closely and on bearings favourable to her gun and torpedo fire." [1]

Much later on a satisfactory system of immediate identification for Allied merchant ships was devised, but, in the meanwhile, as Captain Roskill points out, there were "many other contacts between British warships and ships which sometimes turned out to be friendly merchant vessels and sometimes were discovered much later to have been raiders or enemy supply ships". [2]

The *Pinguin's* total score had been twenty-eight ships of 136,551 tons. Krüder, a particularly resourceful captain, who had clearly managed to get the best out of a good ship and an excellent crew, went down with that ship and most of her crew.

[1] Op. cit., vol. I, p. 385.
[2] Ibid., loc. cit.

VI
Komet • SHIP 45

THE LAST ship of the first wave of raiders was the *Komet* already mentioned briefly on account of her trip round the north of Russia and Siberia and her participation with the *Orion* in the attack on the phosphate ships off Nauru. the *Komet*, like the *Thor*, was a very small ship—only 3,200 tons—the former Norddeutscher Lloyd *Ems*. Her record of sinkings was not outstanding—six and a half ships of 42,950 tons (crediting her with a half of each of the seven ships she sank when working with the *Orion*), but her trip through the north-east passage into the Pacific was a considerable undertaking indeed and will always be something of a political and nautical curiosity.

Her captain was Robert Eyssen, promoted during the cruise to rear-admiral; he had joined the navy in 1911, and in the years between the wars had served two long stretches in the Admiralty in Berlin and had commanded the surveying ship *Meteor*.

Eyssen's little ship, carrying the same armament as the other raiders, sailed from Bergen on July 9, 1940, with orders to pass round the north of the continents of Europe and Asia and operate in the Pacific and Indian Oceans.

It was apparently Eyssen himself who first suggested that the north-east passage was feasible thanks to the policy of the Russian government at that time of maintaining a neutrality which was as helpful as possible to the Germans.

Originally, after the signature of the Russo-German pact of August 1939, Germany had been granted a naval base in the ice-free waters near Murmansk, and had made a certain limited use of it during the first winter of the war. Once the Germans had control of Norway this base lost its value, but the provision of facilities for a voyage through the north-

146

east passage into the Pacific was something of great value which the Russians could still provide for their semi-allies. Russian pilots and icebreakers would be necessary, and the original date upon which the *Komet* was to pick them up was July 15, at Warneck Bay on Vaigach Island, at the south side of the Kara Strait between Novaya Zemlya and the mainland. When the *Komet* sailed it was logical that she should be disguised as a Russian steamer, the *Deinev*. However, after she had left Norway a message was received from the Russians saying that the conditions would not be favourable for another month, and suggesting that the *Komet* should wait in the meantime at Murmansk. The Germans rejected this suggestion, and the ship spent a month in the Barents Sea, drifting most of the time to save fuel, but exercising her crew constantly. In the evenings the crew watched the first of the seventy-nine feature films taken on board, together with twenty-eight other films and 569 books.

By mid-August the ice conditions were reported not unfavourable and the *Komet* was sent to the Matoshkin Straits between the north and south islands of Novaya Zemlya. Here the Russian icebreaker *Stalin* was met; without her the ice would have been impassable. On board were two Russian ice pilots, one of them being Sergievski, Director of the Siberian Seaway.

The first attempt to get through the ice failed abeam of Cape Golotechni, and the *Komet* had to return to Matoshkin, where the crew were allowed ashore in two watches. On August 20 things were easier; what was termed three to six ball ice—that is to say, ice of medium thickness—was found, and, following the icebreaker, the *Komet* was through into open waters in two hours. Once past Cape Dickson another icebreaker, the *Lenin,* took the *Komet* through the Vilkizki Strait to Cape Chelyuskin.

In the ship's war diary Eyssen wrote:

"It was a glorious trip through the Vilkizki Strait, with a blue sky, half moon, midnight sun—everything was there except there was no ice."

After this the *Lenin* and *Komet* lay alongside each other, and Eyssen was invited on board the Russian ship. He accepted the invitation and then discovered that Shevelev, the second ice pilot, was "ill."

The party which followed was supported by Eyssen with difficulty, as the Germans were still on Central European Time and the Russians were on local time. This meant that the German captain found himself beginning a party with zakuska and vodka at what was, to him, six o'clock in the morning.

Four hours after the party had begun the ships were under way again. As six o'clock in the evening fog shut down and the *Komet* followed the icebreaker by means of signals and an oil slick, which the Russians purposely trailed astern.

Five hours later they were through into the East Siberian, Nordenskjold or Laptev Sea, and Eyssen sent a message of thanks to his pilots, as the Russians turned back.

Two days of quiet progress followed.

A fresh icebreaker, the *Kaganovitch,* was met on August 30. The sea began to ice up again, and it was soon a question of whether the two ships would not have to turn back. A snow-squall blew up, through which the German ship slowly advanced, following the searchlight of the *Kaganovitch,* whose dull, yellowish white disc was all that the *Komet* could see of her guide. At this stage the *Komet's* rudder gave constant trouble, and only sixty-one miles were made on August 31. Tantalisingly, away to the south could be seen an area of open water, lying just off the only route. This was the worst part of the trip as far as ice was concerned, but on the next day a different sort of obstacle was encountered, when the Director of the Eastern Section of the Siberian Seaway, Captain Meleshov, came on board and said that he had received a signal from Moscow ordering him to take the *Komet* back to Europe on the grounds that the Americans were watching the Behring Strait and that warships had been reported off Wrangel Island.

Ice-free water was ahead, and Eyssen respectfully but firmly refused to return to Europe or even to wait for further consultation with Moscow. It is known that just before this time the Russian authorities began to change their minds as to the prospect of a quick end to the war, largely because of the reports of their ambassador in London. The attempt to turn back the *Komet* may have been a reflection of this.

Eyssen had his way, and the Russians were left behind with an exchange of compliments. As the *Komet* sailed east her captain began once more to exercise his crew, which he had been unwilling to do under the eyes of the Russians.

It was now summer weather, with a blue sky and good visibility. Eyssen congratulated himself on a passage of 3,300 miles, which had taken only twenty-three days—a record, though he realised he had had luck with the ice and that the whole trip would have been impossible without the ice-breakers. The cost to the Germans of the Russian services, recorded in the SKL's study of the cruise, was 950,000 Reichsmarks—about $300,000.

During the trip with the Russians the *Komet* had stopped being the Russian *Deinev* and become the German *Donau*. Now, with the Russians out of sight, she became the *Deinev* once again, while divers worked at the damaged rudder.

On September 10 the *Komet* entered the Pacific and was greeted by a storm, which was followed, a few days later, by a typhoon. The little ship stood up very well to the weather as she headed towards the Japanese island of Ailing-lap, where Spee had gone in 1914 when he was hiding from the Allied squadrons and the island was German.

On the way there were a number of alarms, but the ships sighted always turned out to be Japanese merchant' vessels or trawlers. As she neared Ailinglap the raider was ordered to meet the *Orion*, but the rendezvous was changed from Ailinglap to Lamutrik. This was done because the tanker *Weser*, which should have brought supplies for the two raiders from Manzanilla, in Mexico, had been captured on September 26 by the Canadian armed merchant-cruiser *Prince Robert*, and it was feared that her captain might not have been able to destroy his confidential papers.

There was still some time to spare before the *Komet* was due at her rendezvous, and she continued south-east, passing between New Guinea and the Solomon Islands, looking for traffic between the Far East and Sydney and New Zealand.

Then, turning back, she was at Lamutrik on October 14,

149

where she replenished from the *Kulmerland,* and so had enough fuel to last until July.

After this Eyssen and Weyher of the *Orion* set off on their joint cruise in company with the *Kulmerland.* Eyssen was depressed because his ship had been five months at sea without sighting an enemy. Despite the fact that he had only been in his operational area for two months, he confided to his war diary that things were "nevertheless really sad."

The cruise of these three ships has already been described in the chapter of this book dealing with the *Orion;* the force broke up on December 22, and for the next day Eyssen planned an E-boat attack on Rabaul, with the aid of a small fast launch which was carried on the deck of the *Komet.* However, the launch's engine broke down and the plan had to be scrapped.

Frustrated, Eyssen went back to Nauru. On December 27 he arrived off the island and signalled to the administrator:

"I will shoot without regards [*sic*] if you use wireless. If you don't use wireless I only destroy your phosphate pier and oil tanks behind and the lighters. Evacuate this area at once diminish casualties. If you dont use wireless your station wont be demolished."

Shortly afterwards the firing began, heavy explosions were seen and the oil tanks set on fire. Later, it was announced in Australia that although buildings and plant had been heavily damaged there had been no casualties.

One of the repercussions of this attack was some friction between the Germans and the Japanese, as the latter did not wish it to be known that they were providing facilities for German raiders in violation of international law. The shelling of Nauru and the statements from the prisoners released on Emirau made it clear that this was what was being done. The SKL, commenting, said that henceforward raiders were to refrain from such operations in the neighbourhood of the Japanese mandated islands; furthermore, it was observed, the *Komet* could easily have got herself sunk during the attack.

Eyssen defended himself by saying that it had been valuable to draw attention to the *Komet's* presence in an area which she was about to leave; in that way the enemy would be attracted to the wrong place.

The SKL admitted something of the justice of Eyssen's contention, but warned him against doing the same thing again.

On New Year's Eve the *Komet* chased a Norwegian ship in vain while heading south-eastwards towards Taumotu, and on the next day Eyssen was promoted to rear-admiral.

The new admiral had been hoping to get supplies sent out to him overland by the Trans-Siberian railway, but the Russians at this period were obstructive, and the *Komet* learned that she would have to rely in the immediate future on supply ships—the *Alstertor* and *Alsterufer*. On January 3 the *Komet* crossed the Equator for the seventh time, and Eyssen proposed to the SKL that he should go to the Galapagos Islands, close to which passed all the ships on their way between Panama and Australia and New Zealand. However, the islands were within the Pan-American neutrality zone, and the SKL told Eyssen to leave their vicinity alone; instead they suggested that he go down to the Antarctic to operate in the Ross Sea against the Allied whaling fleets, as the *Pinguin* had done so successfully on the other side of the Antarctic continent. Eyssen accepted the suggestion, and on February 16 he reached the ice barrier, after hearing a good deal of the radio conversation between Japanese whaling craft. On the next day he found himself in the moonlight entirely surrounded by icebergs, but he did not believe he was in any peril, writing in the war diary:

"The ice is not dangerous, as it is not freezing solid but is broken up by the swell, but . . . there is always danger to the screw and rudder."

A somewhat unexpected result of the *Komet's* sailing through so much ice was that all the marine growth on her bottom had been stripped off and her hull was once more smooth.

Towards the end of February a Japanese factory ship with a tanker and a number of catchers were encountered, but there were no signs of anything British or Norwegian, although the Japanese said they had been present in numbers during the previous season. The factory ship *Nisshin Maru* gave the *Komet* various presents, including coal and acetylene gas. Eyssen reported the situation to the SKL, and was told, on February 28, that he should go to Kerguelen, to take on board ammunition and pick up mail from the *Alstertor*.

The *Komet* made her base in Royal Sound on the island, and Eyssen sent a party ashore to visit the site of a former whaling station at Jeanne d'Arc. Here there was still a good deal of usable material lying about, and the raider's men helped themselves to zinc and copper pipes, screws, nails, coal, wood, glass and upholstery materials. The settlement, which had been abandoned eight years previously, had at one time housed as many as sixty to eighty men. It was presumed by the Germans that the settlement had been made out of date by the factory ships, which could process whales near the spot where they were taken, thus avoiding the necessity of towing them hundreds of miles to a base like Jeanne d'Arc.

Like the *Atlantis* when she was at Kerguelen, *Komet* gave her men a chance to get ashore, to hunt rabbits and gather Kerguelen cabbage, which was found to be very tasty after months of tinned vegetables. On March 12 the *Pinguin* arrived at the island, followed by the *Adjutant*. The *Komet* took on board 1,425 rounds of ammunition and sailed on March 14 for the eastern part of the Indian Ocean, via Area Siberia, where she refuelled from the *Ole Jacob*.

There then followed six weeks of cruising at dead slow speed, without anything happening at all, not even a sight of smoke on the horizon.

On May 8 the *Komet* was off Onslow, Western Australia, at one end of her huge beat, which stretched a third of the way across the Indian Ocean. On the next day she heard the enemy radio announcement of the sinking of a German raider.

Eyssen knew that this must be the *Pinguin*, and that the *Adjutant* would now be on her own. Accordingly he asked SKL if she might be placed under his orders, and received their assent.

The two ships met on May 21. The *Adjutant* was taken in

152

tow to save fuel, while she was fitted with some light weapons—one 60-millimetre and two 20-millimetre guns, together with a range-finder, some magnetic mines set to function in the southern hemisphere, as well as more navigational gear and a smoke-screen apparatus. This having been done, the ships sailed into the Pacific, passing south about Australia and New Zealand. The *Adjutant* was sent to lay mines off Port Nicholson and Port Lyttelton, and the *Komet* sailed north-east across the Pacific to a rendezvous with the *Anneliese Essberger*. This ship had left Dairen for rendezvous Balbo, half-way between New Zealand and Pitcairn Island. Before Balbo was reached, the *Komet* heard a signal from the *Adjutant,* saying that her engines were useless and that she was preparing to scuttle herself.

The *Adjutant* left the *Komet* on June 11, and sighted the coast of New Zealand, mines ready to lay and the ship ready to be scuttled, on June 24. The rising sun on the high, snow-covered mountains of New Zealand reminded the home-sick Germans, one of them noted, of sunrise on Lake Constance. In order to save time Lieutenant Karsten, who was in command of the *Adjutant,* decided to steam straight up the coast until he was abeam of Wellington, rather than make a detour out of sight of land. He began laying his mines, was picked up by a searchlight and laid them too soon—in fifteen fathoms instead of ten.

Heading away from the enemy coast, the little ship could hear the wireless of the planes and ships which were looking for her. Her engines broke down, so that only the medium- and low-pressure cylinders were working, and Karsten set sail to help them out. Three days later, under sail, she met the *Komet* and was finally scuttled.

On July 9 the *Komet* had been a year at sea, and the ship received by wireless five Iron Crosses, First Class, to be awarded at Eyssen's discretion, while everybody on board got the Iron Cross, Second Class.

Balbo was reached on the 14th, where the *Anneliese Essberger* was waiting, disguised as a Japanese, but with no oil hoses. The *Komet* had none either, as she had given hers to the *Orion,* and it was with some difficulty that fire hoses were used instead. Finally, the *Komet* was able to take on board 1,400 tons of oil, enough to last until January 1942. On July 25 Eyssen handed over his war diary and his mail to the tanker and went off in the direction of the Galapagos Islands. This was the area in which Eyssen had wished to operate earlier in the cruise, but had been ordered by the SKL to keep away for fear of causing complications with the United States. Arrived in the area he sighted on August 14 the first enemy ship he had seen for 227 days; the clutch was let in on the second engine, and the *Komet* was off in chase.

According to Eyssen's war diary the enemy ship, of about 5,000 tons, was navigating in a carefree manner and paid no attention to the *Komet* until she had fired two warning shots. She did not then stop but tried to man her after gun. The *Komet* opened fire and in seven salvoes hit her on the bridge; she then ceased signalling and stopped.

This was the *Australind*, of 5,020 tons, from Adelaide to the United Kingdom via Panama, carrying zinc concentrate, dried fruit, jam, honey and piece goods. Her captain and two engineer officers had been killed; the survivors were taken on board and the ship sunk with explosive charges. While this was being done wireless traffic had been normal, and it was therefore concluded that the QQQ messages had been satisfactorily jammed.

The *Komet* steamed closer to the Galapagos, and on the next day sighted a distant ship, identified as Dutch, being either the *Brastogi* or the *Weltvreden*. The *Komet's* full speed at this time was only twelve knots, so that, despite her efforts to chase, the Dutch ship got away without even suspecting that she was being followed.

On the same night the *Komet* picked up a signal from the British refrigerator ship *Lochmonar*, of 9,500 tons, saying that she was about to arrive at Panama. Eyssen saw that she would have to pass near where the *Komet* then was, so he stopped his engines and lay drifting and waiting all the next day, starting up the engines again at night to try to make sure that the *Lochmonar* did not pass him in the darkness. August 16 was also spent in waiting, but on the morning of

154

the 17th a ship came in sight at 0935; Eyssen started up his second engine, sent his men to action stations and gave chase. The ship pursued was of about 7,000 tons, and therefore not the *Lochmonar*. She had a speed of twelve to fourteen knots and headed away towards the Galapagos, replying to the *Komet's* warning shots with her stern gun, whose shells fell short. The ship then stopped and hoisted her flag, which was seen, on approaching, to be Dutch. She was the motor ship *Kota Nopan*, of 7,322 tons, from Macassar to New York with rubber, tin, manganese ore and sago flour. Her crew were thirty-five Dutch and sixteen Javanese.

The new capture was undamaged and a very suitable prize to send home to Germany, but she had on board only 220 tons of oil, which she consumed at a rate of fifteen to twenty tons per day. Eyssen asked the SKL if there was any possibility of getting oil for her long voyage home, either via Cape Horn or the Cape of Good Hope, and in the meantime he began taking out of the prize the most valuable portions of her cargo, in case, after all, he was obliged to scuttle her.

While waiting for a reply from the SKL, on August 19 a new ship came up. The *Komet* opened fire at 8,000 yards and the ship gave the alarm; after some near misses had fallen around her the ship stopped. She was a British ship, the *Devon*, of 9,036 tons, an old coal-burner with 4,570 tons of miscellaneous goods on board, described by the SKL in a later report as a worthless cargo. She was bound from Newcastle upon Tyne to New Zealand. Her crew consisted of thirty-one British and 113 Indians.[1]

On August 24 the British issued the warning that a raider was operating in the *Komet's* area; presumably this was done because the *Kota Nopan* and *Australind* had failed to arrive at Panama. The American authorities were reported disturbed by Eyssen's operations within the Pan-American neutrality zone and American warships were said to be on the way to the Galapagos. Meanwhile, the SKL ordered the *Atlantis* and *Komet* to meet at Balbo, between Pitcairn and

---

[1] Cf. *The War at Sea* by Captain S. W. Roskill, vol. I, p. 547, where it is stated that the *Devon* had intercepted the *Kota Nopan's* raider report but continued to steam straight on to the enemy.

New Zealand, to oil from the *Munsterland*, which left Yoko-hama on August 25. The transfer of cargo continued from the *Kota Nopan*, as Eyssen wanted to make room on board her for his prisoners, and it was still continuing on August 30, when another ship came in sight. The *Komet* showed no sign of interest; the newcomer was quite fast and a chase by daylight would be a long and risky business, but after night-fall Eyssen started off in pursuit. However, the other ship was too fast for him and easily left him behind. Again, apparently, the chased ship never realised that she was being followed.

The *Komet* and *Kota Nopan* then went back south-west-ward towards the rendezvous where they met the *Munster-land* and the *Atlantis*, which saluted Eyssen's flag.

There followed the argument between Eyssen and Rogge over the distribution of the fresh food in the *Munsterland*, which has already been mentioned. The *Kota Nopan* filled her tanks, although bad weather interfered with the process and with the transfer of prisoners and stores.

On September 24 the *Komet* and *Kota Nopan* set off for Cape Horn, and home. As they sailed up the South Atlantic they had hopes of finding enemy ships, but all that they saw were two American vessels—the *Effingham* of New Orleans and a bigger ship of 12,000–14,000 tons, according to the *Komet's* war diary. Both these ships were steering a course for Capetown and passed within 8,000 yards; for a while Eyssen feared that they might report him, but wireless traffic remained normal.

In the moonlight of November 1 a ship was sighted and chased, but once again the *Komet* proved not fast enough, and when, on November 5, Eyssen twice sighted smoke on the horizon he decided that it was not worth while trying to catch an enemy.

The Equator was then crossed for the eighth time, and orders were received from the SKL to discontinue commerce warfare and return straight home, picking up two escorting submarines, *U 561* and *U 652*, west of the Azores. On November 14 the *Komet* had been 500 days at sea, and on November 26 she reached Cherbourg.

The faster *Kota Nopan*, sent ahead independently, had reached the Gironde on November 16.

At Cherbourg the *Komet* was ordered to Hamburg, and on the next night continued her voyage to Le Havre. On the day after that she picked up an escort of three torpedo-boats, five minesweepers of the "M" class and six motor minesweepers ("R" boats). Past Gris Nez, at four-ten in the morning of November 28, British light coastal forces attacked her, and on the next night she was attacked by Coastal Command, one of whose planes, thought by the Germans to be a Blenheim, hit her with a bomb which failed to explode.

Finally, the raider reached Hamburg safely on November 30, and a voyage of nearly 87,000 miles was at an end. There were now no more raiders at sea, but a few days after the *Komet* arrived the *Thor* set out on her second cruise.

The *Komet* herself, later, was to attempt a second cruise. Eyssen, in the meanwhile, was appointed naval liaison officer with Luftflotte IV, and then from August 1942 to July 1944 was in command of the Navy Office in Oslo, being responsible for the movement of shipping and supplies. After this he was sent to Vienna to the Inspectorate of Reserves for the Armed Forces, and in April 1945, in the month before the final collapse of the Third Reich, he retired from the navy.

I

Kormoran • SHIP 41

THE *Kormoran* was the biggest of all the armed merchant raiders, being of 9,400 tons. She was the former *Steiermark* of the Hamburg-Amerika Line, a brand-new ship built by Krupp-Germania of Kiel; despite the fact that she was more than twice as big as the *Thor* and *Komet* she carried much the same armament as these ships and the other raiders, together with six torpedo tubes and 320 mines. On board were two Arado seaplanes and one LS boat—a small motor torpedo boat. The *Kormoran's* diesel-electric engines gave her a speed of eighteen knots.

The commander of the new raider was Captain Theodor Detmers, the youngest of the raider captains, who was thirty-eight when he took up his command. He had joined the navy at nineteen and after serving in the cruiser *Köln* had specialised in destroyers, being captain of the obsolete *G11* in 1935, first lieutenant of the new *Leberecht Maass* in the following year, and then captain of her sister ship *Hermann Schoemann* until 1940.

After Ruckteschell brought the *Widder* home he and Detmers met to exchange ideas. It was decided that the *Kormoran* should break out through the Straits of Dover and the English Channel, rather than north via the Denmark Straits, where at the time planned for the *Kormoran's* sailing—December—there would have been a great deal of ice. This plan was changed just before the *Kormoran* left Gotenhaven (the temporary German name for the Polish port of Gdynia) after an ice reconnaissance by the trawler *Sachsen;* the *Sachsen* said that the ice was bad but not impassable; and, as at this time there were no surface escorts to take the *Kormoran* through the Channel, it was decided that she should go through the Denmark Straits after all, with the passage between Iceland and the Faroes as an alternative if necessary.

For the passage the *Kormoran* was disguised as a German warship, a *sperrbrecher,* with dummy wooden guns and a coat of dark blue-grey paint.

Before sailing, supplies were taken on board for two U-boats—twenty-eight torpedoes, with 400 rounds of 4.1-inch and 3,000 rounds of 20-millimetre ammunition.

The *Kormoran's* operational area was fixed as the Indian Ocean and Australian and African waters, with the South Atlantic and Pacific as alternatives. Magnetic mines were to be laid off the coast of South Africa, with special attention to Simonstown, Durban, Port Elizabeth and East London, and, off Australia, Fremantle, Adelaide, Hobart, Sydney, Brisbane, Wellington and Auckland. Moored mines were to be laid in the approaches to Rangoon, Calcutta, Vizagapatam, Madras and the Straits of Sunda.

On the way to the Denmark Strait bad weather held up the ship at Stavanger, for her final repainting could not be done at sea, and an emergency disguise was prepared for her as the *Viacheslav Molotov,* 7,500 tons, of Leningrad. Finally, after dodging along the edge of the northern ice barrier, the raider was in the Atlantic by December 13. Then she turned south, and on her way it blew heavily, up to Force 10. The ship rolled so much that it would have been impossible to use her armament had there been an emergency, and when Detmers tried to alter his ship's trim by pumping oil from her double bottom into her upper bunkers, he was able to achieve little.

However, the weather improved and with it the visibility. On December 18 smoke was sighted which, to the regret of the German captain, had to be avoided, as the ship was not yet in her operational area. The very day after forgoing this opportunity Detmers was told to start operations at once, as it was not desired to have too great a concentration of raiders in the Indian Ocean during January and February.

As the *Kormoran* sailed on, her engine-room personnel were busy making experiments with the most economical use of her diesel-electric motors, and tests showed that as she stood at that time she had an endurance of seven months without refuelling.

On December 29, with good visibility, Detmers tried to use one of the seaplanes, but the ship was rolling too badly, and owing to a faulty winch, the plane was damaged.

The passing of the Cape Verde Islands was complicated because the area had been assigned for operations to Italian submarines, so that for safety's sake Detmers steered back northwards and then chose a course between the Italian area and the boundary of the Pan-American neutrality zone. Nothing was seen, except a Spanish ship with her flag illuminated and an American vessel.

Detmers states in his war diary that he did not fly a flag at this stage, as he wished to be regarded as "a mysterious vessel." On January 6, he stopped the Greek steamer *Antonis,* which did not give the alarm. She was a ship of 3,729 tons, carrying 4,800 tons of coal on British charter from Cardiff to Rosario. Detmers took on board the crew of twenty-eight, a stowaway, charts, documents, seven live sheep, all the fresh food that he could find, machine-guns and 1,000 rounds of small-arms ammunition. He then scuttled his prize.

Moving over to the Capetown-New York route, all Detmers saw were two American ships, and acting on information received from the survivors of the *Antonis,* he then made for a position 400 miles west of the Azores, between which point and Fernando Noronha single Allied ships were supposed to be sailing.

Again nothing happened, and Detmers signalled to the SKL saying that he presumed that all shipping was moving in convoy. The SKL replied that according to their information there were single ships still to be found west of 25° west.

On January 18, just before last light, a ship was sighted, and the *Kormoran* manœuvred at her full speed of seventeen and a half knots to place herself in a position from which she could come out of the darkness against her adversary, who would be silhouetted against the light. As it grew dark the enemy began to zigzag, apparently in accordance with the Admiralty orders, which had been previously captured by the *Atlantis*.

"In order to minimise the possibility of pursuit by raider or submarine at night, independently routed merchant ships should, when sea-room permits, alter their main lines of advance after dark by at least three points until approximately ten miles from their daylight track. During this period ships should continue zig-zagging whenever visibility is less than two miles."

The ship now being followed was seen at once by the *Kormoran* to be an enemy, as she was sailing without any lights, and, a little later, she was identified as a medium-sized tanker in ballast.

From a distance of four miles Detmers fired starshells, as his searchlights would be useless at that range, opened fire, and with his third salvo straddled the target. This at once elicited a distress signal from the tanker: "RRR *British Union* shelled 26° 24′ N. 30° 58′ W." Five minutes later the *Kormoran* checked fire and headed towards the enemy, which suddenly began to fire with her stern gun, but she had got off only four rounds before the *Kormoran*, reopening fire, had set her after part ablaze. The crew of the tanker left their ship, and as she was still on fire and explosions could be seen taking place, Detmers did not send a prize crew on board. He discovered from the survivors that their ship, the *British Union*, of 6,987 tons, was on her way from Gibraltar to Trinidad and Aruba. Twenty-eight members of the crew were saved, and seventeen lost their lives.

The *British Union's* "RRR" had been picked up by the SKL, which ordered Detmers to meet the *Nordmark* and hand over the torpedoes and stores he was carrying for the U-boats before leaving for the Indian Ocean.

There was now a danger that the *Kormoran* might come into contact by mistake with the *Thor*, and for the time being the SKL told the *Thor* to stay south of the equator and the *Kormoran* to stay north of it, until January 31. After that date neither ship was to attack a vessel unless it was clearly an enemy.

Between the Cape Verdes and the equator, on the after-

161

noon of January 29, *Kormoran* sighted a craft that looked like a refrigerator ship, distant about 15,000 yards and steaming at fifteen knots. At this range there was nothing that Detmers could do, so he pretended that he was harmless and let the big vessel steam towards him; the two ships drew closer together. At 9,000 yards Detmers had his enemy within range. He hoisted an order to stop and fired across the bows of the oncoming vessel, at the same time working up to full speed. The enemy paid no attention, and at 1330 Detmers opened fire in earnest, fourteen minutes after the first sighting.

The enemy ship turned away and gave the alarm, but within four minutes she stopped and her crew abandoned ship. The ship was the *Afric Star*, of 11,900 tons, with 5,708 tons of meat from Buenos Aires and San Vicente to the United Kingdom. Detmers decided to sink her partly because she had been damaged and partly because her appearance was so distinctive. The crew of seventy-two, together with four passengers, two men and two women, all British, were taken on board the raider and the *Afric Star* slowly sank, being finished off with some rounds from the 37-millimetre gun, which was originally an anti-tank weapon, the bigger guns and a torpedo.

The *Kormoran* then left the scene as fast as possible, her wireless operator reporting that although the sunken ship's "RRR" had not been understood by Freetown—the *Kormoran* had been jamming it—other ships in the neighbourhood had heard and repeated it.

After nightfall a dark, shadowy form could be seen through the raider's gun sights. At about 3,200 yards *Kormoran* opened fire with starshell and high explosive; the first salvo was over, but with the second the Germans began to hit. The enemy kept on its course, but, closing to within 1,000 yards, the *Kormoran* opened up with light anti-aircraft weapons. The attacked vessel's wireless stopped and her crew took to the boats.

There was so much British wireless activity to be heard that Detmers decided to sacrifice one of his torpedoes in order to sink the ship at once and thus be able to get away as soon

162

as possible. The ship was hit in the engine-room and sank immediately; two badly damaged lifeboats were picked up, with four British and thirty-nine Chinese on board (five of whom were wounded). Eighteen British and twenty Chinese were missing.

The *Kormoran* went off full speed into the night; the sunken ship had been the *Eurylochus*, of 5,723 tons, from the United Kingdom to Takoradi. She had been off her course and keeping far out to sea to avoid U-boats that were believed to be operating off Freetown.

The raider continued towards her meeting with the *Nordmark* in Area Andalusia. Detmers noted in his war diary that his searchlights had been defective and that there had been no help for it but to use starshells. It would, however, be possible to use the searchlights on some occasions, as they were so faint that they would be taken by an enemy to come from a ship which was much further away than in fact she was. Because of this miscalculation of range due to the feeble searchlights both the *British Union* and the *Eurylochus* had fired over.

From the *Nordmark* the *Kormoran* picked up 1,338 tons of oil and then, like all the other raiders, took her share of the rich booty of the *Duquesa*. For the *Kormoran* there were 216,000 eggs and 100 quarters of beef.

On February 9 the loading of the spoil was finished and the ship went off to the Indian Ocean. From the SKL's account of the cruise it can be seen that at this time Detmers was not feeling very optimistic. On the way towards the Cape of Good Hope, Krüder, from the *Pinguin*, passing him, offered the use of one of his whale-catchers as an auxiliary minelayer, but Detmers refused, saying that he must have something faster and that he proposed to use his motor launch. This, however, at the first attempt, proved impossible, for bad weather prevented the LS boat being used off Walvis Bay. The *Kormoran* was preparing to return as far north as the equator when she encountered a minor disaster. On February 18 some of the bearings of the main engines cracked and it was necessary to cast two more. There was not enough white metal on board for this purpose, and Detmers asked

163

Berlin for 700 kilogrammes of it. The SKL replied that they were sending it at once by submarine and by blockade runner from South America; in the meantime the *Kormoran* was to stay in the South Atlantic, and begin operating on the sea lanes outside the neutrality zones as soon as possible.

There seems to have been a feeling at this time that the South Atlantic was not a good area for the raiders, but in fact, as the SKL pointed out, the *Kormoran, Atlantis* and *Scheer* all did well there.

Meanwhile two shifts of specialists were busy in the engine room casting new bearings; they made fourteen in seven days, for new damage was occurring all the time. On February 24 the *Pinguin* came up to offer 210 kilos of white metal, but for a whole day the two ships dodged each other, not sure of their respective identities and seeing only smoke, and strange lights, which kept on appearing and disappearing.

By March 6 all four engines were working again, but this state of affairs did not last long, as by evening of the same day a bearing had gone in No. 2 engine. On March 10 the equator was crossed going north. Detmers expected great things of this area, as it was here that ships from America to Africa were thought to leave the neutrality zone to cross to Freetown, but nothing was found and Detmers felt that he was running a good deal of danger, as the excellent weather and bright moon damaged his chances of concealment. During the night of March 13 he followed a ship whose lights were not being carried in a typical American way, but he had to give up the chase because of the state of his engines.

Two more bearings had now given way, and Detmers suspected something fundamentally wrong. In his report to the SKL he complained that the *Kormoran* was a new ship, which had to be run in like a motor car, and it was therefore a mistake to use a new ship as a raider. The *Kormoran* had now been at sea for nearly two months and had steamed 10,000 miles without any great result.

U 105 met the raider on March 15, stating that she had been following a convoy with *U 124,* but was now on her way to meet the *Scheer*, which had on board some valves for her electronic gear. Detmers asked anxiously whether *U 124*

164

had the metal for his bearings and was told she had. Meanwhile he gave *U 105* drinking water, fuel and six torpedoes, and took on board one of her men who was ill.

Orders for the *Thor* and *Kormoran* were now being continually changed, as the SKL endeavoured to prevent them operating in the same sector. On March 12 the *Kormoran* avoided a ship which she saw in the neutrality zone and next morning, outside the zone, sighted a tanker which shortly afterwards began to signal "RRR" and position with addition "suspicious vessel *Agnita,*" but this was jammed, and about fifteen minutes later the *Agnita* obeyed an order to stop. She was an armed British tanker of 3,561 tons, with one 4.7-inch and two 3-inch guns, on her way, in ballast, from Freetown to Carupano in Venezuela. She was small and in bad condition and was accordingly sunk as soon as her crew of thirteen British and twenty-five Chinese were taken aboard the raider. The sinking took some time, even though the tanker had been hit by nine 5.9-inch shells.

"Despite the smallness of the ship, we were especially pleased with this success, as it seemed that the spell which had lain over us for seven weeks had at last been broken," said Detmers in the war diary.

On board the *Agnita* was found a very fine chart of Freetown with swept channels and mined areas, copies of which were prepared for the use of the next German submarines to be met. This meeting with *U 105* and *U 106* did not take place until March 28, as the *Kormoran* was now short of fuel and had to steam very slowly. On the way to the rendezvous, early in the morning of March 25 a ship was sighted at a great distance and Detmers brought the *Kormoran* on to an intercepting course, slowly, without arousing suspicion. This stealth was essential because in the present state of the raider's engines there could be no question of a long chase.

The *Kormoran* came within 10,000 yards of the enemy, another tanker in ballast, which began to give the alarm. The *Kormoran* tried to jam her signals and opened fire; the second salvo was a near miss, and the ship hove to and stopped signalling. She was the Canadian *Canadolite*, of 11,300 tons, built by Krupp, Germania, and in ballast from Freetown to

165

Venezuela. She was nearly new, and Detmers decided to send her into the Gironde. Most of her crew were left on board, but the German took her captain, chief engineer, wireless operator and the senior member of the gun crew as prisoners in his own ship.

From March 29 to April 2 *U 105* and *U 106* were supplied. On April 3 the *Kormoran* met the steamer *Rudolf Albrecht*, which had broken out of Teneriffe and brought oil, fresh provisions, potatoes, bananas, oranges, a small dog, a live pig, magazines and English cigarettes.

In return Detmers gave her two cases of beer, a lifeboat from the *Afric Star*, a chronometer and a sextant.

After this transaction the raider's captain was ready to go back to the South Atlantic, but first he wished to take one more look at the area in which he had caught the *Agnita* and the *Canadolite*, for it still seemed promising. Early in the morning of April 9 he sighted smoke on the starboard quarter from a ship which came up so fast that it might be an armed merchant-cruiser. Detmers headed away and towards a rain squall into which, if necessary, he could disappear. But by about six o'clock the enemy was seen to be a freighter in ballast, and the *Kormoran* slowed down to allow herself to be overtaken by the unsuspecting ship. By seven the two ships were within 10,000 yards of each other. Detmers ordered the freighter to stop, adding: "No wireless or be shelled."

After a warning shot across her bows the enemy turned away, and started to use her wireless, which was, however, successfully jammed. Fire was opened and the ship set ablaze amidships. As soon as she stopped wirelessing Detmers checked his fire. The ship which he had attacked was the *British Craftsman*, of 8,022 tons, with 1,500 tons of ballast and a large anti-submarine net which she was taking from Rosyth to Capetown.

Forty-six prisoners were taken on board, and the British ship had lost five dead. Still burning amidships, she was blown up, but continued to float owing to the buoyancy given her hull by the floats of the net defence. Detmers then torpedoed her, and she sank stern first.

The next day Detmers learned that he had been promoted

to captain. Wireless calls for the *Canadolite* were now heard
—proof that the jamming had been successful. Two days
later, on the edge of the neutral zone smoke was seen at six
o'clock in the morning. The *Kormoran* manœuvred to get
between the newcomer and the zone, at the same time edging
herself nearer the oncoming ship, cautiously, so that the
enemy would not be frightened.

At 0740 Detmers sent hands to action stations, but nothing
happened, and the enemy altered course away from the raider.
For three and a half hours the *Kormoran* watched her foe,
gradually manœuvring the range down to 10,000 yards, until
at 0953 he was able to open fire, after warning shots had
been ignored. The ship stopped was the Greek steamer *Nicolaos D.L.*, of 5,486 tons, with timber from Vancouver to
Durban. She was new, with a valuable cargo, but she had
to be scuttled because her bridge and steering gear had been
put out of action by the *Kormoran's* shells.

The German boarding party undid the lashings of the deck
cargo, fired demolition charges in the hull, and then the
Kormoran shelled her, but the ship still floated, on fire forward, on fire amidships and her stern under water, with the
deck cargo floating free. The Greek's distress signal was
thought to have got through, despite jamming, but as it had
given the wrong position of the ship Detmers calculated that
this would add to the confusion of the enemy.

With this sinking the *Kormoran* had disposed of eight ships
of 56,717 tons.

Early on April 17 a large, handsome vessel of 8,000 tons
was sighted steaming at fourteen knots on the same course
as the *Kormoran* and about 27,000 yards away. Detmers did
not dare approach, as a chase would have been a long affair,
during which the enemy would have had plenty of time to
wireless and bring British warships to the neighbourhood,
which was alongside Area Andalusia, where the *Kormoran*,
Atlantis, *Alsterufer* and *Nordmark* were shortly to meet.

When this meeting took place the *Alsterufer* received seventy-seven prisoners and empty shell-cases from the *Kormoran*,
which took on board 200 rounds of 5.9 ammunition and
stores before she left for the Indian Ocean. Her hull was now

painted black to facilitate her passing as a Japanese ship later, but for the time being she was disguised as the Dutch ship *Straat Malakka,* on her way from Rio de Janeiro to Batavia.

There was a violent storm which lasted for four days at the entrance to the Indian Ocean, but by May 14 the *Kormoran* was at another rendezvous, this time at Point Violet, where she found the *Alstertor* and the *Adjutant.* The weather was still too bad for minelaying, and Detmers decided to search the route from the south of Madagascar to Australia. The Point Violet rendezvous had been arranged because the SKL wished another raider to enter the area and take the place of the *Pinguin,* of whose loss they had learned on May 9. Somewhat to his annoyance it would seem, Detmers found himself having to give 200 tons of oil to the *Alstertor,* which he considered a waste; in addition he felt that it was risky to use a raider as a tanker.

In his war diary, Detmers says that he felt that there was nothing more to be done in this area and that it would have to be left alone for at least six months, following the sinking of the *Pinguin.* For this reason he went off to investigate the triangle between the Chagos Archipelago, Colombo and Sabang. On the way he discovered that there was now a minesweeping flotilla in Rangoon and probably in other ports too. This would make his mine-laying of much less value, as the mines could more easily be swept up. Accordingly he cruised on, being able to use his seaplane twice for reconnaissance.

On the night of June 12–13 he avoided an American ship steering for Colombo, and on the 16th sighted a middle-sized passenger ship coming up astern.

"I tried to let him catch me up, so I slowed down," says Detmers in the war diary.

"All went well, then suddenly my bow smoke apparatus started making smoke and the steamer turned away. As we were only 200 miles from Colombo I decided that chase was impossible." The steamer made off, wirelessing.

After six days between Colombo and Sabang nothing else had happened, so Detmers decided to push into the Bay of Bengal, and lay mines off Madras. Two hundred miles from

168

the Indian coast there was smoke on the horizon, and ten minutes later masts and a funnel were seen; action stations was sounded. As the strange ship came nearer she was seen to have a very heavy crow's nest on her foremast, which Detmers thought might be a fire-control position; she was a ship of the *Madura* class of the British India line and a possible armed merchant-cruiser. The *Kormoran* turned away at full speed, and the enemy followed on her port quarter. Gradually the distance between the two ships increased, to Detmers' relief, as it was important that the British captain should not get close enough to see that the raider was disguised as a Japanese ship, for unless he saw this he would think that the *Kormoran* was an Allied ship obeying the Admiralty orders to avoid suspicious vessels. Finally, the British vessel disappeared over the horizon, but she had spoiled Detmers' minelaying plans. Accordingly the *Kormoran* headed away south-east, after having rejected the idea of mining the entrance to Calcutta because of a tornado reported in that area.

Early in the morning of June 26, while it was still quite dark, a faint light was sighted, and then a shadow, which was carefully approached. A warning shot was fired, to which the dark, silent ship paid no heed.

A full salvo followed at 3,000 yards, which immediately set fire to the ship. Her crew could be seen by the light of the flames taking to their boats, but only nine members of a crew of thirty-four could be saved.

This ship had been the Yugoslav *Velebit*, of 4,153 tons, in ballast from Bombay to Mombasa.

The *Kormoran* steered away from the burning and sinking wreck of the *Velebit* on a south-easterly course. By three-thirty that afternoon smoke was in sight again, a little abaft the beam. Detmers took his ship into a convenient rain squall, that she might be unobserved for a while. When he emerged he steered on a converging course towards the strange ship, which showed no signs of suspicion, and at 3,600 yards he fired his warning shot. The steamer answered with a "QQQ" message and her position. This was not jammed successfully, but only the longitude signalled got through, so that all the enemy knew was that there was a German raider somewhere in the eastern part of the Indian Ocean.

The *Kormoran's* first three salvoes hit forward and in the wireless cabin; the ship began to sink slowly and the forty-eight members of her crew, all unhurt, were taken on board. She was the Australian ship *Mareeba,* 3,472 tons, with 5,000 tons of sugar from Batavia to Colombo.

On the next day the *Kormoran* reached the line Dondra Head–Sabang, and Detmers decided to break off operations to repair the ship's engines, clean her bottom, and recamouflage her. The Japanese markings and writing on the ship's side were removed, as it was useless for the modern-looking *Kormoran* to pretend to be a Japanese ship in this area, where the only Japanese were vessels of older types. Moreover, a blacked-out Japanese ship would be very suspicious, and a blacked-out attack by night gave chances for a successful action which Detmers was not prepared to let pass. Finally, the Japanese disguise meant that she had to behave like a Japanese ship. This involved her holding on her course under observation, instead of being able to avoid doubtful vessels. Moreover, if enemy merchant vessels were encountered their suspicions would be immediately aroused by a Japanese vessel altering course and steaming towards them. For these reasons *Kormoran* was now repainted with a black funnel and brown upperworks, as it was observed that white paint showed up a great distance in the moonlight.

The *Kormoran* no longer had a specific disguise which might be easily checked or given away, but simply had the general air of a ship that might be friendly.

On July 21 Detmers decided that instead of minelaying in the Bay of Bengal, where British forces had recently been strengthened, he would continue into Indonesian waters, cruise south of Sumatra and Java and then go all the way down to a point west of Carnarvon, in Western Australia. There was a heavy sea and good visibility as he set off, but the war diary notes that the crew were working in watches round the clock for ten days sieving the ship's store of flour, which was found to be full of worms and beetles, while the coarse meal was unusable.

The rest of the food on board had held out well during the ship's nine months at sea, and the many refrigerated compartments fitted in the ship had proved their worth. The experts of the Hamburg–Amerika Line, when consulted, had recommended taking fresh potatoes in slatted cases, and this had been a good idea, but now the fresh potatoes were finished, and so were the eggs from the *Duquesa*.

"Nevertheless," says the war diary, "the food was still good and plentiful," and it goes on to comment:

"The cook and the baker are extraordinarily important in an armed merchant-cruiser, and both of them on board deserve boundless recognition."

By August 13 the raider had reached a spot 200 miles west of Carnarvon when, at dusk, a ship was sighted about ten miles away. The German's situation was unfavourable, since she lay on the light western horizon and therefore could easily be seen. Detmers decided to keep in touch with the enemy at the greatest possible distance, in the hope of being able to attack at last light. Then, at 14,000 yards, the ship which the *Kormoran* was tracking turned round and steamed towards her, giving the "QQQ" alarm, without a position but with a bearing, which suggested that she was in visual touch with other ships. Detmers suspected that she might be attached as a bait to a convoy and that she was signalling to her escort; she was a ship of about 6,000 tons and clearly fast, so that for both these reasons Detmers decided not to give chase, but turned away westward and then south.

"After seven weeks to have seen a ship at last and to have had to let her go is very bitter," said Detmers in the war diary.

The *Kormoran* went back to the north tip of Sumatra, after giving up the idea of mining the approaches to Carnarvon or Geraldton, on the ground that there was not enough traffic off those ports to justify the measure.

In its comments on the *Kormoran's* operations the SKL deplores the fact that mines were never laid, especially as an auxiliary minelayer could have been used without excessively exposing the *Kormoran* herself.

Ten days' cruising on a northerly course brought the ship within sight of land for the first time since she had left Norway, nine months previously, and the crew gathered on deck to see the summit of Mount Boea Boea, on the island of Engano off the south-west coast of Sumatra, brilliantly lit by the setting sun and looking like "a South Sea fairy-tale" according to the war diary.

The next ship to be seen by the raider was found on September 1, 150 miles south of Ceylon, suddenly emerging from a mist at about 20,000 yards. She was a modern vessel of the *Waigani* type, of 10,800 tons, and was probably faster by about one knot than the *Kormoran*, Detmers reckoned, thinking of his ship's foul bottom. He also calculated that the two ships would probably pass each other at about 15,-000 yards. "Unhappily too far off for an attack," commented Detmers in the war diary.

"If turned towards him," he continued, "action would be at maximum range and it would be difficult to catch him, for he would have plenty of time to call for air cover from Ceylon, only 150 miles away. I decided to follow him and try to get him that night, or the next day. I thought him to be a transport in the service of the British Admiralty."

However, the British ship disappeared in a rainstorm and touch was lost; Detmers tried to use his plane, but could not. Of the use of a plane by raiders he said in his war diary:

"Without a catapult it is a weapon of opportunity which can only quite infrequently be employed."

On September 3 the SKL informed Detmers that they intended to send *Thor* to relieve him in the Indian Ocean about the end of December. In the war diary Detmers commented on the small degree of success which he had had in this area so far. He added that he thought traffic was keeping well to the north and close to British bases, so that it could only be attacked at great risk and without regard to the limitations imposed by his operations orders.

This, he felt, had been the lesson of the sinking of the *Pinguin*.

"At the present time," he went on, "the task of the armed merchant-cruiser in the Indian Ocean is that of a police nature, preventing the use of the shortest routes." Personally, he said, he thought that it was a thankless role, for he could only stop ships by making short sorties during new-moon periods into the southern edge of the zone, where enemy traffic was to be found.

The *Kormoran* reached the equator on September 23, near the spot in which the *Pinguin* had been sunk, and at nightfall a light was seen. Half an hour later the *Kormoran* was near enough to signal and get the answer:

"Greek ship *Stamatios G. Embiricos*."

The *Kormoran* sent a boarding party, and only when it arrived did the Greek captain discover that the ship which had stopped him was German, and by that time it was too late for him to use his wireless. The captured ship was of 3,931 tons, in ballast from Mombasa to Colombo. She had been converted from oil- to coal-burning in 1937 and now had only twenty-three days' coal in hand. There was thus no question of using her either as an auxiliary minelayer or as a prison ship, and accordingly she was scuttled. In transferring the Greek prisoners to the raider one boat, with twenty-four men in it, drifted away and was not found until 1300 on the next day. The *Kormoran* had now disposed of twelve ships of 68,283 tons.

On September 25 Detmers again criticised his seaplane in the war diary, saying that only seven flights had been possible, whereas, had the ship been fitted with a catapult at least forty could have been made. As it was, the swell, generally across the wind, made take-offs very difficult, and Detmers never had what he described as "the nice feeling that a fat steamer was not getting away from him just over the horizon." It is to be noted that Detmers considered his plane solely from the point of view of reconnaissance and apparently did not contemplate using it for attack.

It was now time for another self refit, and replenishment from the *Kulmerland*, which had left Kobe on September 3 with 4,000 tons of diesel fuel, lubricating oil, white metal and provisions for six months. The replenishment and refit duly took place after the *Kormoran* had steamed across the Indian Ocean to Point Marius, which was on the fringes of

Area Siberia, opposite Perth in Western Australia. The *Kulmerland* also took off the *Kormoran's* prisoners, to hand them over in the Society Islands to a blockade runner, which was on her way from Darien to Bordeaux.

When the replenishment was finished the raider was now stored and fuelled up to June 1, 1942.

Nothing more was ever heard directly from the *Kormoran*. Her last war diary, sent home in the *Kulmerland*, said: "Hope to be in the operations area during the next new-moon period," but in fact the SKL learned afterwards from one of the survivors, Dr. Habben, that immediately after writing this Detmers changed his mind and decided to lay his mines off Perth. On his way he learned that a big convoy was to leave there escorted by the British cruisers *Cornwall* and *Dorsetshire*, and he decided to head for Shark's Bay, further north along the same coast.

Then, on November 24, Sydney radio was heard in Berlin asking:

"Details of the action and the name of the ship from which survivors have come."

On the last day of the month the SKL learned that the Australian cruiser *Sydney* had been six days overdue at Fremantle on November 26; she had been returning from convoy duty and it was believed that she had sunk an enemy raider, but her fate was still uncertain.

Then came the next intercept:

"A British tanker has taken on board German seamen from a raft, and others have been sighted in lifeboats, of which two have arrived in Western Australia. Apparently *Sydney* was on fire when last seen by the Germans."

At this date the *Kormoran* was the only German raider at sea so that the SKL realised that she had been lost. Later on they received the story of what had taken place in the letters of survivors from Australia. Amongst these survivor prisoners-of-war was Detmers himself, but the SKL seems to have got the first news from Dr. Habben.

The preliminaries of the last fight of both the *Sydney* and *Kormoran* began at four o'clock on the afternoon of November 19, when the raider's look-out sighted smoke

174

ahead. Very rapidly it was clear that a light cruiser, which was the *Sydney*, was heading directly for the *Kormoran*, who immediately turned away at full speed, reaching eighteen knots. The escape course which Detmers had chosen led straight into the sun and against the sea and wind. The *Sydney* followed, working up to high speed; to the Germans she appeared to be doing about twenty-five knots. She was signalling hard with her searchlight; the *Kormoran* hoisted the Dutch flag. The *Sydney* kept on flashing, and the Germans answered with flag signals, as was usual in merchant ships. Detmers is described as having let this exchange of signals develop "quite coolly;" some of the signals which he made were intentionally hoisted in a garbled form, and sometimes in reply to the *Sydney* he hoisted simply "Not Understood."

All this gained time. The *Sydney* did not open fire, but she was coming up fast astern and was soon within quite a short distance of the raider. Detmers had considered carefully, long before, the problem of what to do if he found himself faced by an enemy warship of superior strength, with no chance of escape, and he now set himself with deliberation to carry out his plans.

At 1730—an hour and a half after the first sighting—the *Sydney* had come up level with the *Kormoran* and was about 900 yards away, on the raider's starboard side. It seemed to the Germans that the *Sydney's* captain thought their ship to be a quite harmless Allied merchant vessel. The Australian cruiser's seaplane catapult, which had been swung out as though the plane were about to be launched, was swung inboard again, and through their glasses the Germans could see that only half the guns' crews appeared to be at action stations.

The exchange of signals between the two ships had now reached the point at which the *Sydney* was demanding the raider's secret call sign, in her character of a Dutch ship.

There was now nothing for the *Kormoran* to do except fight. The order to unmask the guns was given, and carried out in the record time of six seconds, while the Dutch flag

175

was hauled down and the German war flag and the captain's pennant were hoisted.

The war flag had not quite reached the masthead when the Germans opened fire with one round. The shell fell short, but the second salvo, from three guns, hit the *Sydney's* bridge and fire-control positions.

As the *Kormoran* fired her second salvo the *Sydney* opened fire herself, but her shells went far over; the *Kormoran* fired again, and hit *Sydney's* B turret, blew off its roof, and apparently damaged the training gear of A turret; thus half the cruiser's armament was out of action.

The Australian's seaplane catapult was swung out again, but the seaplane was at once destroyed with a direct hit; at this fantastically short range it was almost impossible to miss anything. A torpedo hit the *Sydney* forward, and her bow dipped in the water. The cruiser's speed fell, while the *Kormoran*, with her 37-millimetre anti-tank gun and the 20-millimetre anti-aircraft guns, swept her decks and prevented her from manning her torpedo tubes and anti-aircraft guns. The German light guns could easily be seen taking heavy casualties amongst the fire-control personnel. The *Sydney's* fire-control system was clearly out of action, and she was reduced to independent firing from the guns of her two after turrets. These scored three hits. The first passed through the funnel, exploded on the raider's disengaged side and filled the wireless office with splinters, killing two men. The second shell burst in the auxiliary boiler-room and oil bunker and put out of action the ship's fire-fighting equipment. The third shell destroyed the transformers of the main engines, while a fourth shell, although it failed to explode, injured members of the crew of No. 3 gun. The effect of all this damage was to start a heavy fire in the engine-room, and in a black chaos of pouring smoke and frequent electric flashes and short circuits as the electrical gear failed the *Kormoran's* engine-room personnel tried to put out the fire, but none of them were ever seen again.

As the result of her damage, the *Sydney* had now dropped astern, but she could see by now that the *Kormoran* was out of control and she tried to ram her. *Kormoran's* No. 5 gun

176

kept on firing, and the *Sydney* then turned away, steaming slowly at about five or six knots; as she went she fired four torpedoes, the nearest of which missed the *Kormoran* by 150 yards. The *Sydney* had turned now, but her turrets were apparently jammed, for they were trained on her disengaged side, while the Germans kept her continuously under fire and hit her again and again on the water-line; the Germans' 5.9-inch guns were firing salvoes every four or five seconds, and altogether fired about 500 rounds.

By six o'clock, just a half an hour after the action had started, it was growing dark; the *Sydney's* port quarter was heavily ablaze and there were continuous explosions coming from her. At a distance of 10,000 yards she was out of reach of the *Kormoran's* guns and steamed on slowly towards the horizon. For hours, as they strove to save their own ship, the Germans could see the huge fire on board their enemy, until an hour before midnight, when it disappeared. It was probably then that the *Sydney* sank.

The *Kormoran* was nearly as badly ablaze as the *Sydney*, and with her fire-fighting gear out of action there was very little that her crew could do. Detmers, realising this, ordered everybody away but the guns' crews. Some of the boats had been destroyed by fire, so that recourse was had to rafts and rubber dinghies, while two steel lifeboats were got out of No. 1 hold—by hand, as the auxiliary machinery was out of action.

As the crew left the ship it was seen that about twenty men had been killed in action; then about sixty more were drowned as a big rubber dinghy sank while the ship was being abandoned. The Germans tumbled over the side, knowing that the flames were nearing the stored mines. At one o'clock in the morning Detmers hauled down his flag and pennant and got into the last boat; twenty minutes later the mines exploded and the *Kormoran* sank stern first.

The weather became worse and the men in the boats, in the dinghies and on the rafts were separated from each other. One boatload was picked up by a coasting steamer, which passed on the news, and the R.A.N. and R.A.A.F. set out in search of the survivors, from both sides, of this battle to the death. All the Germans were found, but some of them took six days to reach shore. On one raft there were fifty-seven men in an area of twenty-five by ten feet, taking turns standing or sitting, as no one could lie down. By the time they reached shore all the survivors had suffered greatly from heat and cold. Afterwards they all, including Detmers, reported that in captivity they had been well treated by the Australians.

Clearly it was a terrible mistake on the part of the *Sydney's* captain that she came so close to the *Kormoran* and allowed herself to be taken by surprise. Long after the war the British official historian of the war at sea dealt at length with the incident, for it was a heartbreaking example of a tragic waste of a fine ship and a fine crew, the lessons of which will be of enduring value as long as men make war upon the sea.

Captain Roskill wrote: [1]

". . . the situation in which her *(Sydney's)* captain found himself was liable to occur in every contact with a suspicious ship, until a firm system of checkmating a raider's bluff by calling the shore authorities had been established. And, of course, the ability of the shore authorities confidently to tell a patrolling warship that the ship she had intercepted must be an enemy was absolutely dependent on having accurate knowledge of every true Allied merchant ship's position, all over the world, at any given time. Such knowledge was not easily amassed and kept ready for instant use in time of war, and the system was, in fact, not perfected until later. Yet, granted the difficulties of piercing raiders' disguises, the very close approach made by the *Sydney* during the exchange of signals was certainly injudicious.

"As early as January 1940 one of our own Q ships whose gun and torpedo armaments were about the same as the *Kormoran's* was intercepted off Sierra Leone by the *Neptune,* a sister ship of the *Sydney,* which was unaware of her true identity. The cruiser approached, and remained for some time steaming at slow speed, within a few hundred yards

[1] Op. cit., vol. I, p. 549.

of the Q ship whose captain later reported to the Admiralty that, had he been a German, he 'could have disabled (the *Neptune*) with two torpedoes and swept her upper deck.' But such complete secrecy enveloped the work of the Q ships that the report was never circulated to the Naval Staff and the fate which the *Neptune* escaped actually overtook the *Sydney* more than eighteen months later. The unheeded warning of the Q ship had not been the only pointer to the danger of making a close approach to a suspicious ship. The engagements between the raider *Thor* and the armed merchant-cruisers *Carnarvon Castle* and *Alcantara* in July and December 1940, and the loss of the *Voltaire* in April 1941, had amply demonstrated the capacity of the enemy to hit back hard and suddenly; the Admiralty had issued several warnings to that effect. Yet, in February 1941 the *Leander* also made a close approach to a suspicious ship which, had she been a German instead of an Italian raider, might well have brought on her the *Sydney's* fate.[1] The truth is clear. Though a comprehensive system of plotting the positions of all friendly merchant ships and the issue to them all of secret call signs are essential to success in anti-raider operations it will always take time to establish such measures on a world-wide basis. Meanwhile the difficulty of identifying an intercepted ship will inevitably remain. But to make a close approach to a suspicious ship, on a favourable bearing for gun and torpedo fire, is to court disaster."

[1] This is a reference to the Italian banana vessel *Ramb I* sunk by the *Leander* seven days after leaving Massova. In her very brief career she met with no success.

II

Thor • SHIP 10 SECOND CRUISE

RIGHT UP to the end of the war the SKL was studying the raiders' voyages, one after the other, and issuing as secret documents accounts and appreciations of what they had done. This preparation for winning another war went on until the war which was then in progress had been lost and it was never completed.

Accordingly, details of the cruises of the later ships in the second wave are harder to obtain than in the case of those already described.

After the *Kormoran,* there were five other ships in the second wave. Of these two never left European waters, one being sunk and one damaged on their way through the Channel. The three remaining vessels were the *Thor,* whose first cruise had lasted from June 1940 to April 1941, and two new raiders, the *Michel* (Ship 28) and the *Stier* (Ship 23).

In addition, during 1942 three Japanese armed mechant raiders also made their appearance in the Indian Ocean. The small number of these ships, in view of the size of the Japanese merchant fleet, is surprising. So, also, is their comparative lack of success.

During May and June the *Aikoku Maru* and the *Hokoku Maru* operated to the east of Madagascar, looking for Allied shipping which they hoped would have been driven out of the Mozambique Channel (between Madagascar and the mainland) by Axis submarines. On May 10 they captured the *Genota,* and at the end of the month reconnoitred Diego Suarez, then just fallen into British hands, with a seaplane. On June 5 a seaplane from the raiders bombed the British steamer *Elysia,* of 6,757 tons, which was then finished off by the raiders' guns, and on their way home towards

Japan they sank the *Hauraki,* of 7,113 tons, on her way from Fremantle to Colombo, when she was 780 miles south-east of the Chagos Archipelago.

In November of the same year the *Hokoku Maru* and another raider were back in the Indian Ocean, and on the 11th, some 1,500 miles west of Fremantle, they attacked the Dutch tanker *Ondina* (6,341 tons) and her escort, the 650-ton Indian minesweeper *Bengal.* The *Bengal* carried one 12-pounder gun, and the *Ondina* one 4-inch manned by an Australian able-seaman, four Royal Navy ratings, three army anti-aircraft gunners and one Dutch gunlayer. The Japanese ships carried six 5.5-inch guns each, so that they had, roughly, a combined broadside of 640 lb. against the 43 lb. of the two Allied vessels.

At 0534 the raiders were sighted by the *Bengal,* which immediately steamed towards the bigger enemy, hoping to cover the flight of the tanker. The tanker, however, did not attempt to escape, but also attacked the enemy with her single gun, mounted at her stern.

After two hits from the *Bengal* the *Hokoku Maru* caught fire, and following an explosion sank an hour after the action had begun. The *Bengal* did not have time to watch her triumph, for the second raider was shelling the *Ondina,* and the minesweeper went to her rescue, firing with her one gun until she had only five rounds of ammunition left. She then withdrew behind smoke, hoping that the Japanese ship would follow. This did not happen; instead, the raider continued to attack the tanker, whose gun ran out of ammunition. Her crew thereupon abandoned ship and were machine-gunned in the water—"for fun," said one of the survivors; "if it had not been for fun they could not have missed us."

The Japanese crew, in khaki shorts and shirts, leaned over the side and watched the men struggling in the water, then fired two torpedoes at the *Ondina* and went off to pick up the survivors of the *Hokoku Maru.* After this had been done she came back, fired another torpedo, which missed, and then went away. The survivors of the *Ondina* then went back to their ship, corected a 35° list, put out a fire, and a week later brought their ship to Fremantle.

181

The *Bengal* also reached safety, via Diego Garcia. One of her crew afterwards wrote:

"Those who took part in this action will never cease to marvel at the result. To think that a small ship with only one 12-pounder gun should engage two raiders, both more than ten times her size, and so enable the tanker to escape, sink one raider and then get away herself is almost miraculous."

One may add that it is not only "those who took part in this action" who will never cease to marvel at its result.

In July 1943 Japanese raiders made another foray into the Indian Ocean and sank the American steamer *Samuel Heintzelman* (7,176 tons) off Western Australia.

Finally, in March 1944 the two Japanese heavy cruisers *Tone* and *Chikuma* sank the motorship *Behar* (7,840 tons), took her passengers and crew prisoners and murdered most of them. For this Vice-Admiral Sakonju and Captain Majuzumi were brought to justice after the war.

·   ·   ·   ·   ·   ·

When the *Atlantis* and *Kormoran* had been sunk in November 1941, for the first time since March 1940 there was not a single German raider at sea.

The *Thor*, first of the raiders to attempt a second cruise, left Kiel on November 30, 1941, under cover of very bad weather, which made it impossible for searching planes to find her, and by stages descended the coast of Europe to the Gironde, where she arrived on December 17, to sail finally on January 14, 1942. Her commander was Captain Gumprich. Once more bad weather helped the raider's escape, but the storms were so bad that she herself was forced to shelter in the southern part of the Bay of Biscay. After repairing the damage done by the weather, the ship steamed out into the Atlantic and headed southward. On two occasions she turned away to avoid ships which she sighted, for Gumprich planned to reach the edge of the Antarctic before beginning operations.

As the raider neared her area of operations air reconnaissance became possible, but there was no trace of an enemy ship. It was not until February 25, when the *Thor* was just on the Antarctic Circle, that she picked up short-wave radio-telephone signals which revealed whaling activity in the neighbourhood. Despite a search, however, nothing was found. Information as to the activities of the ship at this time is confined to a list of dates and positions in February and March and the note against them "air reconnaissance."

Having given up the search for the whaling fleets, the *Thor* was on her way north again and was in the vicinity of Capetown when on the evening of March 13 she was sighted by the British cruiser *Durban,* which challenged her and received the reply that the raider was the British freighter *Levernbank.* The cruiser was satisfied with this reply and both ships went on their way.

The next morning another British warship appeared, the armed merchant-cruiser *Cheshire,* which also challenged the *Thor,* also received the answer that she was a British ship and was also satisfied with the reply.

When news of these two sightings became known and it was clear that the ship concerned could not possibly be British, there was an official enquiry by the Admiralty, which established that neither of the British warships had any means of telling that the *Thor* was not the ship she claimed to be, partly because they were unwilling to break wireless silence to ask questions of the shore authorities. The challenging ships had not persisted in their cross-examination of the raider on the ground that such questioning was often inconclusive and that even British merchant ships did not understand the procedure.

After this double blunder efforts were made to tighten up the system of challenge and reply, especially the seeking of information from the shore, but as Captain Roskill states in his comments on the action between the *Sydney* and the *Kormoran,* already quoted, it was some time before the efficient identification known as "Checkmate" was working.

On her way back northward, by March 23 the *Thor* was seeking the *Regensburg* for replenishment, but when funnel smoke was sighted at five-thirty-five on the morning of that day it did not come from the *Regensburg* but from a Greek steamer, the *Pagasitikos,* which was stopped and sunk by torpedo after her crew of thirty-two men and one woman had

183

been taken off. The sunken ship had been a small vessel of 3,942 tons. On the next day the *Regensburg* was sighted and replenishment took place. The cruise went on through the Indian Ocean until, on March 28 at eleven-thirty in the morning, masts were sighted and the *Thor* headed to intercept; the enemy turned away and a three hours' chase followed, but the *Thor* was not fast enough and had to give up.

Two days later the seaplane found another Allied merchantman and led the *Thor* up to her after a whole morning's hard steaming during which the aircraft destroyed the aerial of the merchantman by bombing. This ship was the British S.S. *Wellpark*.

After seven hours' pursuit and manœuvre the *Thor* opened fire at three minutes past two in the afternoon; the aircraft also attacked, but was driven off by the *Wellpark's* anti-aircraft guns.

Shortly afterwards the *Thor* began to hit the enemy, so that she stopped, and her crew abandoned ship. The *Wellpark* was scuttled and the *Thor* went on. On April 1 the *Thor*, whose captain seems to have had more success with his seaplane than any of the other German commanders, was again informed of the presence of an enemy by air reconnaissance. The plane had flown off early in the morning, and at about eight o'clock sighted a British freighter; she returned to the *Thor*, and was hoisted on board while the raider headed to intercept. At noon the plane was flown off again to make sure of the position of the British ship, and at 1330 was back once more, her duty done. The ship, the *Willesden*, of 4,563 tons, was finally seen by the *Thor* at 1635, and just under an hour later, no suspicions having apparently been raised aboard the British vessel, the plane flew over her and tried to destroy her aerial, at the same time dropping two bombs.

The *Thor* opened fire, and the *Willesden* returned it, but there was little she could do, and by 1752 her crew were in the boats. After hoisting in her aircraft, the *Thor* came up and sank her victim with a torpedo, after a pursuit that had lasted more than twelve hours.

A similar raider-seaplane combined operation took place

vo days later, when the Norwegian steamer *Aust*, of 5,630 ns, was sighted by the plane, intercepted by the raider, elled and her crew obliged to leave their ship, which was en finished off with demolition charges. In this chase the aplane was damaged, but was quickly repaired.

On April 10 *Thor's* radar, the first installed on board a aider, picked up a ship out of sight. The *Thor* followed her ll day, and at nightfall fired out of the darkness at 1,700 ards. The ship stopped almost at once, and thirty-two mem- ers of her crew were rescued from the water. This was the *irkpool* of 4,842 tons; later she was sunk by torpedo.

Another sighting from the air was made on April 16, and n this occasion the plane took a photograph of the sus- ected ship and brought it back to the *Thor,* whose com- anding officer was expecting a possible meeting with either e tanker *Doggerbank* or the *Michel,* now at sea under the ommand of Ruckteschell, the former captain of the *Widder*. he ship could not be identified, and after the aircraft had ade one more flight—its fourth of the day—pursuit had to e given up after nightfall for fear of attacking, by mistake, ither of the German vessels.

All this had been going on in the South Atlantic, in the icinity of the Cape of Good Hope; now the *Thor* received rders to move to the Indian Ocean, with instructions to void the areas in which Japanese submarines might be perating.

The passage to her new station was quite peaceful. On 1ay 10 she was about 1,500 miles off the coast of Western Australia when the seaplane sighted the liner *Nankin*, of ,131 tons. The plane successfully snatched away the enemy's erial. When the ship stopped Gumprich put a prize crew n board her, and took her off to another rendezvous with he *Regensburg*. After this the *Regensburg* and *Nankin* headed or Japanese-held ports and the *Thor* went back to her op- rational area, where, on June 16 in the evening, the primi- ive radar, which seems to have been an almost continual ource of frustration, had one of its good days and gave a ontact at 10,000 yards. Steering a convergent course, the

185

Thor got to within a distance of 1,800 yards of the ship, which at that distance could clearly be seen to be a tanker.

The first German salvo put the enemy's steering gear out of action and she began to steam around in circles, burning from stem to stern. In the flames many members of her crew perished, either on board or in the blazing waters, which were covered with burning oil. This ship had been the *Olivia*, a Dutch ship of 6,307 tons, on her way from Abadan.

According to the Germans a survivor gave information which enabled Gumprich to capture two Norwegian tankers, the *Herborg*, of 7,892 tons, on June 19, and the *Madrono* of 5,894 tons, on July 4, which were sent to Japan with prize crews. Four survivors of the *Olivia* later reached Madagascar in an open boat.

There was one more success for Gumprich before he was ordered to Japan—the sinking of the 5,187-ton British freighter *Indus* on July 20, after a gunnery action in which both ships suffered casualties, half the crew of the British vessel being lost. This action took place midway between Perth and Lourenço Marques. Before sinking, the *Indus*, which had fought well, managed to get off a raider report which was heard and repeated by both Melbourne and Kilindini. The sinking of the *Indus* brought the *Thor's* total sinkings or capturings on her second cruise up to ten ships of 56,037 tons in six months.

The *Thor* went to Yokohama, and after a long refit and a spell in dry dock she was met by another German vessel—the tanker *Uckermark*, which had begun life some three years earlier as the *Altmark*, and had been renamed after the famous incident in Jossingfjord in February 1940, when she had been stopped by the destroyer *Cossack* and 299 prisoners taken by the *Graf Spee* had been liberated. This had happened within Norwegian territorial waters, and as the *Altmark* was nominally a merchant vessel, she had not been taken away by the British as a prize.

After this affair the *Altmark* spent ten months at Kiel being refitted and armed (with three 5.9-inch and six anti-aircraft guns of various sizes), and received her new name. In March 1941 she was at sea helping to supply the charnhorst and *Gneisenau* in their big raid on the North Atlantic convoys. While in attendance on the *Gneisenau,* the tanker was sighted by the British battleship *Rodney,* but the *Uckermark* was able to take advantage of the *Rodney's* preoccupation with the *Gneisenau* to escape by herself.

After this she made for St. Nazaire and remained in that port for a year, except for one sortie to La Pallice. She was still at St. Nazaire when the big raid took place in March 1942, but survived that wild night undamaged.

Finally, after another refit, she sailed in August 1942 for the Far East. At La Pallice she took on board stores for the raiders—oil, ammunition, twenty torpedoes and two Arado seaplanes for the *Thor.* Her first attempt to get to sea past the British blockade, with an escort of three torpedo boats, was unsuccessful, and she was driven back, slightly damaged, by planes of Coastal Command. In the following month, at the new moon, she sailed again, and after supplying the *Michel* in mid-Atlantic safely reached Batavia and then Singapore, where she loaded oil and rubber for Yokohama.

The voyages of the *Uckermark* and the other supply ships were part of a considerable effort made by the Germans to supply their raiders at sea and bring back from abroad materials scarce or non-existent in the Reich.

At the beginning of the war there had been fifteen German merchant ships in Asiatic ports which it was planned to use as supply vessels and blockade runners, and between December 1941 and June 1943 twenty-two ships had been despatched from Europe to the Far East, of which seventeen reached Japan. In the period from December 1940 to October 1943 thirty-seven blockade runners had been sent from the Far East to Europe; six of these were recalled, and seventeen reached German-controlled ports safely; thirteen were intercepted and sunk or scuttled, while one was taken intact by the Americans in the neutrality zone during the autumn of 1941.

Between December 1940 and November 1942 losses of 5 percent were incurred, but in 1943 only two out of thirteen blockade runners reached their destinations safely, so

greatly had the Allied blockade improved because of t[l]
increase in the number of aircraft and ships available f[c]
patrol duties. But amongst the material brought to Ge[r-]
many by the blockade runners was 45,000 tons of natur[al]
rubber urgently needed for various purposes for which bu[na]
—the German *ersatz* or synthetic rubber—was unsuitabl[e.]
In addition the blockade runners carried quantities of q[ui-]
nine, iodine, opium, tin and wolfram.

Dealing with the period up to December 1941, the Br[it-]
ish Official History gives a list of thirty-six German supp[ly]
ships which worked with raiders and U-boats, as well [as]
twenty-two captured ex-Allied and neutral ships used by t[he]
raiders as supply ships.

Out of these fifty-eight ships, twenty-five were sunk [or]
captured by the end of 1941 and twenty-four between th[at]
time and the end of the war. One more ship, the *Winneto[u]*
was also lost in the Far East.

The simultaneous presence of the *Thor* and the *Ucke[r-]
mark* in Yokohama seemed to the German authorities worth[y]
of celebration, and a lunch was held on board for Germ[an]
and Japanese newspapermen on November 30. After lun[ch]
the guests were taken on to the forecastle of the *Thor* to [be]
photographed, while Gumprich and those officers who we[re]
off duty said good-bye to their guests and got in a boat [to]
cross the basin in which *Thor* and *Uckermark* were lyi[ng]
side by side. They were on their way to the supply sh[ip]
Leuthen, the former *Nankin*, and the dockyard gates. T[he]
officers on duty remained on the forecastle of the *Th[or]*
talking with the journalists as they posed for the photogr[a-]
phers.

Just before two o'clock there was a detonation in t[he]
Uckermark which sounded like the report of a 6-inch gu[n]
followed immediately by a much louder explosion. Hu[ge]
light-coloured flames sprang from the tanker, and in [no]
appreciable time both ships were on fire. A third explosi[on]
blew away the *Uckermark's* bridge and damaged the *Tho[r's]*
superstructure. Part of the tanker's bridge torn away by t[he]

xplosion was dropped partly on the ship and partly on the
quayside and some of the crews rushed across it to safety.

Both ships began to sink and everyone who could made
or the shore or jumped into the water. Flaming oil spread
cross the surface of the dock basin and caught up with the
men as they tried to swim away. The boat with Gumprich
and the officers on board turned back to the sinking ships
and began picking up people as fast as it could, but the
spread of the oil could not be stopped. The *Leuthen* was on
fire as well, and the whole surface of the basin was covered
with burning oil. Not until ten o'clock that night did the
flames die down. It was then possible to see that the three
German ships, together with a Japanese merchantman in
the same basin, were totally destroyed, while forty-three men
had been lost from the *Uckermark* and thirteen from the
Thor.

The cause of the disaster appears to have been the explosion of a spark in the fume-laden air within the *Uckermark's*
oil tanks, probably having been caused by a gang of workmen who were carrying out repairs.

III

Michel • SHIP 28

THE *Michel*, Ship 28, started her maiden voyage as a
raider from Flushing, on the evening of March 13, 1942.
Within a few hours she was in action as she made her way
westward towards the Straits of Dover, escorted by five
torpedo boats and nine minesweepers. Before midnight the
minesweepers were exploding mines laid by the British in
the German-swept channel and the engines of British motor-
torpedo boats could be heard close by; just before four o'clock
in the morning the track of a torpedo was sighted and a
starshell seen, but there was no other trace of the enemy until
the raider and her escort were in the Straits themselves. Then

189

M.T.B. engines were once again clearly heard. One of the German minesweepers fired a starshell, which showed that the *Michel's* convoy was being attacked on the seaward side from both ahead and astern.

At the same time, the British were picked up on the radar of one of the torpedo boats, and in great clouds of smoke, lit by the flashes of light weapons, the convoy turned inshore. One British M.T.B. caught fire and two others were thought by the Germans to have been hit. Within four minutes the action was over, but as the convoy steamed on starshells kept bursting overhead as it was shadowed down-Channel.

This shadowing lasted forty minutes, then, once again, mines started exploding all around the German ships, and when dawn began to break at 0650 off Le Touquet two small silhouettes could be seen coming from seaward, closing rapidly. The Germans fired starshells and spotted several M.T.B.s heading towards them, followed by four destroyers. Both sides opened fire at about 3,500 yards, and the British kept on a converging course until the distance between the two groups of ships was only about a mile. The two groups then continued on a parallel course, the Germans being straddled by British shells, but not hit. The German torpedo boats fired their torpedoes, but all except one stuck in their tubes, and the British were able to turn away under cover of smoke as the German fire got too heavy.

The *Michel* had sailed just one month after the *Scharnhorst*, *Gneisenau* and *Prinz Eugen* had made their successful dash up-Channel from Brest, and since that event what was possible had been done by the British to prevent such a thing from happening again, but it was not until the next raider tried to break out that the arrangements worked well.

In the early morning of March 14 six motor-torpedo boats and three motor gunboats had left Dover to intercept the raider, whose southward passage along the Dutch coast had been reported.

At the same time five British destroyers, *Blencathra*, *Fernie*, *Calpe*, *Windsor* and *Walpole* were ordered to patrol east of

achy Head to catch the German ship if she got past the
.T.B.s and M.G.B.s.

Soon after leaving Dover the British light forces came
der heavy fire from the German shore batteries and three
them were damaged. After a while the whole force re-
rned to harbour, and it was now the destroyers' turn. They
et the *Michel* and her escort twenty-nine miles south of
ungeness, and in the action which followed the *Windsor*
d the *Fernie* were slightly damaged. There were no British
sualties, and although eight members of her crew were
led, the *Michel* was safe. She steamed on to Havre and
en to the Gironde, finally leaving European waters on
arch 20, in the direction of the Azores. Her captain was
uckteschell, from the *Widder,* and about half her crew
ere also from that ship.

The *Michel* had been laid down before the war as the
lish freighter *Bielskoi* at Copenhagen, a ship of about
000 tons. Before she was launched she fell into German
nds and was very largely reconstructed. Her armament
as slightly different from that of the other raiders—four
9-inch, three 4.1-inch guns, with light automatic weapons
d torpedo tubes. She carried a new and fairly primitive
dar as well as gear for the detection of the enemy's radar.
addition to the conventional seaplane for spotting pur-
ses she also carried two LS boats, each of which were
med with two torpedoes and were able to make forty
ots in good weather. The masts and derricks of the ship
ere arranged in such a way that they could easily be struck
moved to other parts of the ship to make identification
ore difficult; her funnel was also movable and fitted with
device for making smoke, so that she would appear to be
coal-burning vessel instead of the diesel-engined ship which
e was.

The *Michel* steamed south, taking great care to follow a
ack prescribed by the SKL, for if she strayed from it there
as a danger that she might be taken for an Allied merchant
ip by a U-boat and sunk. Her first operations area was to
the South Atlantic between the Equator and 15° South
beyond this area the *Thor* was at work.

Arrived on her station she was replenished by the tanker *Charlotte Schliemann,* which had broken out of Las Palma after lying there ever since the outbreak of war. The raider then went on to capture two Allied tankers, the *Patelle* (British—of 7,468 tons) on April 19 and, two days later, the *Connecticut* (U.S.—of 8,684 tons), both on their way to the Cape. The *Connecticut* was the first victim of the *Michel's* LS boats.

The practice of Ruckteschell was to follow his prey unseen for as long as possible to determine their speed and course and then lower the LS boats after dark. These used their greatly superior speed to pass out of sight and sound of the tracked ship, get ahead of her and then lie silently in wait, with their torpedoes ready. If all went well for the Germans the first their enemy knew of their presence was when the torpedoes struck.

On May 1 there was another opportunity for the LS boats, when early on a fine morning there appeared a large British steamer, the 10,000-ton *Menelaus* of the Blue Funnel Line. The first of the LS boats was carefully lowered into the long swell of the South Atlantic and the raider ordered the British ship to stop. The master of that vessel, Captain J. H. Blyth, refused and went on to give an example of what a determined and intelligent man in command of a well-found ship could do when confronted by this kind of emergency.

The first point to notice is that the British ship's look-out had been excellent, and as soon as the *Michel* had been seen the suspicions of *Menelaus'* captain led him to keep his distance. When the *Michel* opened fire he started off at full speed, giving the alarm as he went.

With clouds of smoke pouring from her single tall funnel, the *Menelaus* headed away; her engineers and her stokers, giving the performance of their lives in conditions which were tropical on deck and infernal in the boiler room, extracted from the vessel a knot and a half more than her official full speed, and began to draw away from the raider. But the fifteen and a half knots of the *Menelaus* were as nothing to the forty knots of the LS boat which came bounding after her, almost hidden by double arching bow waves. The German torpedo boat came closer, flying the White Ensign and the International Code signal: "Stop."

In a report to his owners, Captain Blyth told the story:

"At 5.25 a.m. (apparent time ship) 1st May 1942 Course 282 degrees, speed 14 knots in Lat. 25.19 S Long. 13.21 W. Sea smooth, wind North force 1. Visibility clear, dawn breaking, a vessel bearing 102 degrees distance about 8 miles called up on a flashing lamp. The following signals were exchanged:

Raider's Signals	Our Signals
What ship is that?	*Menelaus* GFXC
WBA (stop do not use radio etc. Disobey and I open fire) also several long and short flashes.	What do you want? Who are you?
Naval patrol service. WBA several times.	

"I disregarded the WBA signals and instructed the Chief Engineer to open engines full out, give all speed possible and maintain highest possible boiler pressure. At the same time instructing Wireless Operator, Mr. R. J. Seaman to send out QQQ signals with our position. Raider immediately replied on wireless RNR 1 TU (Thank you, received your message) and jammed further sending on 600 metres. Wireless was immediately switched over to short wave and signals sent out on that; also all confidential books were placed handy on bridge for throwing over the side with weights. Raider at 5.55 a.m. swung off about six points and commenced to attack by shelling. She fired 18 or 20 shells, the last six being two salvoes of three each (this looked to me like control-fire) all shells falling between a half mile and one mile short. She then immediately resumed her course and carried on the chase again. I ordered guns to be manned but not to open fire until I gave the order. I did this as I decided that to save my ship I must endeavour to make it a long stern chase. Our QQQ signals being out if I could make the chase last long enough the Raider would give up as he knew his position had been given out. At about 6.30 a.m. Raider being then about six miles astern an object was observed in water about 2 miles S.W. of him. This turned out to be a motor-torpedo boat coming along at about 35 knots in our direction, signalling was observed passing between the Raider and this motor boat. When motor boat drew level with us about 2 miles off on port side it was observed that she flew White Ensign and her crew were dressed in duffle suits. She signalled to us continually WBA—also 'New reg. . .' Remainder of signal was obliterated but ended with word 'stop'. This I interpreted to mean 'New regulations require you to stop' and she proceeded on about 1½ miles ahead of us, kept in the position and hauled down her White Ensign.

"While the motor boat was coming up, the Raider turned around showing us his stern for about a quarter of an hour. We observed from our bridge, however, that the distance between us did not materially increase although we were full out making about 15½ knots. By this I decided he was coming full speed astern and at the same time trying to work a bluff so that I would stop for the motor boat and allow her to board me. At about 7.00 a.m. the Raider then being about 5½ miles astern a splash was observed from stern of motor boat 1½ miles ahead of us. I immediately crossed her wake as I formed the opinion she was laying submerged floating mines ahead and thereby endeavouring to turn us towards Raider. Raider at this time was observed to swing out another motor boat on his derrick and lower to his rail but he did not put this into the water that we could see nor did he slacken speed. At about 7.20 a.m. motor boat turned around and came down at full speed about 35 to 40 knots on starboard side about 1¼ miles off and when one point abaft our beam swung stern on and fired one torpedo. Helm was immediately put hard a port and ship swung for torpedo to pass by. I could not see trail of torpedo in water and motor boat carried on to Raider. The Raider being then about 5 miles astern turning to North and opening fire again, firing about eight shells from her port broadside, the last three being a control salvo. These shells all fell astern, about two ships' lengths short. At 7.30 a.m. Raider abandoned chase turning and heading E.S.E. with her motor boat close alongside . . ."

The LS boat had been commanded by Lieutenant Otto Krink, who had been with Ruckteschell in the *Widder* and who had been recommended by his captain for the Iron Cross for his conduct early in the cruise. This recommendation was cancelled following the *Menelaus* fiasco, and Krink left the *Michel* as soon as she reached Japan. In carrying out the attack Krink made a number of mistakes on this occasion which resulted in the only abortive attack of the whole cruise, according to a statement which he made to an officer of the *Menelaus* some seven years after the war ended.

In the first place, as he realised after the event, he had continuously misjudged the speed, course and range of the British ship, and for this reason his torpedoes missed, including two which had been fired in the dark before the *Menelaus* had sighted the enemy.

In addition, when he closed the *Menelaus* in daylight, pretending that the LS boat was British, he was careless in his disguise. Thus he and his crew wore duffle coats on a warm morning, and over them they wore Merchant Navy life-jackets—not those of Royal Navy pattern.

Moreover, when signalling the Germans repeatedly spelled "patrol" with two "T's" and the imitation White Ensign which they flew was so poor a copy that it failed to take in the people of the *Menelaus* even at a distance of one and a half miles.

Ruckteschell had not pursued the British ship, for he feared the arrival of an Allied cruiser. Accordingly he picked up his LS boats and left the area as quickly as possible. He headed south for the area in which the *Thor* had been operating before she left for the Indian Ocean.

After finding the *Charlotte Schliemann* with the help of the seaplane, Ruckteschell transferred his prisoners on May 8. On May 20 he came up with the *Kattegat,* a Norwegian ship of 4,245 tons, which he at once attacked. The *Kattegat* surrendered after a few rounds and without getting through a raider warning; her crew was taken off and she was scuttled.

A fortnight later, on June 6, the *Michel* found the American Liberty ship *George Clymer* (7,176 tons), which had been drifting, broken down, about 600 miles south-west of Ascension. Picked up by the *Michel* just as her engines were in working order once again, she was followed and attacked at night by the LS boats, which hit her with two torpedoes. However, the American did not sink, but wirelessed with determination about her plight. To her appeals the radio station at Capetown answered: "A cruiser is coming to pick you up."

Ruckteschell had apparently been told by the SKL that the only British warships in the neighbourhood were either ancient "C" class cruisers with an armament no better than his own or else armed merchantmen of the same type as those with which the *Thor* had so severely dealt. Accordingly he decided to lie in ambush for the British cruiser and treat her as the *Kormoran* had treated the *Sydney*. First, however, he had to keep away from the sinking American until the enemy came up; he could not use his plane since the enemy would know that it could only come from a hostile ship nearby. So Ruckteschell waited just over the horizon, disguising himself as a British merchant ship coming to the rescue of the Liberty ship. When he felt that the time had come he steamed back to where the *George Clymer* had been. There was nothing there, but far off on the horizon was what he thought to be the tripod mast of the British cruiser, just disappearing after having picked up the American survivors.

In fact the ship which he saw steaming away was the old antagonist of the *Thor*, the armed merchant-cruiser *Alcantara*, which had found the *George Clymer* still afloat but in so badly damaged a state that she could not be towed into port, and was therefore sunk.

A week later, at nightfall, Rucksteschell picked up the freighter *Lylepark*, of 5,200 tons, of Glasgow, on her way from New York to the Cape with 8,000 tons of warlike stores on board, and steered towards her on a collision course. Just as the British look-outs sighted him he opened fire. The *Lylepark* was hit at once in the charthouse and elsewhere amidships, and with the second salvo a fire started on the boat deck; after this there was nothing to do except abandon ship. While this was going on the *Michel* kept up her fire. The entire crew left the ship except the British master, Captain C. S. Low, and his chief officer, who decided to try and avoid captivity. One lifeboat had been left floating alongside, damaged, and into this they lowered themselves down the falls of the boat, which sank as they got in her. The two officers swam away, and the chief officer almost at once found a raft, but it was some time before the master, nearly worn out, was as fortunate. As Captain Low struggled to a precarious and momentary safety the raider steamed slowly by, watching the *Lylepark* burning brightly. Low was still determined not to be taken prisoner; by dawn the *Lylepark* had sunk, the *Michel* had gone, and Low had discovered that the fresh-water tank on the raft was nearly empty. Just then another raft came alongside, empty, and securing it to the first raft, Low found that its water tank was full. It was now bitterly cold and raining hard. On the next day the weather had improved and Low saw an aircraft in flight. He fired rockets, but the plane paid no attention and went on to land on an aircraft carrier, whose smoke was just visible on the horizon. Then another plane took off and within a short while he was being picked up by a boat from the British escort carrier *Archer*.

The *Archer* took Low to Freetown, where after a week there arrived the liner *Avila Star,* having on board his chief officer and his second officer. Low arranged a passage for himself in this ship, and sailed for Liverpool; however, on the night of July 5 the *Avila Star* was torpedoed north-east of the Azores. The lifeboat in which Low was supposed to get sank at once, before it could be loaded. He got in a second boat, which was destroyed as soon as it touched the water by another torpedo fired at the sinking ship, and Low was thrown into the water, wounded in the shoulder and the arm. After swimming as best he could through the water covered with oil he was picked up by another boat, which shortly afterwards sank. Those in it were taken on board other lifeboats, and finally picked up by a Portuguese destroyer.

Twenty-two members of the crew of the *Lylepark* had been taken on board the *Michel*, which on June 12 was ordered to refuel again from the *Charlotte Schliemann* and then, after transferring her prisoners to the *Doggerbank* (formerly the *Speybank* captured by the *Atlantis* in January 1941), to operate in the direction of the Gulf of Guinea.

The meeting with the *Doggerbank* took place according to plan. This ship was nearing the end of her second round trip between Europe and the Far East, operating as a blockade runner and minelayer. In March 1942 she laid mines off Capetown despite the fact that she was sighted by an aircraft and by an auxiliary vessel on patrol. This success she owed to her impeccable camouflage, garnished with captured American lorries as a deck cargo, and to her knowledge of the Allied system of recognition signals. It may have been upon these mines that the steamers *Alcyone* and *Soudan* sank and the destroyer depot ship *Hecla* was damaged. The *Doggerbank* continued in this dangerous service until March 1943, when she was mistaken by a German submarine for an Allied merchant vessel and sunk.

The *Michel* was now in the neighbourhood of Ascension on a route to which Allied merchant vessels had been diverted by the Admiralty to keep them away from the areas in which the U-boats were working.

In three days she sank the old Union Castle liner *Gloucester Castle,* of 8,006 tons, the U.S. tanker *William T. Humphrey,* of 7,982 tons, and the Norwegian tanker *Aramis,* of 7,984 tons. This last ship was torpedoed during her attempt to escape by the LS boats of the raider and then finished off the next day by gunfire.

The *Gloucester Castle* had left Birkenhead for Capetown on June 21. On board she had twelve passengers, all women and children going out to join relatives at the naval dockyard, Simonstown. For the first part of her voyage she travelled in

198

convoy and then continued independently. She was alone on the evening of July 15, about 1,300 miles south-east of Freetown. It was hot and sticky and quite dark.

Suddenly there was a bright flash close at hand on the starboard bow, and a crash. The ship was hit by a 5.9-inch shell just below the starboard wing of the bridge. A great number of other hits followed, some by heavy shells, some from automatic weapons.

The wireless office was hit at once and both operators killed and the aerials were shot away, so that no alarm could be given.

The dining saloon was wrecked, and petrol stored on the foredeck just outside it went up in flames. Within ten minutes, when the shelling ceased, the *Gloucester Castle* was listing heavily to starboard and all her boats on the starboard side had been destroyed.

As the boats on the port side were being got away the ship righted herself for a moment, then listed heavily to port and sank.

A motor boat came from the *Michel* and began picking up survivors. Out of 154 people, sixty-one were saved—including one woman, a girl of eighteen and two young boys.

Once on board the raider, the prisoners were sent below and forbidden to come on deck for several days, as the *Michel* was looking for further prey. Already on board the ship were prisoners from other ships sunk by the raider; when the prisoners were permitted on deck there was little that could be seen, as the ship's armament, fire-control, radar, etc., was kept under canvas covers when the ship was not in action.

At the top of both masts look-outs were permanently on watch sitting in chairs and sweeping the horizon with extra large binoculars, which, like the chairs, were fixed to the masthead. Food was described as not too bad.

After about three weeks in the raider the prisoners were transferred to the *Charlotte Schliemann*, where they were stowed in the hold forward of the oil tanks. "The hold was rat-infested; no sanitary arrangements were provided. The food was mostly unfit to eat," wrote a survivor.

Under these conditions were living some 300 prisoners, and

199

their lot seems to have been typical of all the prisoners taken to Europe or to Asia by the supply ships of the raiders.

The *Charlotte Schliemann* now spent a month stationary in the South Atlantic, with occasional daily kicks of her motors to make up for drift due to wind or current. On September 1 the tanker started off for Japan, and soon after having left the tropics the prisoners were freezing in their quarters in the holds.

On reaching Japan, the women and the boys were put in a civilian internment camp, and the rest of the survivors spent nearly three years working as coolies.

The fact that the *Michel* was able to sink three ships in three days made it clear that, for a short time at least, this was an excellent area of operations, but Ruckteschell believed that two raiders could do better than one so that when he did meet another raider—the *Stier* (Ship 23)—he proposed to her captain, Gerlach, that the two ships should work together. Gerlach had been doing well off Fernando do Noronha, however, and he rejected Ruckteschell's suggestion. The latter thereupon decided to go to the area south of St. Helena, where on August 11 he sank the British freighter *Arabistan*, of 5,874 tons, in ballast from Capetown to Trinidad. Once more he refuelled from the *Charlotte Schliemann* and then entered the Indian Ocean, on the way sinking a brand new American cargo ship, the *American Leader*, of 6,778 tons, on her way from the Cape to Punta Arenas, on the Straits of Magellan.

This having been done, the *Michel* received a message from the SKL ordering her back into the Atlantic to meet another oiler and a blockade runner; carrying out these orders, she met the British freighter *Empire Dawn*, of 7,241 tons, on September 11, and sank her after sunset in a surprise gun attack similar to that which she had made on the *Lylepark*. Despite the fact that the *Empire Dawn* signalled that she was stopped and abandoning ship Ruckteschell kept up a heavy fire and half the British ship's crew of forty-four were killed; this affair was the subject of one of the charges of which Ruckteschell was found guilty on his subsequent appearance before a War Crimes Tribunal.

On September 22 Ruckteschell stopped the blockade runner *Tannenfels* on her way from Japan to the Gironde and put on board her his prisoners, and on the next day refuelled from the *Uckermark*, which also supplied additional torpedoes. Finished with the *Uckermark*, the *Michel* returned to the Indian Ocean, while the tanker remained at the rendezvous, waiting for the *Stier*.

Five days later Ruckteschell picked up a message from the *Stier* saying that she had been severely damaged in the course of an action with an enemy vessel and needed help.

In fact she was so badly damaged that she had to be scuttled, her crew being taken on board the *Tannenfels*.

The entire month of October passed without event for the *Michel*, until she received an order to go down into the Antarctic to try to repeat the heavy blow which had been struck by the *Pinguin* against the Allied whaling fleets.

But that blow had been struck two years previously, and Ruckteschell did not believe that the Allies would let such a thing happen twice, especially as the entry of the United States into the war had made them so much stronger. Accordingly a message was sent to the SKL urging that the orders be changed and the *Michel* allowed to work in the Indian Ocean. The SKL agreed to this, and the raider moved on to an area between Australia and the Cape.

Here another blockade runner was met, the *Rhatokis*, on her way back from the Far East to France. This ship never reached home, however, for off the coast of Spain she was sighted on New Year's Day 1943 by aircraft of Coastal Command, which called to the scene the British cruiser *Scylla;* as soon as the cruiser arrived and opened fire the *Rhatokis* scuttled herself.

On her new beat the *Michel* sank three more ships, the *Reynolds* (British, of 5,113 tons), the *Sawokla* (American, of 5,882 tons), and the *Eugenia Livanos* (Greek, of 4,816 tons); on December 11, four days after the latter had been sunk, Ruckteschell received the order to return home to Germany.

After steaming in a big arc far south of the Cape, the *Michel* sank one more British ship, the *Empire March*, on December 27, 300 miles east of the barren rock of Gonçalo de

Alvares; the British ship had been on her way from Durban to Trinidad, following a new route just laid down by the Admiralty.

Ruckteschell found nothing else; but when he was roughly abeam of St. Helena he received orders to turn back into the Indian Ocean and thence continue to a Japanese port. This decision had been taken by the SKL after the interception of the *Rhatokis* had made clear the greatly improved efficiency of the Allied blockade of the coasts of Europe.

Finally, on February 7, after 324 days at sea, the *Michel* once again sighted land and went on to Batavia, where a Japanese pilot took her into the port amongst the wrecks of the ships which had been sunk a year previously, when the Japanese conquered the island.

Afterwards the Germans were to complain of the discourteous manner in which they were received by the Japanese, and it would seem that the Japanese treated their German allies as little better than spies.

After another stop at Singapore the *Michel* continued to Japan, where she was met at Kobe by Admiral Wenneker, the German naval attaché, and Gumprich, the former commander of the *Thor*. For the first time Ruckteschell heard of the disaster to the latter ship, learned that his vessel was now the only operational German surface raider, and learned that because of the *Rhatokis* affair she would not be able to return home.

A refit which the *Michel* needed was taken in hand by the Mitsubishi yard. Before the *Michel* was ready to sail again, Ruckteschell, a sick man, was relieved by Gumprich and sent to hospital in Peking, where he remained until the end of the war in the Far East, when he was repatriated and convicted as a war criminal.

When the refit was finished Gumprich took the *Michel* to sea through the Indian Ocean and to the west coast of Australia. Early on June 14, on the edge of the Roaring Forties, which were living up to their name, the *Michel* met the Norwegian freighter *Hoegh Silverdawn* (7,715 tons) on her way from Fremantle to Abadan. Without warning the German opened fire, first with his guns, and then with two torpedoes, and by the light of starshells continued to fire as the Norwegians began to abandon their flaming ship; in the horror of the sinking and the storm the Norwegians believed that Gumprich was deliberately trying to destroy the lifeboats. Only one boat survived, and that was damaged by machine-gun fire; under the *Silverdawn's* captain it sailed across the Indian Ocean into the Bay of Bengal, and was brought to shore exactly one month and one day after the *Hoegh Silverdawn* had been sunk, 130 miles south-west of Calcutta. The voyage had been 2,865 miles long and of the *Hoegh Silverdawn's* company the brave Norwegian captain brought thirteen men safely to Calcutta in the oxcarts of peasants.

Having made this savage attack on June 14, Gumprich attacked and sank another Norwegian ship, the *Ferncastle,* by means of four torpedoes from the LS boats. Here again the suspicion must be that Gumprich deliberately tried to destroy the survivors of the sunken vessel, but he failed, for one boat-load of survivors was picked up, after eleven days at sea, 1,300 miles west of Fremantle.

Gumprich guessed that he was known by the Allies to be in the Indian Ocean (for his last victim had managed to get out a warning before she sank). He therefore retired to the southward, towards the 43rd parallel, where he awaited orders from Berlin. No orders came and Gumprich after a long and vain wait steamed slowly back towards Japan, via Batavia.

This decision not to attempt to bring the raider home appears to have been taken by the SKL after the sinking of the blockade runner *Portland* by the French cruiser *Georges Leygues* on April 13. The *Portland* had left Bordeaux on March 28, and had immediately been picked up by aircraft of Coastal Command. These called Allied warships to the spot, but the *Portland* was able to avoid them by using her gear for the detection of enemy radar, and made her way toward the Equator, where she was met by the *Georges Leygues,* which, after lying under Vichy control for more than two years at Casablanca, had not yet been fitted with radar. Accordingly she was able to approach the blockade runner without warning, and sink her as soon as she was within range.

On the night of October 17–18, 1943, the *Michel* was sixty

203

miles off Yokohama. In bright moonlight and in a flat calm the American submarine *Tarpon* was running on the surface when she sighted the German ship, which she took to be a Japanese naval auxiliary.

For an hour the *Tarpon* followed the German, trying to place herself in a position for a successful attack. Her time came at 0156, when she fired four torpedoes, two of which were seen to hit. The *Michel* stopped and listed to port and then, getting under way again, headed straight for the submarine. The *Tarpon's* captain, Commander T. L. Wogan, took his boat deep and went right under the enemy, coming up again to find her stopped and firing wildly round the horizon. The *Tarpon* fired three more torpedoes; two missed, but the third blew the stern off the raider, which did not, however, sink until 0230, when she was torpedoed once again by the *Tarpon*. There was an explosion, and when the flame and smoke subsided the *Michel* had disappeared.

It was not until some months later, when the blockade runner *Burgenland* was captured, that the Allied authorities knew which the sunken vessel had been, and knew that the last of the German surface raiders had been sunk.

IV

The End of the Raiders

SHIP 23, the *Stier*, was the last of the raiders to put to sea unscathed, but the hard fight which she had and the losses which were inflicted on her escort showed that since the *Scharnhorst, Gneisenau* and *Prinz Eugen* had made their escape up the Channel much had changed.

The *Stier*, formerly the *Cairo*, a 4,418-ton ship of the Deutsche Levante Line, sailed from Rotterdam under command of Captain Gerlach on the afternoon of May 12. For the occasion her disguise was simple—she purported to be the *Sperr-brecher 171,* one of the armed merchantmen used by the Germans to sweep magnetic mines and give close cover to the coastwise convoys which were essential to the life of Festung Europa.

As she left the estuary of the Maas the raider was escorted by the four torpedo boats *Kondor, Falke, Iltis* and *Seeadler,* vessels of 800 tons, armed with 4.1-inch guns, which had been sent up from Brest for the purpose, as well as by sixteen motor minesweepers. By ten-thirty that evening the formation of the convoy was as follows: six motor minesweepers, a distance of one mile; ten more minesweepers, a distance of 600 yards; and then the *Stier* with the four torpedo boats. As the convoy moved towards the Straits of Dover the Germans received radar warning that M.T.B. attacks were to be expected. At two o'clock next morning there was the noise of motor-boat engines to be heard to starboard, the side of the convoy towards the English coast, and astern, but when starshells were fired there was nothing to be seen. Just before three the convoy entered the Straits and came under fire from the British 14-inch guns mounted ashore outside Dover. Two or three salvoes were fired, which fell about 300 yards short, and once again the noise of the M.T.B. engines would be heard. By the time the German ships were about five miles west of Ambleteuse it was clear that they were to be attacked. The convoy continued with a speed of thirteen and a half knots, and by 0325 was abreast of Gris Nez, when the mine-sweepers ahead began firing starshell and their 20-millimetre guns to port—that is to say inshorewards, which seemed to Gerlach to mean that the British had worked their way around between his convoy and the friendly shore. Indiscriminate firing without any clear target went on for thirty minutes, with all ships joining in. There was mist and poor visibility, but the 5.9 starshells from the *Stier* managed to break through the darkness and show the silhouettes of enemy vessels on both sides of the convoy.

Having thus been discovered, the British M.T.B.s to port came closer and then followed the convoy on a parallel course with all their guns firing; the Germans returned their fire, but apparently without effect. While this was going on to port of the *Stier*, the M.T.B.s from starboard also began to close in. They were engaged by the *Falke*, which was hit several times by 40-millimetre shells, while one of the M.T.B.s caught fire and stopped, lying ablaze in the water.

Five minutes later the port column of M.T.B.s attacked again, and one of them was clearly hit and put out of control. The *Seeadler* closed and illuminated her by searchlight in order to finish her off—there were no more starshells available; a few rounds and the British M.T.B. was on fire. The manœuvring which this action had entailed meant that the third torpedo boat, the *Iltis*, on the starboard side of the *Stier*, had had to slow down to keep station, and while she was steaming at only three or four knots she was hit by a torpedo which had been fired from the port side, narrowly missed the *Kondor*, passed the *Stier* and, crossing over to the starboard line of German escort vessels, exploded, breaking the *Iltis* in two. Both parts of the ship sank within three minutes.

The *Seeadler*, having set her opponent on fire, changed course to resume her position behind the minesweepers. At 0408 another M.T.B. was sighted, which disappeared before the German guns could be brought to bear. One minute later the *Seeadler* was hit by a torpedo on the starboard side abeam the after funnel. She also broke in two and sank immediately.

The two surviving torpedo boats took the *Stier* into Boulogne and then went out to sea again to pick up survivors. Eighty-eight Germans were rescued, as well as three British from *M.T.B. 220*. The total German losses were about 200.

The *Stier* left Boulogne at nightfall on the same day for Le Havre, and thus gradually worked down the coast of France until she reached the Gironde on May 19.

Later that month she escaped from European waters and came to her first operational area off Fernando do Noronha. The ship had hardly settled down to her normal routine, and her crew were still worrying because the ship was so full of stores that it was difficult to move about, when on June 4 she had her first sinking. The British steamer *Gemstone*, of 4,986 tons, was sighted, and the *Stier* came up to her out of the sun, with such success that she was not seen until she opened fire at 8,300 yards. After the freighter's crew had been taken off she was sunk by torpedo. Although there had been no sign that her "QQQ" alarm had been picked up, Gerlach was in a hurry. The *Gemstone's* cargo had been iron ore from Durban and Capetown to Baltimore. Gerlach noted that her captain, on being questioned, had told him nothing of importance, but that he had stated that he thought that he was being attacked by a U-boat, even after the *Stier* had fired on him, so hard was it to find out what was happening in the glare of the sun.

That night three planes flew over the raider; at the sound of their engines Gerlach hove to, so that the bow wave and wake of his ship would not show.

On the morning of June 6, at 0915, a ship was sighted on the edge of a rainsquall. Gerlach sounded "V" (. . . —) on his alarm syren, which sent the men below to their action stations. The tanker was a Panamanian, who turned her stern to the raider and opened fire with two guns. A chase started, which was not ended until the raider had fired 148 rounds of 5.9 ammunition, and hit the tanker aft with a torpedo. She was the *Stanvac Calcutta*, of 10,170 tons gross, in ballast from Montevideo with sealed orders, which Gerlach guessed meant that she was on her way to Aruba to load. Of her crew of fifty-two, thirty-seven were rescued; her captain and wireless officer had been killed by the *Stier's* first salvo. Because of this there was no "QQQ" signal, though the action lasted until the tanker had been hit forty times.

Two days after this a ship was seen which was taken for a warship, and avoided; two days later still, on June 10, the *Stier* had her first tanker rendezvous, with the *Charlotte Schliemann*. Oiling was difficult; the couplings of the hose pipes required modification, and then when everything was going well it was suddenly discovered that the tanker was pumping oil which contained 98 per cent water. This proved to have been due to a mistake by the chief officer of the tanker, whom the incensed Gerlach fined the sum of 150 Reichsmarks.

Winter weather now set in, with storms and bad visibility. Gerlach determined, after oiling again on July 15, to ask permission to go to the west coast of South America, for he felt himself handicapped by lack of exact knowledge as to where U-boats were working in the South Atlantic.

On July 7 smoke was sighted, but the ship making it was travelling at such speed that the raider was unable to get within sight of her. Two days later the raider, repainted light grey, deciphered a signal from the British freighter *Tordene*, which gave a course which would bring her close to the *Stier*. The raider, accordingly, got herself into a suitable place for an interception and lay stopped in the dark, waiting. Nothing happened.

Throughout this period it was impossible for the raider to use her seaplane for reconnaissance owing to bad weather, and accordingly the search had to be abandoned. On July 18 the *Charlotte Schliemann* was met again. At this stage, Gerlach states, he became acquainted with the fact that Allied ships steaming by themselves were changing their course every twenty-four hours in accordance with orders taken from a series of sealed envelopes which were only opened after the ship was at sea.

The ship's war diary remarks at this stage that prisoners were receiving reduced rations—on the same scale as people in Germany doing no work.

On July 28 there took place the meeting with the *Michel* previously referred to, but according to Gerlach the other raider and her accompanying LS boat, which was in the water, did not go through the correct identification procedure, and a lot of delay was caused.

Ruckteschell came on board, and the two captains conferred, speedily reaching agreement as to the futility of remaining in their present operational area. On July 31 they started off together, moving northward, twenty kilometres apart. As they went they practised exercises between the two ships and carried out drills on board. Gerlach notes that his gunnery officer had brought his crews to such a pitch of efficiency that even the reserve crews of the main armament, made up of officers, petty officers, clerks and anti-aircraft gunners, could get off a minimum of fourteen rounds per minute, while the crack crew achieved a figure of eighteen and three-quarter rounds in one spell.

Still nothing was seen, and weather continued bad. On August 6 Gerlach told the SKL that he thought that there was no more regular steamer traffic in this area, which was traversed only by a few fast ships which the raiders would find it difficult to overtake.

Gerlach suggested that he either be sent to the Freetown Narrows, where the distance between South America and Africa is least, or closer in to the east coast of South America. If the SKL did not wish this done he proposed that he either try his fortune against the fast steamers or else go round the Horn to the west coast of South America.

On the 9th the two raiders parted at two o'clock in the morning; six hours later the *Stier's* look-out sighted a ship with one funnel and three masts steaming on a parallel course. For a while Gerlach held his ship so that the newcomer was just in sight from the masthead, while he himself was out of sight from the bridge of the enemy. Then he began a stealthy approach, drawing ahead of the enemy and then gradually nearing her. After a while he was in a position to cross her bows, but as he began to do this he saw with surprise that the enemy, instead of turning away, was heading straight towards him. The *Stier* turned to port and the two ships headed to pass each other on opposite courses. When they were about 17,000 yards apart the *Stier* opened fire and the enemy gave the QQQ alarm. With the fourth salvo the raider began to hit and the enemy was set on fire aft. She replied to the *Stier's* fire with one gun aft, but the range was far too great for her to hit.

After twenty salvoes the merchant ship stopped; she was the *Dalhousie,* of 7,250 tons, in ballast from Capetown to Trinidad. Because the alarm had gone out Gerlach was again in a particular hurry and finished off the freighter with a torpedo just as another ship came into sight. After some moments of doubt this was identified as the *Michel,* who had turned back to see what was happening.

The *Stier* now headed south and began to search the Capetown–River Plate route.

On August 14 the SKL called up the *Stier* and told her that the *New York Times* stated that an American cruiser had been sent to look for German raiders on the east coast of South America; this news strengthened Gerlach's desire to proceed at once round the Horn to the west coast of that continent, but permission from the SKL was still not forthcoming. Instead, the ship, after a run south and then north, went to Gough Island, 300 miles south-east of Tristan da Cunha, to investigate the possibilities of using it as a temporary base, in the same way that Kerguelen had been used in the Indian Ocean.

The engines were now slightly over-heating and full speed was only ten knots. It blew very hard from the W.N.W.— Force 11 to 12, and with revolutions for ten knots the ship's speed of advance was only three knots.

At this stage Gerlach entered in his war diary a series of complaints, starting with the fact that he had been sent to an area in which there appeared to be almost no ships, and going on to say that all three ships which he had seen he had sunk, and that despite these sinkings and two heavy actions in the Channel the ship had been awarded only twenty Iron Crosses, Second Class, after being 100 days at sea.

On August 20 he heard that ten survivors had been picked up from the *Arabistan*, sunk by the *Michel*. He noted in the war diary:

"The auxiliary cruiser must in every case make sure that no man of a crew prematurely escapes to friendly territory—otherwise the enemy will get substantially accurate, if exaggerated, details of the auxiliary cruiser."

Gough Island was reconnoitred and judged a suitable place for a self-refit, and enough oil was supplied by the *Charlotte Schliemann* to last until November 28, by which time, said Gerlach, his ship must be in the Gironde. In making this estimate he calculated his fuel consumption as follows—at a speed of fourteen knots, fifteen tons per day; thirteen knots, ten tons per day; ten knots, six tons per day.

Oiling from the tanker went very well on this occasion, unlike his experience with the same ship earlier in the cruise, and seven minutes after passing the first line pumping began, the two ships drifting in the swell.

Two days later wireless was suddenly heard loud and clear,

and the *Stier* stopped. Gerlach did not want to blunder on a ship until he knew for sure what she was. On the next day, temporary repairs having been made, the seaplane was hoisted out to reconnoitre, but nothing was seen despite excellent visibility.

September 1 was the third anniversary of the outbreak of war, and Gerlach complained that no message had been sent from the Fatherland to give his crew the feeling that they were in touch with home; he also returned to the charge on the subject of decorations, saying that this would have been a suitable occasion to award them and thus make easier his task of command.

All that was heard from the SKL was the news that the British steamer *Industria* had left Capetown for Montevideo on August 22.

In 1952 Krink, the former lieutenant from the *Michel*, stated that during the cruise of that ship she received notification of every ship leaving Capetown, together with their destination, speed and very often course. It should be borne in mind that Krink was speaking ten years after the event, and in other statements which he made at the same time showed his memory was sometimes at fault.

Gerlach made some calculations from which he concluded that the British ship had passed him about thirty-six hours previously, and that he did not have the fuel needed for a chase of three or four days which would have been required to catch her up. If he had had the news two days previously, he noted, he would have been in an excellent position to intercept.

Early on the morning of September 4 the look-out in the crow's nest reported a ship in sight; she was in the sun, and could not be identified, but had two masts and one funnel. It was, however, seen that she was steaming at twenty-one knots. The *Stier* headed towards her, and from a distance of 24,000 yards could see that she was a very large passenger ship. A little later she was identified as the 29,000-ton French liner *Pasteur,* operating under Allied control. Because of her very high speed there was no chance of the *Stier* getting within range of her, and there was nothing for Gerlach to do but to edge away and hope that his ship had either not been noticed or taken for an innocent vessel. No alarm was heard from the *Pasteur*, and she was soon out of sight.

The *Stier* at this time was beginning to run short of coal—she needed twenty tons a week to provide fresh water and run the auxiliary engines—so that Gerlach was relieved to hear that he was to meet the supply ship *Brake* at the beginning of October. In the meantime he was to meet the *Michel* again, as well as the blockade runner *Tannenfels* on her way from Japan to a French port. As he headed for the new rendezvous, Gerlach steamed west again, having passed round Tristan da Cunha.

There was an alarm on September 12, when a ship was heard close by loud and clear, but it was a dark night, with a new moon, and nothing was to be seen. Another alarm followed on September 18, and the *Stier*, with the use of her radar detector and hydrophones, started to track the unseen ship, but after twenty-four hours gave up, contact having been lost. As the *Stier* headed for the rendezvous with the *Tannenfels* a ship's fair was held on September 20, with a lottery and auctions, as a result of which over 3,000 marks were raised for the Nazi winter relief fund. Gerlach noted the sum with approval, for he had suggested that five marks per head would be a sufficient contribution, and in fact ten marks per head had been received.

The *Michel* and the *Tannenfels* were met during the next two days with the *Tannenfels*, cleaning his ship's sides at rendezvous with the *Uckermark*, and Gerlach decided to spend two days with the *Tannenfels*, cleanings his ship's sides at the water-line and doing some much needed painting. On the *Stier's* deck was a Japanese seaplane, a gift brought by the *Tannenfels* and received with no enthusiasm by the Germans, who noted that the plane was without bomb racks and radio and could not be made flyable in less than three or four weeks.

On the morning of Sunday, September 27, the *Stier* and *Tannenfels* were lying stopped, and painting and scraping was still in progress over the side of the raider. At eight in the morning the wind began to get up, and there was rain in the offing. The ship's executive officer gave orders for the men to come inboard as it was judged better to run no risk of the ship being caught in bad visibility with part of the crew over the side, "although long observation had appeared to establish the area as one through which no ship ever passed," comments the war diary. As the men finished their particular jobs they came back on deck, so that by ten minutes to nine only one boat and a few men on stagings over the side were still at work. Visibility had fallen to about two to two and a quarter miles.

Describing what followed, Gerlach wrote:

"At 0852, just as I left the bridge to go below, I heard a shout: 'Ship in sight to starboard.' The alarm was given as the ship seemed a large enemy steamer. The signal was hoisted: 'Stop at once.'

"I ordered: 'Full speed ahead,' and then: 'Steady on your course.'

"Two minutes after the alarm had been given the anti-aircraft armament reported:

" 'Permission to open fire.'

"And one minute later the main armament was also ready."

The *Stier* opened fire at 0856, and four minutes later the enemy replied. Gerlach stated afterwards that she replied with four or five guns, with good fire control, and that her total armament was one 6-inch and six 4- or 4.7-inch guns, as well as light anti-aircraft weapons. He was sure that she was an auxiliary warship, "a patrol vessel, or even an armed merchant-cruiser."

In fact she was an American freighter, a Liberty ship, the *Stephen Hopkins,* armed with a single 4-inch gun, and she proceeded to fight one of the great single-ship actions in the history of all time. The American sea services grew up in the tradition of the frigate actions of the war of 1812 and the privateers of that war and the War of Independence; now a very different sort of war was being fought by an American navy which was to emerge from the struggle the greatest sea-power in existence, but on that day in late September 1942 in the mist and drizzle of the South Atlantic with the Germans and the Americans fighting each other at a range at which it was impossible to miss, the American seamen were back at their beginning again.

The *Stephen Hopkins* turned hard aport and the *Stier* turned hard astarboard, so that her foe could not escape; the *Tannenfels* meanwhile jammed the American's alarm signals. As the *Stier* turned she was hit by two shells; the first jammed her helm hard astarboard, so that she began to turn in a circle, while the second passed through the main engine room and exploded, cutting off the supply of oil to the engines, so that they stopped. The way on the ship, however, carried her round in a half-circle, so that she could open fire with her guns on the port side. Gerlach tried to fire his torpedoes, but could not, because all the electrical gear in the ship was out of action.

The German guns, however, kept up a good rate of fire, despite the fact that the power-operated hoists from the magazines were out of action and shells and charges had to be brought up from below by hand. The American ship was soon on fire in several places, and stopped. At 0910 the *Stier* checked fire for a few minutes, as a rain squall blew down on the two ships, hiding them from each other. When the *Stephen Hopkins* was in sight again, Gerlach reopened fire for a space of about five minutes and secured more hits. By 0918, according to the German war diary, fire was checked finally and both ships lay side by side crippled and stopped. At 1000 the American ship sank. Gerlach had been taking stock of his position; in ten minutes he had been hit fifteen times. Oil leaking from shattered tanks was drifting about the engine room on fire, and all the fire-fighting gear in the ship was out of action. The fire spread out of the engine room and fastened on everything combustible—bunks, mattresses, chairs, benches and the like. Hand fire-extinguishers were brought to the scene, but within a few minutes they were empty and the burning oil spread on through the ship.

Boats and tubs and buckets, lowered over the side and filled with water, were laboriously hoisted on board again by hand and still the fire spread—towards Number 2 hold, where there were stored nineteen torpedoes. The flooding valves for this hold could not be reached, but the torpedo officer carried out a brave rescue of the crews of his tubes shut up in the 'tween

214

decks on the water-line, their way of escape barred by the fire.

By 1014 the engines were working again, but the rudder was still almost completely jammed; within ten minutes the engines finally broke down. Gerlach called his officers to the bridge, as the heat drove the men away from the auxiliary steering gear; all agreed that the ship could blow up at any moment. At this stage light coloured flames were seen coming from the torpedo hatch on the forecastle and the decks were on the verge of being red hot.

It was decided to abandon ship, and boats and rafts were lowered or thrown into the water, while the *Tannenfels* manœuvred as close as she dared. The ship was abandoned amidst cries of "Sieg Heil" and cheers for the Führer and the Fatherland.

The *Tannenfels* picked up the men in the water, and they had just reached her deck when the *Stier* blew up and sank. Stock-still, and without a word, the raider's crew watched her go.

Altogether she had lost three men killed and thirty-three wounded. As for the survivors of the *Stephen Hopkins*, fifteen survived after a boat journey lasting thirty-one days to the coast of Brazil. The other forty-two perished. The *Tannenfels* and the men from the *Stier* reached Bordeaux on November 8.

The fight of the *Stephen Hopkins* was nearly unique in the history of the war at sea. The disparity in strength between her and the *Stier* is not to be expressed simply by stating that the German vessel could fire on her broadside 400 lb. of shells while the American fired 31 lb., for in addition to this was the fact that the *Stier* had a fully trained naval crew while the *Stephen Hopkins* was a merchant vessel with an "armed guard" of naval reservists manning her armament. Moreover, the raider was equipped with an up-to-date fire-control system of a sort that was far too elaborate and complicated to fit in a D.E.M.S.—Defensively Equipped Merchant Ship.

The *Stephen Hopkins* had good fortune, but her crew could not know that. They could only know that within a very short time all of them, or nearly all of them, would be dead; they could not know as they ran to their action stations that their great courage would be rewarded and that the last but one of the German raiders was to accompany them and their own ship to the bottom of the sea. Nothing in the tradition and history of any sea service, naval or mercantile, can surpass the story of the *Stephen Hopkins*.

Nearly a year after her return from her first cruise the *Komet* sailed again. She left Flushing at midnight on October 7–8, 1942, disguised as a *sperrbrecher* ostensibly moving out to pick up a convoy.

With her went an escort of motor minesweepers, four of which struck mines almost simultaneously off Dunkirk, in an area which four hours previously the Germans had swept clear. Obviously British ships or planes had freshened the minefield after sweeping had taken place, and equally obviously they might well have done the same thing all the way down the coast. Accordingly the *Komet* put into Dunkirk to await developments. More minesweeping went on and early on the morning of the 12th the raider was able to leave for Boulogne. All went well on this stage of the journey, as it did the next day when the ship went from Boulogne to Le Havre.

From Le Havre onwards the *Komet* was escorted by four torpedo boats; she sailed at six-thirty on the evening of October 13, and by two in the morning of the next day had passed Cherbourg. At 0205 she reported that she was in action with surface forces off Cap de la Hague. Twelve minutes later, after two heavy explosions, she was sunk; all her escort vessels were damaged and all sustained casualties. What had happened was this:

Early in October the British had suspected that an attempt would be made by the enemy to get an important ship to sea and a force of destroyers, minesweepers and M.T.B.s was made ready. For three nights a careful watch was kept; nothing was seen, and it was feared that the strange ship had escaped. Accordingly plans were made to catch her further westward, but before she left the Channel. Five "Hunt" class destroyers—*Cottesmore, Quorn, Glaisdale* (Norwegian), *Esk-dale* and *Albrighton*, with eight M.T.B.s, left Dartmouth and stationed themselves north of Cap de la Hague. This was Group A.

Four other "Hunts," *Brocklesby, Fernie, Tynedale* and *Krakowiak* (Polish), were also waiting six miles west of Guernsey. They constituted Group B.

Group A sighted the *Komet* just before one o'clock on the morning of October 14 and almost at once set her on fire, together with two of her escort vessels.

The *Komet* blew up with a heavy explosion, and sank, leaving oil-fuel fires on the water, while the two escort vessels also continued to blaze.

In the attack, the British *M.T.B. 236* was hit.

As the surviving German escorts continued on their way they were attacked off Sark by Force B, despite covering fire from the German shore batteries. A torpedo boat was hit and a minesweeper was blown up.

British casualties in the whole operation were two wounded, while the *Brocklesby* was superficially damaged.

After the sinking of the *Komet* the Germans made one more attempt to get a raider to sea. In January 1943 Captain Ernst Thienemann, who ever since the beginning of the war had been responsible for fitting out the armed merchant raiders, was appointed to the command Ship 14—the *Togo*, of 5,600 tons and seventeen knots' speed, a former vessel of the Deutsche Afrika Line. The decision to try to send this ship to sea was one of the last taken by Raeder prior to his being replaced in command of the navy by Dönitz, and he took it without any great expectation of success, for he was convinced by then of the very nearly absolute efficiency of the Allied air and sea watch on the Channel.

Thienemann first took his new command from Rügen, in the Baltic, to Christiansand, in Norway, to finish her working up and to wait for suitable weather. The tide for the breakout would have to be high, as only thus would the *Togo* be able to get through the shallow swept channels in the coastwise minefields, and the moon would have to be new.

When she finally did sail she ostentatiously headed northwards as though she were attempting to enter the Atlantic through the Denmark Strait, as the earlier raiders had done. On her first night out, as soon as it became dark, she turned round and headed south, straight into a heavy storm in the Heligoland Bight. This storm, Thienemann knew, would tear mines from their moorings by the score and until more sweeping had been done it would be necessary for him to return to harbour. He found shelter at Sylt, and finally, with an escort of minesweepers, sailed once again on February 7. Off Rotterdam one of the minesweepers was herself mined and got into port with difficulty. The *Togo* kept on, Thienemann being always concerned by the fact that his ship was moving through extremely shallow waters—so shallow that she ran aground once and then a second time before she reached Dunkirk. After the first grounding she got off within three-quarters of an hour, running her own engines full speed astern. The second grounding was a much more serious affair, and it was soon clear that there was no chance of getting her off until the next high tide. That meant that she had to stay on the sandbank off Dunkirk during most of the daylight hours of the next day.

Four heavy flak batteries were brought to the shore, 300 yards off which the *Togo* lay, and protected her against an attack which never took place. The next night the raider floated off, but there was not enough darkness left for her to get through the Straits of Dover unseen. Thienemann bitterly regretted having to remain in this extremely dangerous neighbourhood, but there was nothing for him to do but to take shelter in Dunkirk itself.

On the next night, February 10, however, the *Togo* was able to leave Dunkirk unscathed, and with an escort of twelve minesweepers she had got as far as Gravelines on the way to Calais when she came under fire of the long-range guns above Dover. For forty minutes she steamed on at top speed under their fire; thirty-three salvoes were fired, but although they were well placed no hit was scored. The German heavy guns also joined in, with counter-battery fire. When the guns ceased the R.A.F. attacked and scored one hit on the *Togo* forward of the foremast, causing considerable damage. She turned towards Boulogne at what was now her top speed of six knots to land her wounded, and

218

was the target for further air attacks, without suffering further damage.

When the *Togo* was picked up by British radar off Gravelines, five "Hunt" class destroyers were sent to intercept her south of Beachy Head, and six M.T.B.s also sailed from Newhaven, but these ships searched in vain, for the raider had already turned back.

The following day she spent in Boulogne. Air-raid warnings were on almost constantly, but there was no attack until five-thirty in the evening of the 12th, when fifty-six British aircraft were reported over the town. No damage was done, but following another R.A.F. visit on the 13th the *Togo* left Boulogne at three-thirty in the morning of the next day, on her way back to Dunkirk. The British long-range guns opened fire again. Once more, according to the Germans, the enemy fire was well directed, and once more every salvo— there were twenty-three of them this time—just missed.

The *Togo* reached Dunkirk at eight-twenty-three on the morning of the 14th, and just over twenty-four hours later Thienemann received orders to take her back to the Baltic. It was clear to the SKL, now controlled by Dönitz, for Raeder had resigned on January 30 following his dispute with Hitler, that there was now no chance of a safe passage down the Channel. The British would have plenty of time to concentrate planes and ships with which to attack her as soon as she left the shelter of German-controlled waters; in fact, she was attacked before she could even leave Dunkirk.

Four hours after Thienemann received orders to bring his ship home eighteen bombers appeared over Dunkirk, and although they scored no hits on the ship some of their near-misses damaged the lock-gates of the port, so that it was impossible for the *Togo* to leave until they had been repaired. These repairs were completed by February 26, but a thick fog prevented the ship from putting to sea. The fog did not, however, prevent the R.A.F. from returning, and during that attack a bomb hit the after part of the ship, went right through her without exploding, and then burst in the water beneath her bottom. The after part of the ship was flooded, but her screw and steering gear were still in working order, so that she was able to sail on the next day, when she again ran aground twice on the sandbanks outside the port. She was able to get off under her own power on both occasions, and as she headed back home she was attacked by eight British M.T.B.s and M.G.B.s, who were, however, driven off by her escort.

So she just succeeded in getting back to Germany, and except for the *Michel* in the Far East the days of the raiders were over.

The Identity of the Mystery Ships

EACH OF the armed merchant raiders had at least four identities. There was the ship's original name as a merchant ship; then there was the name she received when she became a raider; with this went a yard number prefaced HSK when she was undergoing conversion, and another number prefaced Ship *(Schiff)*, which was generally used in signals and official correspondence; finally there was a letter allotted to each ship by the British Admiralty when she was known to be at sea. These letters, A, B, C, etc., were given to the ships in the order in which they were discovered and not in the order in which they went to sea. Thus the first ship to go to sea was the *Atlantis*, but she was Raider C, while the second ship, *Orion*, was Raider A, but the *Komet*, the sixth ship of the first wave was Raider B.

Order in which ships went to sea	Ship no.	Name as raider	Previous Name	HSK no.	British Admiralty letter
		FIRST WAVE			
1.	16	*Atlantis*	*Goldenfels*	II	C
2.	36	*Orion*	*Kurmark*	I	A
3.	21	*Widder*	*Neumark*	III	D
4.	10	*Thor*	*Santa Cruz*	IV	E
5.	33	*Pinguin*	*Kandelfels*	V	F
6.	45	*Komet*	*Ems*	VII	B

Order in which ships went to sea	Ship no.	Name as raider	Previous Name	HSK no.	British Admiralty letter
		SECOND WAVE			
1.	41	Kor-moran	Steiermark	VIII	G
2.	10	Thor (second cruise)	See above		
3.	28	Michel	Bonn (ex-Polish Bielskoi)	IX	H
4.	23	Stier	Cairo	VI	J
5.	45	Komet (second cruise)	See above		
6.	14	Togo	Name unchanged		
*	5	Hansa	ex-British Glengarry		
*	49	Coburg	ex-Dutch Amerskerk		

*These two ships were prepared as raiders but not sent to sea.

Tonnage Sunk by the Most Successful Raiders of the Two World Wars

FIRST WORLD WAR

Emden	101,182	tons
Möwe, 1st cruise	65,590	tons
2nd cruise	119,600	tons
Wolf	39,391	tons plus
	73,988	tons sunk by the mines which she had laid.

SECOND WORLD WAR

Atlantis	145,697	tons
Thor, 1st cruise	96,547	tons
2nd cruise	42,791	tons
Pinguin	136,551	tons
Scharnhorst and *Gneisenau* (operating together)	115,622	tons

ACKNOWLEDGEMENTS

My gratitude and thanks are due in the first place to the departments of the Admiralty and the Air Ministry which have made available to me facilities without which the writing of this book would have been impossible.

Reg Holmes, of the Department of the Chief of Naval Information, made it possible for me to receive information generously given by Commander Malcolm Saunders, R.N., of the Historical Section and Lieutenant-Commander P. K. Kemp, R.N. Admiralty Archivist. L. M. MacBride, the Chief Information Officer of the Air Ministry, has also given essential help.

Major-General R. E. Vyvyan, C.B.E., M.C., Editor of the *Journal* of the Royal United Service Institution, kindly permitted me to use the lecture given to members of the Institution by Commander E. V. St. J. Morgan, D.S.C., R.N., entitled "Sea Raiders in 1939-45 War." Her Majesty's Stationery Office has allowed me to quote from *The War at Sea*, by Captain S. W. Roskill, R.N., and Captain W. C. Chambliss, U.S.N., was good enough to furnish information as to the fate of two of the raiders sunk by American ships.

Messrs. Alfred Holt (The Blue Funnel Line) gave me full details of remarkable defence of their vessel, s.s. *Menelaus,* and William Kimber & Co., Ltd., have allowed me to use material from *The Swastika at Sea,* by C. D. Bekker and published by them, dealing with the unsuccessful attempt by the last of the raiders to reach the Ocean.

I am also grateful to Messrs. Longmans, Green & Co., Ltd., for permission to use information contained in *Union Castle Chronicle,* by Marischal Murray, published by them.

As usual the staff of the Reference and Photographic libraries of the Imperial War Museum have given much friendly and imaginative assistance.

Without all this courtesy and help it would never have been possible to have written this book, but, of course, the responsibility for the facts and opinions which it contains is my own.